THE STRANGE

AMERICAN WAY

Letters of Caja Munch
from Wiota, Wisconsin, 1855-1859

WITH

An American Adventure

Excerpts from "Vita Mea" an Autobiography
Written in 1903 for His Children
                    by Johan Storm Munch

Translated by HELENE MUNCH *and* PETER A. MUNCH

AND WITH AN ESSAY

Social Class and Acculturation *by* Peter A. Munch

Southern Illinois University Press   *Carbondale and Edwardsville*

Feffer & Simons, Inc.   *London and Amsterdam*

F
590
.N658

Contents

Foreword

These are the letters of a young woman who, as a newly married minister's wife, accompanied her husband to the Middle West, where he had received his first call to become the pastor of several newly organized congregations, and where he spent four frustrating years attempting "to bring the Word of God to the widely scattered and sorely misguided Norwegian settlers." My father often talked about these letters, which his mother had written home to her parents in Norway and which had since been preserved in the family as a cherished treasure along with other documents and mementoes from my grandfather's adventurous life.

Until recently, I had never seen the letters but knew some of their contents from stories told and retold in the family circle. Both of my paternal grandparents had died before I was born, and after the death of my grandfather in 1908, my grandmother's letters were kept, first by my father's eldest sister, *Fru* Else Holtermann (born in Wisconsin and frequently mentioned in the letters), and after her death in 1929 by the youngest sister, Dr. Christine Munch, who guarded them jealously and never let them out of her house.

In the family circle, an aura of sacredness surrounded the letters. I grew up in an atmosphere of family integrity and loyalty, not only in my own home but also in those of my uncles and aunts. From the walls of our living room, large family portraits in heavy frames, ministers for five generations, looked down upon us, following our every move with their eyes, austerely but kindly. Indeed, they were a part of our warm family circle as vividly and naturally as my brothers, my sister, and myself. And in my father's study, a large enclosed bookcase with lumpy, greenish glass panes in the rickety doors

housed a modest library which had been handed down through the
generations, and whose titles and authors, in cumulative fashion,
reflected the changing times as each new generation had added its
taste and style, from the Rationalism and Enlightenment of my
great-great-grandfather's time, through National Romanticism, to the
more ecclesiastical atmosphere of my grandfather's home. A particularly precious gem in this book collection, often shown to visitors,
was a small leatherbound volume, handwritten in a Gothic script so
fine that it takes a magnifying glass to read it. These were the
sermons of my great-great-grandfather Peter Munch, pastor at Vaage
in Gudbrandsdalen, later at Land, where he died in 1802. On a blank
page in this book, my grandfather had written:

> This book was given to me as a memory of my grandfather,
> Peter Munch, the faithful servant and true witness to the Lord.
> So as I, in my infirmity, apply myself to offer the testimony
> of faith in our Lord Jesus Christ to many, so is it here my
> prayer to God that in my lineage there shall never lack a man
> who vows himself to the Lord in His holy office.
>
>   Kristiania, March 1884
>   J. St. Munch
>   Servant of the Gospel
>   *Soli deo gloria!*

All these things were powerful symbols of family solidarity, and
wherever we went on visits to uncles, aunts, and cousins, there were
similar symbols tying us together in a shared identity. Among them
all, my grandmother's youthful letters ranked high in symbolic significance.

My interest in my grandfather's sojourn in America was reawakened shortly after World War II, when I myself became a migrant
and went to Wisconsin, where I was engaged in sociological studies of
Norwegian settlements for the University of Wisconsin. In fact, one
of the communities that I had chosen for more intensive studies was
just north and east of the rather extended area served by my grandfather, and it was a self-evident thing that my travels should include
a trip to Wiota, in Lafayette County, where my grandparents had
their home from the fall of 1855 until spring 1859, and where two of
their children were born. The old stone church, where my grandfather preached, is still standing and is now believed to be the oldest
Norwegian Lutheran church in America in actual use. It was built in

1851 but was not quite finished when the Munchs arrived: "One sits on rough boards put up on stumps, and you can see the sky through it in many places."

It was there, in the archives of the Wiota Lutheran Church, that I came across the very interesting church records, including the minutes of some apparently rather stormy congregation meetings, which revealed some of the reasons why Pastor Munch returned to Norway a year earlier than originally planned. Stimulated by this discovery, I wrote to my father, Pastor P. A. Munch, who was then living as a retired minister in a rural community in eastern Norway, and inquired about my grandmother's letters, requesting a copy of them for my own perusal. Nothing, however, came of this, partly for reasons which only later came to light. This was in 1949.

Fourteen years later, in 1963, as I was making plans for a field trip to the South Atlantic island of Tristan da Cunha, I received news from Dr. J. C. K. Preus, of Minneapolis, Minnesota, that he had fortuitously obtained possession of a copy of my grandmother's letters. He had not, however, received them from the Munch family. During a visit to Norway in 1955, Dr. and Mrs. Preus had spent an evening in the home of *Domprost* Johs. Ø. Dietrichson in Oslo: "Among other things that made the evening memorable for us was the reading by the *Domprost* of excerpts from some pioneer letters which we understood were from his grandmother, *Fru* Gustav F. Dietrichson of Rock Prairie (Luther Valley) ."

Because of his well-known interest in the Norwegian Lutheran Church in America, particularly its early history, and because of the apparent family connection—Mrs. Gustav F. Dietrichson was a sister of Pastor Adolph C. Preus of Koshkonong—Dr. Preus later obtained a copy of the letters from *Domprost* Dietrichson and then discovered that they were not from Mrs. Dietrichson but from Mrs. Johan St. Munch, my grandmother. It was Dr. Preus who brought the letters to the attention also of Dr. Kenneth Bjork, of the Norwegian-American Historical Association, which in turn led to my wife's and my own engagement in the translation of the letters for publication.

It was now even more important for me to see the original letters and, if possible, to obtain a good facsimile of them. Dr. Preus kindly let me have his copy, so at least we had something to work from, although it was only a photostatic print taken from a carbon copy of a poorly typed transcript which later proved to contain a number of errors. Obviously, these were the same letters of which my father had spoken. But the whereabouts of the originals was shrouded in mystery.

By this time, both of my parents and my aunt had passed away. It had been assumed in the family that the letters were safely in the custody of my aunt and, although it became increasingly difficult in her later years to find out exactly what family documents she actually had in her possession, nobody worried about it because it was expected that whatever she had was bound to come to light some day. However, when she died in 1959 as the last survivor of that generation, it appeared that she had completely denounced her family and had willed her entire estate—lock, stock, and barrel—to the young pastor then serving her congregation. Enquiries by members of the family concerning heirlooms and family documents led to negative results. No one in the family seemed to know what had happened to my grandmother's letters, and it was assumed that they were lost to the family along with pieces of furniture from my grandparents' home and other heirlooms. It was even feared that they might have been thrown away. Nor did any one in the family to my knowledge have a copy of the transcript. One can imagine my excitement, therefore, when I learned that at least one copy of the transcript, whatever its origin, was in existence and had come into the hands of Dr. Preus.

It was at this point that a dig into some more recent family correspondence brought back to light a long forgotten incident. It appears that my enquiries about my grandmother's letters in 1949 had brought about a minor family feud, as may happen in the best of families. My mother, Mrs. Cathrine Munch, née Bull, who usually expressed herself mildly in such matters and often found herself playing the role of a mediator and a damper upon the stronger tempers of the Munchs, described it as "a regular family brawl," and my father, in his often quite flowery language (and with an obvious allusion to the Wars of the Roses), declared: *Der er brand i Rosernes leir!*—or, as one would say in America, "The prairie is on fire!"

At that time, in 1949, my father and his youngest sister were the only survivors of a large family of nine children. What happened was that when my father made enquiries in my behalf about his mother's letters, he learned that his sister had donated the letters as well as other family documents to the University Library in Oslo. This piece of information was not kindly received by my father, in the first place because it had happened without his knowledge and consent, in the

second place because he had always maintained that family documents "should be preserved for the family" and not be "buried in a
library," but perhaps most importantly because this, in his view, was
a breach of family loyalty. The underlying tacit assumption was that
the letters, like any other family heirlooms, "belonged to the family,"
no matter who had custody of them, and could not be disposed of by
any individual by gift or by sale except within the family.

This notion was certainly not peculiar to the Munch family.
Although it has yielded in recent decades to a more individualistic
attitude (as witnessed by the fate of Caja Munch's letters), at least in
the nineteenth century and well into the twentieth it was a commonly accepted principle, not only in the familistic tradition of the
professional and proprietor class but also in the peasant tradition of
Norway as seen particularly from the continued assertion of allodial
right (*odelsrett*) to landed property among the peasants. This principle, that no "family property" should go "out of the family" without
the consent of other members of the family, was part of the unwrit-
ten conventions of the familistic tradition, and it is doubtful that it
would be upheld by any legal court except in the case of allodial
rights to landed property, which has been legally recognized in
Norway.

The situation in the Munch family was further aggravated when
my father asked permission to borrow his mother's letters, as well as a
"journal" kept by his father over the years, and this was opposed by
his sister and denied by the University Library, who apparently acted
on the assumption that my aunt had the exclusive right of disposal
over the documents. "And these are my own mother's letters!" he
exclaimed.

In this connection, it was disclosed that, two years earlier, my
aunt had made arrangements with the University Library to produce
a typewritten transcript of Caja Munch's letters in three copies, one
for herself and two for interested parties outside the Munch family,
this time also without the knowledge and consent of other members
of the family, including my father. It was from this transcript that
my aunt had presented a copy to *Domprost* Dietrichson. Another
copy was given to the private archives of the Koren family. Both of
these families, the Korens and the Dietrichsons, had a genuine interest in the letters because of the persons and events mentioned and
described there. Undoubtedly, there would have been no objections
to the presentation of copies to these families had other members of

the Munch family been consulted, especially if my father, as the next of kin, had also been given an opportunity to acquire a copy. Now the University Library belatedly offered to lend him a copy of the transcript—against proper security. This, in my father's opinion, was adding insult to injury.

But more was to come. The University Library, trying to tread gently between the feuding parties of the family Munch, had made the offer to my father in an attempt to soothe the ruffled feelings but thereby inadvertently revealed the fact that they indeed had a copy of the letters to lend. When the copies were made, the Library had—apparently unknown to my aunt—retained a fourth copy for its own manuscript collection. This threw my aunt into a rage as she had explicitly stipulated *three* copies only and had later donated the originals to the Library on the condition that she should remain in control of their distribution. Indeed, "family brawl" is an appropriate description of it. It is perhaps fortunate that neither my father nor his sister apparently knew that still another copy of the letters, "because of their great historical interest," was later presented to Professor Henning Larsen, then of the University of Iowa, during a visit to Norway. (Professor Larsen's father, Professor Laur. Larsen, is briefly mentioned in one of the letters.)

It is quite obvious that this lovely feud had an invigorating effect on my father, who was eighty-three years old when this was going on. He gave an unrestrained piece of his mind both to his sister, who had disposed of the letters in this manner, and to the director of the manuscript collection of the University Library, who had refused to let him borrow the original documents—and he seemed to enjoy every minute of it. *"Quel bruit pour une omelette!"* he used to say.

At the same time, the whole episode is sociologically and historically interesting as an example of the drama—the comedy and tragedy—of social change, with old values fighting for survival until they are broken down and crushed under the relentless pressure of the new. My father was in fact carrying the banner of family integrity and family rights, in full accordance with the traditions of Norway's professional class, against a new and modern age in which the family no longer plays a significant part in ascribing identity and status to its members, and where history no more belongs to specific families but to the "public." To him, the family documents, including his mother's letters from America, represented family history and were therefore important symbols of family identity and pride, and his effort was to preserve these symbols for the family. He did not claim possession of his mother's letters or any other family documents for himself; it really did not matter to him who actually had custody as long as they remained "in the family." He even conceded the right of his aberrant sister to keep a fair share of family heirlooms as long as she discharged her obligation in loyalty to the family. It appeared to be a small victory as well as a reassurance to him, therefore, when he was informed that, as a result of the whole affair, the University Library had returned his mother's letters to his sister.

This was the apparent situation when my father died in 1954 at the age of eighty-eight. And so, five years later, when my aunt's entire estate went out of the family, it was assumed that the letters were lost. We had forgotten to take into account that my aunt, too, was a Munch, with a strong mind fully to match that of her brother—although, how could anyone who knew her ever forget? It appears that if an offer was indeed made to return the letters to my aunt, as my father was led to believe, she must have refused to accept them and confidentially persuaded the University Library to keep them. Obviously, she was not going to let the family interfere with her dispositions.

So the donation was confirmed, and Caja Munch's letters from Wisconsin are now in the manuscript collection of the University Library in Oslo—no longer a symbol of family identity and of a vanishing tradition but a part, perhaps only a minor part, of the historical record of a people, its struggles, failures, and achievements, on both sides of the Atlantic Ocean.

The collection is not complete. At least two letters are missing, and parts of one or two more have been lost. Besides, Caja Munch sometimes makes references to letters written by her husband, which have not been kept. Only two letters written by Pastor Munch during his stay in America have been preserved, and they are included in the following translation.

Formally, the letters are mostly addressed to Caja Munch's mother, Mrs. Thalie Falch, or to both her parents. But they are obviously written as family letters and were even, by previous agreement, sent on from Hovland, near Larvik, to Pastor Munch's widowed mother, who was living in Christiania (Oslo). Before they were sealed and sent off, the letters were read by Pastor Munch, who added his remarks and an occasional postscript. Yet it is clear that as Caja wrote, it was her mother she had in mind.

The letters are long and detailed, each written with interruptions over a long period of time, sometimes weeks or even months, before it was completed and sent. They are written on both sides of large double sheets of very light paper, with hardly any margin at all. Caja Munch's handwriting is fairly close, and she appears to have had almost a compulsion about filling the sheet completely. Afterthoughts are often added in what little margin there is, in one case even across the lines of the other writing.

Among the professional class of Norway around the middle of the last century, letter writing was still an art consciously cultivated. The preferred style in private letters seems to have been a mixture of solemn literary style and oral diction, often juxtaposed in striking contrast, and with a fair sprinkling of wit. Caja Munch obviously does her very best to live up to the standard. She appears to be quite style conscious, offers apologies for her "miserable" writing, and repeatedly asks that her letters not be shown to strangers. But unconsciously, in her childish spontaneity, she has created a style of her own, which in the original Norwegian stands out in clear contrast to her husband's more mature and literary—but also, perhaps, more conventional—style. In Caja's hand, the conscious art of letter writing turns into a rather charming, almost naïve chatter of a young girl writing in confidence to her mother.

Peter A. Munch

Southern Illinois University
December 18, 1969

Letters of Caja Munch
from Wiota, Wisconsin, 1855–1859

The Voyage to America *and*
The First Year in Wiota, 1855–1856

Mrs. Caja Munch to her Parents, Mr. and Mrs. F. W. S. Falch

[Hamburg, August 1855]

I will go ahead and write to you, my dear Parents, while I am still in Hamburg, although it may turn out to be an awful lot of nonsense. But it makes me happy, and I believe you will not mind paying a few pennies postage to please me. Besides it will now be a long time before you hear from me again.

Please give my love to Sophie Pehrson and thank her from me, it was so nice of her to be standing so long in the rain waiting for us. She was the last person I saw in Laurvig. Tell her that the woolen cap and poncho have been, and will still be, very useful. I am going to write to her also.

September 1 [1855]

Time has almost come when I have to bid you farewell, my beloved Parents, but first I must tell you that last night we went to the theater and saw the opera *Robert le Diable;*[1] oh, how delightful it was. I shall cherish this experience for a long time. There was a lady from Riga, who did her part excellently. I have never heard such singing and such a voice before; she performed so beautifully the aria which Nanna has. Indeed, I shall never forget it. We had our seats in the parquet, for one *Ort*, eight *Skilling* each, the theater was big and rather nice.[2]

Well, Munch is waiting for me to finish as he wants to give the letter to Wage for further delivery. A cordial good-bye, my dearest beloved Parents, brothers and sisters, friends and ac-

quaintances, may God keep you and protect you. Do not think
of us too much, and do not worry in the least! Everybody
congratulates us on the ship *Rhein* and praises its fine quality in
every respect; Munch went on board again yesterday, and he saw
a great many delicious things being brought aboard, hams,
canned goods, and I don't know what. The captain was nice,
and everything is in order.

Farewell, then! It is so hard for me to close. Please write to
New York to Heierdal's address. Once again farewell! My dear,
dear Parents, brothers and sisters! God be with all of you.

Your own Caja

Tell Falkenberg that Brose has been of great assistance to
us, and thank him from us.

Emil sends many regards to parents, brothers and sisters, he
will write from New York.

Mrs. Caja Munch to her Parents, Mr. and Mrs. F. W. S. Falch
With a Postscript by Pastor J. St. Munch
to his Mother, Mrs. Else Munch, née Hofgaard

Chicago, October 17, 1855

At the moment I am sitting in Pastor Unonius's home,
where we are staying all by ourselves for the time being. But
nothing more about that now as I have to start from the beginning.

Before we left Hamburg, we spent a few very pleasant hours
at Wage's. He is married to Amalie Rieffel. They had just
returned from a long tour of Norway. I shall never forget the
kindness shown us by these people. They presented us with two
bottles of aquavit from Trondhjem, one bottle of bitter orange
essence, and, as a rarity, a piece of Norwegian wort-cake; they
sent us their calling cards, took care of the letter to you, and
assisted us with odds and ends. By their help, I also managed to
exchange the gold watch and got instead a rather large but, I
hope, good watch to the value of 6 *Spd.;* the gold was not worth
any more, and the watchwork was worn out, it was a trustworthy
man. Our last stay in Hamburg, then, was the most pleasant,
and all is well that ends well.

We went on board Saturday night, but the ship stayed in the
harbor until Sunday morning. Then a steamer pulled us out

between beautiful country estates while the music was playing. A strange feeling came over me at that moment, which it is impossible for me to describe; believe me, it was strange to see the different moods of all these people, some danced and were happy and gay, while others sat in the corners and wept. The weather was fine but with no wind; the steamer left us after a while, and in the afternoon we had to drop the anchor, but not for long. Soon we had a splendid wind and set off with lightning speed through the Channel.

I hardly think this passage took us as much as two days. But then we got by turns calm, good wind, and head wind, now and then a "small" storm as it was called, but I for my part thought it strong enough. Chairs, tables, food, bottles, and everything danced around in the room and crashed to pieces if it was not extremely well secured. One could neither stand up, walk, nor lie down. It was just on a Sunday a fortnight after our departure, the weather was beautiful in the morning, and on that very day I got well from my seasickness, it disappeared suddenly; I dressed up nicely, and we had an undisturbed little devotion in our cabin, but then it started.

At Pastor Dietrichson's, October 26 [1855]

Oh, Mother, I don't feel like writing about our long sea voyage, it was so boring, I don't like at all being on the ocean. Furthermore, our traveling company was less than fortunate, all of them Low Germans except a doctor and an American; but for these two, I believe we would have become sick with mere boredom. The American was a wealthy young man, who had taken a trip to Europe for his own pleasure. He understood some German but spoke mostly English; Munch learned quite a bit from him, I some. He was very much like Uncle Constantin in figure and size but most of all because he loved to have fun. One day I put on his overcoat and cap, and he my hat and coat besides a very long black beard, which looked queerly out of place, you can imagine it drew a general applause.

The doctor was a revolutionary, who once had taken part in a disturbance in Germany and had spent several years in jail as a prisoner of the state. He was always in a fight with our captain, who was not a pleasant or well-bred person at all.

The rest of the party were Low German craftsmen, one lumberjack with his wife and three adopted children, who had been to America before and therefore put on an air and had Yankee manners. Next there was a butcher family with two children, a resolute boy who was my best amusement on the whole trip; he called me Aunt and was my steady companion. The other child was a little girl, two months old and with long golden rings in her ears. Then there was a stupid, boorish carpenter, who also had been to America and was now returning with a wife of sorts and an old father, who once during a storm got so scared he appeared amongst us in his underpants. These people played cards and smoked tobacco all day, ate herring with their fingers, and were ill mannered in every respect. The butcher's wife nursed her baby under our noses and never thought a thing of it. The captain was apparently of the same class and with a good portion of vanity; but a competent sailor he was and navigated us safely to our destination while at the same time other vessels had suffered in storms and bad weather.

The food on board was excellent, three courses for dinner every day; for instance, fresh soup that had been kept in hermetic tins, or wine soup, then roast or ham with stewed vegetables, and then pudding or confectures. I must say that this was really my only meal, for mornings and evenings I could not take any more than a piece of cake and a glass of water or wine, although we had fresh bread every day, salami and cheese and cured ham and what else there was; but coffee and tea without cream I simply could not drink. We had powdered milk which was stirred in water, but that was dreadful both in taste and smell. Then there was luncheon, but there I was present only when they served sardines and soft boiled eggs.

During my seasickness I made good use of the wine as this was all I had the first few days until at last I was forced to eat. Yes, I threw it up, and Munch forced me again until at last I felt better, but I was never really well on the ship. I must praise Munch's patience with me; every day he pulled me out of my berth, I had to get up, he got me dressed and, when the weather permitted, took me up on deck and then settled me against the mast since I could absolutely not keep my head up. Oh, what a time, but worse for Munch who always had to be with me, usually in a stuffy air, which, by the way, was present all over the ship.

Our only diversions were some large fish, porpoises, and whales, and sometimes other ships to whom we signaled and talked to each other at a distance of several miles. In the evenings, all the ones who were well generally gathered on the deck and sang with all their might, sometimes I could participate also.

I would like to describe to you one full day. In the morning, Munch and Emil got up first and brought me a cracker and whatever else they thought would please me as I was very particular. Then they went up on deck while I dressed, reeling from pillar to post, and usually did not manage to get ready before the steward rang the bell for breakfast, after which we again went up on the deck and were awfully bored. I would knit a little on a poncho, receiving some assistance from my good friend, the American. Munch read, or wrote with great difficulty on a translation of a German medical handbook. But time went slowly until the steward finally, at 3:30, rang the bell for dinner, which went on in a very amusing way. We could never put down our plates, one had to balance it with one hand and eat with the other, sometimes we had to use cups. However, we could never be quite certain that we did not get dishes and food all over us. When we had finished eating, we usually took a nap, which could last until evening, but note that we seldom finished our dinner until after 5. Afterwards they played cards, but I was busy just hanging on.

Before we went to bed, I often had a good laugh at Munch. To be able to stay in the upper berth he had to pile up mattresses or any other thing he could put his hand on in front of him in order not to come head first out of his berth again. During the night, there were many amusing episodes. We could hardly ever sleep, and to forget about all the annoyance, we gave ourselves over to merriment, took a nip of wine, knocked on the wall to our neighbors, the doctor and the American, who were always ready to have some fun. When the weather was nice and I slept well, it never failed but that I was dreaming about you, my dearly beloved ones at home—oh, some disappointment these dreams have caused me! Yes, even after I was fully awake and heard the roosters crow on board in the morning, and some canaries sing, I did not know what to believe.

Upon our arrival in New York, the captain opened three bottles of champagne, and we drank toasts in Norwegian, Ger-

man, and English. But after this we got the sad news that we had
to be in quarantine as we had nine dead on board, and there
was no doubt but that we had cholera. One sailor died after a
short time, and many were ill. To our dismay, Emil also had an
attack, but with the doctor's wonderful help he recovered completely, and he has been very well since.

First cabin class passengers were allowed to go on shore, but
we were very far from New York. However, the weather was
nice, the church bells were ringing for it was Sunday morning, so
when the captain asked me if I wished to go on shore, we
decided to do so and dressed up nicely, I myself in black silk, the
gentlemen in all their trappings. The captain ordered one of the
boats put out, but it was not the Norwegian sailors to be
rowing[?]. We were put ashore at Staten Island, from where we
sailed with one of the thousand steamboats to New York.

Believe me, it was strange to stand on firm ground again,
and I don't think I have ever been so tired as I was that night
after having walked around in New York the whole day. We
walked in one street only and did not even get to the end of it.
But this street is more than one German mile [about seven
miles] long and New York's only attractive street. Here are
houses of marble and iron, so big and splendid I never thought
anything could be like it. That day we had dinner in a basement
and ate some horrible raw meat. But afterwards we went into
New York's best restaurant, where we had agreed to meet the
captain and the American (so that we could return to the ship
together) — the doctor was with us all the time. Here we enjoyed
hot chocolate and cake of the most delicious kind and beautifully served in small silver pots; yes, everything around us contributed to making it attractive—only nice people, the room
elegantly illuminated by several hundred gaslights. In the middle of the room was a huge staircase leading down to another
hall just as magnificent, and in the middle of this room was a
basin, in which goldfish and turtles were swimming, and
through glass tubes and beautiful things the water sparkled
fresh and clear up in the air.

From there we went on board, once again by a steamer.
The next day a steamboat arrived with a ferry [barge?] to get
the passengers' luggage, and with the customs personnel to check
it. You can imagine we were worried, for they started with the
lumberman's luggage, broke his box open, picked up every item,

lifted up the bureau, opened every drawer, and investigated everything. Oh, oh, I thought, here I get work to do. But after Munch had talked with the man, to our big surprise, not a thing was opened.

November 3 [1855]

Dear Parents-in-Law!

My time is very occupied, wherefore I can only add a few lines and therein include my best greetings and congratulations on the occasion of the 31st Oct.[3] Thank God I am well and doing fine after having overcome the inconveniences from New York. Today Dietrichson and I will go to Wiota, where I will officiate tomorrow, while Caja will stay here with Mrs. Dietrichson. I shall be back the day after tomorrow. Next time you will get a more complete letter from me. May all of you keep well!

Yours, J. S. Munch

Dear Mother!

From the Falchs I trust you have received the pencil-letter from New York. Now I have had so much to do with travels to Dietrichson's annex parishes, where I have been officiating together with him, that I did not have the time to write. But next time I shall give an account of everything. I am quite well—a wonderful thing. The scenery here is ugly. God be with you and all my brothers and sisters.

Yours, Johan

November 3 [1855]

Beloved Parents!

My letter is certainly getting old enough, but now it must be sent off. I can well imagine that you may be a little worried about us, but nevertheless we are doing very well. I have been waiting for Munch and Emil to write also, but as this never seems to happen, you may have to be content with mine only. Munch is certainly to be excused because of his many sermons and travels, but on Emil's account it is only laziness or lack of energy.

Since I wrote last you have had your birthday, my dearest

Mother, God bless you and make you happy with all those around you, for I know very well that your happiness depends most on seeing my dear Father and your big and little children cheerful and content. Yes, God will surely some day bless and gladden such a wonderful mother, He always shapes everything to the best for us, although His ways are incomprehensible. If we only could work diligently on ourselves to make us worthy of a small share of the goodness of our Father in Heaven.

I spent the day of the 31st in peace and quiet with this blessed parson's family. Here is peace of heart and a true Christian devotion to God's will! Oh, how wonderful it is to meet such people. Dietrichson is a marvelous speaker, eager for the promotion of true Christianity, for which he certainly has rendered great service here in America. At the same time, he is very gentle, friendly, and exceedingly merry in his home; I have had many a hearty laugh from all his funny stories and jests. His wife is really also a very amiable Christian person, mild and calm, although it is not easy for her sometimes, brings up her children with good sense and in true Christianity, and looks faithfully after her house, which is not always quite simple as it is terribly difficult to get a maid; indeed, last summer she had only a mere child to help take care of her little baby so she even had to do the scrubbing herself. The least pay for a maid is 1 *Spd.* per week, and more often it is 1½ up to 2 *Spd.*, and they seldom hire for more than one week, then they just leave, and one is very lucky if one can find another. This can be very uncomfortable at times but is actually a small matter, especially for me who am lucky enough to know what it is to be busy, so this problem does not worry me. I wish to God that you would not need any more help than I do since from now on it will be a difficult time for you. But assign the heaviest tasks to your grown-up daughters and save yourself a little, sweet Mother mine.

November 4 [1855]

I really should return to telling you about the rest of our journey, although I find it most uninteresting. We thus went along with the ferry to New York, found a place to leave our luggage, and then went out into the city to meet the Norwegian

consul, Heierdal,[4] but unfortunately he was out of town for a
few days. The best thing for us to do then was to go in search of
living accommodations on our own, and we arrived at a German
Bordinghaus [boarding house], where a strangely masculine
woman gave us a friendly welcome. Here we got two rooms or
whatever I shall call them, for they were so small that one of us
had to wait until the other had undressed; this was no place to
stay except to sleep, so we went down to the drawing room,
where they also sold wines and something of everything. The
woman told me not to feel disheartened but to find myself a seat,
for here in America all were equal. I found a place as far away
from the crowd as possible with Munch and Emil, one on each
side, and we got some newspapers to read.

Soon the gong rang for supper, a table was set with butter,
bread, roast, potatoes in a washbasin, and for each place setting
there was a large bowl with something in it which at first I took
to be meat soup, but on closer scrutiny it was found to be tea
ready brewed. So we enjoyed this as much as possible as everything was very clean. Afterwards we returned to the drawing
room, but when we saw one ruffian worse than the other come in
to have drinks, we preferred to retire and went to bed.

The next morning, straight away we went to check on our
baggage, and here we ran into the rest of our traveling compan-
ions, who were busy taking care of their luggage and buying
tickets to go on the immigrant train that same afternoon. Since
these people were going the same way as we were as far as
Chicago, and we were just like lost sheep in this big city without
knowing a single person, and furthermore since they assured us
that it was absolutely necessary to accompany one's luggage if
one wanted to keep it, we decided that the only sensible thing to
do was to travel with them.

Thus we left the big city of New York on hard wooden
benches, without having seen a thing and with a dismal impression from the whole sojourn. Munch was a little impatient as it
was not very comfortable; one single fish-oil lamp illuminated
the whole big car, where at least 50 people not exactly of the
most refined kind were gathered. But now I had my time since I
was not on the water; I made him a bed of coats, and all of us
fell asleep.

However, this joy did not last for very long. We were soon

turned out as we were about to cross the Albany River.[5] Oh, what a night! We were driven like cattle without knowing where we were going, darkness around us, between steam engines and boxcars, I tore my dress as it was caught in the rails, Munch cut his finger carrying the black suitcase which we had brought with us in the car, and we were afraid of losing each other. I found it so totally absurd that I broke into laughter. This Munch and Emil could absolutely not comprehend, so they were a little annoyed with me.

Finally we got on board a steamer, it was dark here too; however, we found a corner and had just got ourselves settled down when once again they called *"heraus—heraus!"*—and we were across the river. Several men with lanterns came and pulled us hither and thither, for they were [land] speculators. Finally, with some of our company, we came to another German [boarding] house and found lodging for the night as the railway [train] was not to leave until the next day at 11 o'clock. Here something horrible was served to us in the morning; I fussed, but Munch and Emil ate remarkably well. At this station we got better cars, and we stayed undisturbed in one and the same car for more than 24 hours. We then felt rather comfortable, surrounded only by acquaintances from the ship, if only the smell hadn't been so bad, and the seats had been somewhat softer!

Our food on the whole trip consisted mostly of bread, a piece of ham, and a little cheese and wine which we had hurriedly bought in New York. To be sure, even in the middle of the night, big men and women came into the car with coffee for us in large tin pails; a couple of times when they did not look too dirty, we bought some of it, for we had to have something to relish, and with us emigrants the train did not stop long enough to enable us to procure anything of the kind.

Finally we reached Niagara and crossed the bridge, much more quietly than on the ground itself. I only wish that it should have been Andreas Munch instead of myself who had seen these two wonders of art and nature, then you would perhaps by his description have been able to form an idea about it. There are two bridges, one above the other, the lower one for driving, the upper one for the railroad only. On each side of the river are two enormous towers of granite stones which support the whole structure. The bridge itself hangs in, and I believe consists in part of, fine steel wires which have been entwined so many times that they have reached about the thickness of a log of timber. It looks beautiful, though, and what caught my eye were two flower beds at each end, laid out on the bridge itself, even arranged as a small garden with a bench in the middle.

At this station we bid farewell to the emigrants and their pleasant company and bought tickets for *Pasagertrainet* [the passenger train], whereby we also had time to make a trip to the waterfall, which is some distance from the bridge. Indeed, steamboats go up under the bridge and almost clear up to the cataract. There is not at all a strong sough from the fall, for it is not high but marvelously wide; it is actually divided into two falls by a beautiful patch of woods, through which again run several small waterfalls with lovely little bridges across. Far out in the cataract itself is a tower, which can be reached by a bridge; we were on the other side and could not get there.

After this very interesting walk we had a good supper and then proceeded into the far more comfortable passenger cars, but these were already so crowded with people that we barely obtained some poor seats. Sleep was out of the question, besides they put so overly much in *Stowen* [the stove]; indeed, it is unbelievable how hot the Americans want it, we most certainly would have fainted if we had not been able to open our window —you see, there is a window by each bench and a *Stowe* in the middle of the car.

The 5th [November 1855]

Well, beloved Parents, this will never see the end, and I will rather send this now with this mail and continue next time, for I am sure you are longing for a letter, just as I am very dearly longing to hear from you, for we have not been able to receive a letter from you, probably because Heierdal was out of town. Oh, Mother dear, it will be a long time yet to wait! The address you will find on the enclosed little slip.

Munch preached for the first time on his birthday in Chicago. The next day, the 22nd, we arrived by railroad here at Pastor Dietrichson's. The following Sunday, the two pastors traveled together to Dietrichson's annex parishes, they left on Saturday and did not return until the early morning hours of

Wednesday. All Saints' Day Dietrichson preached here in his own main church. Munch, Emil, and I took Communion from him, and he said such a wonderful prayer for us which I shall never forget.

Saturday, the 3rd, all our three gentlemen went to Wiota, from where they are not expected to return until tomorrow night. We are all in good health, the air is fresh and sweet, certainly milder than in Norway, there is no sign of winter yet. Here one is not at all in the wilderness, all around are big cities, and everything is obtainable for money, but expensive it is. Some day this week we are all going together down to *Beløit* [Beloit] to buy some necessities and to have ourselves daguerreotyped; but these [the daguerreotypes] will not reach you until next spring with a Norwegian who is leaving America. In Chicago I carried a baby to the font for christening, Munch was the godfather, and it was baptized by Pastor Unonius.

Farewell, dearly beloved Parents, brothers and sisters! God keep all of you in good health and contentment. Thousands of warm greetings to friends and acquaintances

from your well contented Caja Munch.

Munch asked that this letter be forwarded to Christiania. For you, dear Mother-in-Law, I have no worries, nor for Caroline and Jette, because you love me and will surely not make fun of my pitiful letter, but I will ask you most sincerely not to let any stranger read it. You, my dear Jette, are probably the one who most likely can take care of that. God give that all of you, my dear ones in the capital, were in good health. How do you feel now, Jette? And my sweet little Johan? Now he will probably forget Aunt Caja. My heartfelt greetings also go to all of you. I am longing awfully to hear from everybody, Grandmother, aunts, uncle, cousins, and all, all who remember

your affectionate Caja.

Farewell! Kiss little Emilie from me. All the daguerreotypes are hanging on the wall here and have met with general admiration.

We have unpacked here and have found only Munch's lampshade broken; but then Munch and Emil fastened, nailed, and supported the boxes all the way. Had we not traveled as emigrants, we surely should have lost everything. More later, my time is very short.

Mrs. Caja Munch to her Parents, Mr. and Mrs. F. W. S. Falch

Wiota, the Kronborg Farm, November 25, 1855

My beloved Parents!

It is Sunday evening, Munch left yesterday morning for his annex parish, Dodgeville, and will not return until Tuesday night. In the meantime, Emil and I are alone at home, and we are very comfortable in our new residence with an old nice bachelor, Even Kronborg, who lives right across from the church and the parsonage and has offered us free lodging until our own house will be ready to move into, perhaps after Christmas.

I wish of my whole heart that you, my kind Father and Mother, could look in on us and see how cozy it is here, only not just now; for I cannot deny that presently it is somewhat lonely, but wait until my dear Munch is at home, for to me he crowns it all. However, time will pass, for Emil and I have a lot to keep us busy these days. We are in every respect our own servants, although there are three confirmants who have offered to help me, most likely because it is something new, otherwise they are usually not that willing. But we have no room for a maid, and besides it is not at all necessary, for I hire help for washing, and our housekeeping business goes like a breeze; moreover, our host Even has been a servant in Norway and is as good a cook as anybody, and he is so helpful and pleasant he does not know what all to do for us.

We have two very nice rooms all to ourselves, in one of them is a cooking stove which serves me perfectly both as a kitchen stove and as a baking oven. I have smartened up the room with our four chairs, which are much admired, my chest of drawers stands in our bedroom with my dear Grandmother's spread on top because it has got a few nails in it here and there during the voyage; above it, all my very dear daguerreotypes are hanging, amongst which I miss very much Grandmother and everybody there, besides little Johan and brother Oskar. In the cupboard next to the stove I keep my crockery and kitchen utensils, very nice and rather complete. We got almost all of it in Beloit and, thanks to Dietrichson, on six months credit, which is a good help to a newcomer; however, Munch isn't quite penniless. We had some left over from our voyage, although that took quite a lot, and then he received 39 dollars in offerings here in Wiota the first time he preached, besides for ministerial functions far more than expected. Oh, I hope that by God's help all will go well here. Munch will, if we can judge from our short stay so far, get along very nicely with his congregation, they really compete in doing all that they possibly can for us and assist us in every way. Four men, each with two horses, came all the way down to Dietrichson's for our baggage and ourselves.

We left the Dietrichsons last Friday in our own *Boggi* [buggy], a type of vehicle that looks like our little *Svenskevogn* [Swedish carriage]; this is the most common conveyance here and almost always with two horses in harness, which they claim is the safest as the horses ordinarily are rather skittish. One always rides with four wheels, and all vehicles drive in the same tracks, otherwise one would not be able to get anywhere, for such roads as we have here you can not possibly imagine, one can really describe it as riding "over stock and stone." Nobody drives after dark or when the weather is bad.

The 28th [November 1955]

Dear Mother mine!

I am so happy, so happy! At last I received your dear letter. God bless you for every word, it made me feel so good; I have tried not to let on how great my longing has been, but now it is all over. God be praised and thanked for every word from my dear home! And would God in Heaven make it so that everything continues to be well there!

The—I don't know.

Time and days run so fast for me, dear Mother, and I have so much to write about; it is already a long time since I finished my last letter at Dietrichson's, which I hope you have received by now. I paid the postage since I found it much cheaper from here, 48 cents only; now I shall not pay for the next one I send, and then you must tell me the difference. I know Munch has paid 1 *Spd.* and more for letters from here.

If I only could recall how far I had come in my previous letter, and what I have written and not written; however, I believe I had mentioned Niagara. I am sending you, Mother, a small twig picked close by the fall from a couple of big trees that were standing there; isn't it the same type as our Copenhagen tree?

From Niagara, as mentioned, we went by *Esprestrain* [express train] after having tried in all possible ways what it means to travel as an emigrant; however, I do believe that it was thanks to this that we were able to keep our baggage, for most of the people we know of have sometimes lost half of theirs, and Munch and Emil had to do some repairs on our boxes at each station. They were thrown around so that the pieces flew in all directions, once the bottom almost fell out of the crate where the bureau was, and in the end the iron hoops were the only thing that held the casks together.

We got an acquaintance from the ship to look after our baggage from Niagara as far as Chicago, where we met once again safe and happy, although not without having been exposed to some danger, for no sooner had we got some small space in the overcrowded passenger cars, where we were to spend the night in the most terrible heat without any rest at all, when there was a stop and we had to get out in the dark and walk some distance in deep sand alongside a big ditch, with smoking steam engines and fire on all sides, to move into another railroad car. Another engine had been coming full speed against our train, but since this one did not have any cars behind, it steered right out into the sand, and in the rush it tore the rails apart; thanks to this our lives were saved since this way our train had time enough to stop. Indeed, it is dreadful how many people lose their lives on the railroads here. They are, however, much more careful now as there is a big fine for every human life lost by carelessness.

In Chicago we were put up once again in a small room in a German boarding house because the hotels asked one and a half dollar a day for each person; but we did not stay there long. Munch left at once to locate the Swedish minister Unonius, who was not at home; but he received an equally good assistance from a true Norwegian, Torkelsen, who took care of us so all our sorrows were forgotten. Here came one Norwegian after the other and invited us to see them, so we were not at home one single day; one day we were even invited out to three different places at the same time. You can imagine how wonderful it was for us to find so much friendliness and to meet again with our countrymen, it is a feeling which is hard to describe. Here I met a shoemaker who was married to a girl from Qvelsogn.[6] I have forgotten her father's name, but it was one of the old acquaintances up there whom Father certainly knows, she went to confirmation together with Sophie and knew us all very well. They were wealthy people and exceptionally graceful. We had a good dinner there, and Munch bought himself a pair of inexpensive boots from him.

When Pastor Unonius returned, we had to move to his house, and Munch simply had to preach before he left, which just happened to take place on his birthday, and he was also godfather for the first time while I for the first time presented a beautiful little girl at the font. Now this is old hat to me, for I have later carried two children to their baptism for farmers here in our congregation and have become godmother to a little boy at Fleischer's, who lives next door to Dietrichson and is in charge of the Norwegian printing press over here.

We left Chicago on the 22nd of October and arrived by railroad the same afternoon in Beloit, where Pastor Dietrichson met us with horses and buggy and received us with a *cordial* welcome. Our baggage, which had arrived ahead of us, he had already sent to his house. That same evening, we arrived at his parsonage where we indeed were taken care of in all ways possible. Right off, Munch and Dietrichson were *Dus*,[7] likewise his wife and I, and all four of us are very good friends. Munch accompanied and assisted Dietrichson in his annex parish, and they traveled together on a trip to Wiota, where also Emil went along. Munch delivered a sermon for Dietrichson and conducted Communion for him and his wife, and we took Communion from Dietrichson.

Indeed, we stayed for more than a month with these kind people, it was really hard to leave them. I got all our dirty clothes washed there. One day they drove with us to Beloit to buy coffee, sugar, crockery, a stove and all such things of necessity. The same day, we also picked up Holfeldt and his wife, who arrived from Quebec, where he makes money in the summer, but every winter they have their lodgings with the Dietrichsons.

Now it became even livelier in the house with so many people together every day. The following day was Mrs. Dietrichson's birthday, she received many beautiful gifts, and from me a poncho which I had finished during the voyage. It so happened that the Fleischers had a christening on the same day, so all of us went to their place for roast goose, turkey, chicken, and fresh [vegetable] soup with meatballs for dinner, and with this we had a delicious red wine. Then the whole party went over to Dietrichson's. Among us was also a Norwegian by the name Suckow, who could sing and play the guitar; he commenced at once on mine, and now started a general singing and gaiety. Later on, Holfeldt produced champagne and cherry wine, in which toasts were given to the hostess, to us and others, and the day ended happy and cheerful.

Often during the following days did we have a small glass of wine since Holfeldt had quite a supply of good things! Yes, we had some merry days together in all innocence, brought about for the most part by Dietrichson and myself. Furthermore, Pastor [A. C.] Preus came here for a couple of days to see Munch, also a nice and pleasant man. We are invited to his home for Christmas, but I doubt that anything will come of it.

You can't imagine what a good bargain I have made with Holfeldt's assistance. You see, he had upon request bought a gold watch at 25 dollars for Pastor Preus's wife, but since we brought one for her, she did not really need this. I, however, could very well use one as my silver watch, which I had exchanged for a little more than 6 dollars [in Hamburg], had a defect and went 26 hours in a day. Holfeldt noted this, too, whereupon he offered to exchange watches if Munch would pay him 20 dollars by next Christmas, which after much consideration he consented to do. It is seldom that such a chance occurs, so now I have the most beautiful and *excellent* gold watch standing in a small case on my bureau with a small gold key by its side. Do you think we did the wrong thing, Father? We should first of all, maybe, have considered our debt. But such an opportunity does not often come one's way.

After several days of gratifying company we left our good friends, the Dietrichsons, and went to our own present home with another good friend, Ole Monssen (take note of this name, for he is a remarkable man in our congregation). However, we did not arrive that same day on account of poor weather and road conditions, but took shelter for the night in a town called Monroe, where we passed by, and came to Wiota on Saturday, where dinner had been prepared for us at a nearby blacksmith's; [8] but we left soon afterwards to continue to our present place of residence with Even Kronborg, where Munch then wrote his sermon and officiated the next day in our church. I was present also and carried a baby to the font, although it was very cold; the church, you see, is not quite finished yet, so one sits on rough boards put up on stumps, and you can see the sky through it in many places. But the location is attractive on a hill right across from the parsonage. All of the grounds next to and between the church [and the parsonage] belong to us. A little brook runs through, in which there are even some small fish; its spring is only a little ways from where the kitchen door is going to be, comes right out of the ground so we will always have nice fresh and cold water, a great blessing, isn't that true, Father? We will try to get a *Springhus* [spring house] over it so that I can keep my milk and other things there in the summer. We can very easily keep ducks and geese since they will have plenty of water. Our garden will probably be on a sloping *Batum* [bottom] that stretches from the parsonage down to the stream, beautiful and good prospects, but the weeds are supposed to be bad. The Dietrichsons have not been able to keep a decent garden here, but Munch and I do not give up at the first obstacle. The front of the house faces the church and the hill below, with a raised level for driving between the house and the slope. Here, then, will be the main entrance to the big palace, which consists of three rooms on the first floor and two upstairs, one of which is now being finished with some assistance from Munch, and a big cellar. A kitchen is going to be built next to this and should be ready not later than the end of July, but then we will have a nice kitchen and pantry built in stone. Yes, you may be sure we already have wonderful friends who are arranging things for us. I shall send you a small drawing of it all so that you can have some idea about it. Munch can make a better one later.

Our congregation consists, of course, of all kinds of people, but as an example of one of the good ones, I will tell you what Ole Monssen *visibly* has done for us in this short time. He came down to Dietrichson's to pick us up with his horses, paid room and board for us in Monroe, gave Emil a pair of good mittens as his hands were cold, paid 22 cents to have a new crystal put on

Emil's watch, treated us to apples and beer in another town.
When his horses had to have water on the way, he bought for
this purpose a new painted pail with iron hoops, which he gave
us. Sunday he drove us to church and afterwards home to his
place, he lives quite a ways from us, is married for the second
time to a very attractive widow and has many children; furthermore he is a man of several thousand. We were extremely well
treated in his home, stayed overnight, and went the next day by
sleigh to another important man in the congregation, Ole Brun-
volla, where the congregation meeting was to be held, which
Munch will direct from now on; till now they have always ended
up with quarrels and disputes, but now it is pleasant to see how
peaceable they are, and Munch gets approval of everything he
wants, I believe even the most stubborn ones have quite a bit of
respect and esteem for him. May God provide that it always may
go so well!

A couple of days later, Ole Monssen came driving over to
our place with two bushels of wheat flour, the two hindquarters
of a young heifer, two piglets for roasting, a big jar of lard, eight
pounds of butter, 3½ dozen eggs, a big jar of cream, a large sack
of potatoes, another one with carrots and onions, two *Rabbitter*
[rabbits], or hares as they are called at home, but smaller, and
quite a few thick candles; later on he brought us more cream
and a bag of nuts. All this from one man. In addition we have
been given butter, lots of pork, chickens, *Rabbitter, Qvæls*
[quails]—some kind of bird bigger than a thrush—potatoes,
cream, bread, cake, beets, cucumbers, and many other small
items. As you see, dear Mother, we are not suffering but have
provisions in abundance. The only thing Munch has bought is
some good dried fish for a change, and a piece of beef, which I
scraped, pounded, and made into some extra good meatballs
while Munch was in Dodgeville—to his great surprise; indeed, I
am praised quite frequently for my cooking, but it is no trick to
prepare when there is so much to make from, and indeed, we
have been living very luxuriously, usually a hot meal three times
a day, for we just had to eat so that the food should not be
spoiled. We have had ragout of hare several times, real fresh
soup with meatballs, ground beef steaks, creamed chicken, quail
fried and stewed, delicious roasted piglets, roast beef, and often
apple compot made from dried apples, some of which were given

to us, and some we bought, and many other good things. Cakes
are frequently given to us, I have made flead-cakes and several
other cookies, completely without a scale or measure; but we
don't take it so seriously here, everything is done in a hurry.

Yankee housewives are sometimes real ladies, and at other
times, when they cannot get any servants, they themselves tend
to the most ordinary chores. Their food consists of pork, coffee,
and pie morning, noon, and evening. The Norwegians have
consistently adopted this, and we are really tired of it, especially
since these dishes are not at all our favorite ones. We have
regularly been served this every place, and we have already been
quite a bit around in the community, partly on business and
partly to get acquainted; I have faithfully accompanied Munch
everywhere.

Surely you would not have recognized us had you met us on
one of these trips, riding in what they here call a *Lombervogn*
[lumber wagon], which looks just about like our box carts, but
twice as long and with four wheels; we sit on a board with arms
around each other to keep from falling out; the shaking is
terrible because there is no snow yet and the ground is frozen
hard.

We cannot say that we ever live in quiet, because either
there are people coming here to talk and visit with us, and then I
always have to make coffee and arrange for some food, or somebody will bring their "team" to take us to their place. Just
recently, Munch was taken to a sick person several miles from
here in the middle of the night, it was an unpleasant trip, so
dark and cold, but he is in good condition after it as well as after
all his other strains. For here is really not one day free. I believe,
however, that this is just a life for him, and I hope to God that
we will continue to be as comfortable as human beings can expect to be.

Today a man arrived to talk to Munch about getting him to
take over a new settlement not too far from here. I went with
Munch up there some time ago when he had a service for some
of them in a small sitting room. There were 68 taking Communion besides several christenings. For an altar they used a plank
which was put down on the floor. The minister was surrounded
by people all around, and he had just enough space to stand up.
Among the children there were two who had to be christened by

the emergency ceremony as they took ill due to the crowd and the heat; furthermore there was nobody who could sing, so I had to start them out on the Amen and other things.

Indeed, here in America one really gets to see and hear a lot of things one neither could have imagined possible nor would ever have heard of before. God help all those who here wander upon the path of delusion. Here are so many sectarians and persons who call themselves ministers and try to tempt the people that it really takes a steadfast faith for the ordinary man if he is to keep his Christian belief. We visited a Norwegian Methodist church in Chicago, where two persons stood on a platform and preached all but the Word of God. They banged the chair, threw themselves to the floor, and screamed at the top of their voices; finally, to give more force to his speech, one of them shook his head for a full half hour so violently that he turned blue in the face. Yes, it is really sad for many of our Norwegians over here, and there is certainly a great need for ministers.

Should the Norwegian, Barmand from Drammen, come over here next spring, please, dear Mother, do not send Munch's coat or money for it as he once gave the coat to Bernt, and we don't need it; but if you would rather send me some incense, which we cannot get here, and also the double volume of hymn music, and if there should happen to be some new book published; for everything else is much easier to get here than at home. I do regret, however, that I did not bring with me a small coffee kettle, because here you find only tall tin pots; but I have now learned to brew in these, and I make a fairly good coffee. Furthermore, I miss a pudding form and a *Goro* [wafer] iron as such things are unknown here. Americans never have soup, they don't even know what it is, meatballs arouse great curiosity; on the whole, they never use any kind of gravy or prepared food. Fruit porridge with cream they don't even know how to eat, but they enjoy it with delight. Such items are of course impossible to send, although I know you would love to do so, my sweet Mother, but we will survive without them; besides, I can do as Mrs. Dietrichson and cook the pudding in a tin pail, but she had to stand and steady it until the pudding was cooked.

Munch has twenty-seven confirmants to teach every Wednesday, some of whom are almost as big as he is but hardly able to read one Norwegian word. They have attended an English school, which here is regarded as the most distinguished thing to do, so he has to serve fully as a schoolteacher. Emil is also going to start in an English school, which is being conducted right across from the parsonage; one goes to classes absolutely free. Eventually I am sure he would like to go out and earn some money, for which there is plenty of opportunity here, even for as much as a dollar a day; but I believe he himself wants to write and give you more information. Beloved Parents, you must not in the least be concerned about Emil; with God's help he will do very well here. Munch believes it will be the best for him if he would go and live with an American as soon as he gets an opportunity, that way he would both learn the language well and also how to run a farm in this country, which only these people do to any degree of perfection, and he could then earn as much as 20 dollars a month. This would always be something for him which he later on could invest in land either here or at home, because he does not need anything for his own personal use, especially if he would stay near us, which I hope he can, as there are lots of Americans around here. (Even Kronborg, with whom we live, wants to sell his farm. Munch has talked to Emil about it, convenient and easy and suitable for him) .

I hope that we, too, will have the opportunity to learn the language. In any case, you will surely find it very broken, for here I regularly hear everything mentioned by its English name, for which I already have given you some proofs. *Team* you must interpret as two horses, but ask my dear Sophie, she will be sure to know. Greet her a thousand times and ask if there is a possibility of getting a letter from her, I should so much like to have one.

                                   The 17th [December 1855]
It is soon Christmas, beloved Parents, indeed, much sooner than I had thought. God bless all of you both before, during, and after! and bestow upon you many happy, blessed days, and give you peace in the Name of Jesus!

By now you must have started the usual balls, where I suppose the general talk will concern itself with our well-being. Nanna and Lagertha, I am sure, know the answers by heart, it should be an excellent topic for the good gentlemen who are short of conversation. You are probably having your usual *Trou-bel* (exertion) preparing for Christmas, I can see you in my thoughts. Please take a little care of yourself, dear Mother, get your healthy daughters going, they can take it better than you can; but you are too concerned about them, I am sure that is so, for if you were with me here, I would not be allowed to do the things I have managed over and over again; however, I feel perfectly well doing it, and I flourish and am in good health all the time, just as much as Munch and Emil. In fact, all three of us have gained weight, especially Emil.

Yesterday it was decided in the Congregation Meeting that we should continue to stay with Even for the winter because the plastering in the parsonage could not be done properly as long as the walls were so cold, and we are comfortable here. Some time in January, I shall get a milch cow from Ole Monssen, probably for a small payment. Here the cows give three to four times as much milk as at home, although they are mostly kept outdoors all winter; the only animals which have a roof over their heads are the horses, for the others they only throw some straw over a couple of bars, under which they take cover during the night and in bad weather. Oxen are often used for driving, and they keep a lot of them, yet one has to pay 100 dollars or more for two of them. They are seldom mean, in spite of their size. Horses and cows are even more expensive. Munch could surely not get himself a good horse for less than 100 to 150 dollars; he is just now over at the place of an American to look one over.

Outhouses are rarely seen here (not even the most needed ones can be found). Hay, straw, and grain are kept in stacks. The wagons are made of wood only and can stand all kinds of weather. No, here they usually (although there are exceptions) put up only a square house of logs and smear mortar or some-thing on the inside. The whole house, therefore, consists of one single room, with windows in all four directions and a stove in the middle of the floor. Here lives the family, whether big or small, day and night; here all kinds of work is performed, not to mention that they sometimes suckle two or three urchins at the same time right in front of our eyes, but they clean them up also —hush!

The Dietrichsons and we once had dinner in a house like that, and several times later we have been to parties in this fashion. This, of course, is the only company we have here, so we may be a little peculiar if we return some time among cultured people, they may be staring at us as if we were strange animals. It has even happened twice that we had to spend the night with them. One time the man and his wife were lying on the floor, Munch and I in their bed, and Emil and a son, who goes for confirmation, in another bed. Another time the man, his wife, and a sister were in one bed, and Munch and I in another. Isn't it jovial? But as I said, here everything is possible, and anything goes.

January 1, 1856

Beloved Parents!

The day, indeed, has drawn to a close, but such a strong longing came over me to talk to you although I am so far, far away from you; God be praised that I am able to think and to write! Have thanks for every treasured memory from the old year! God give that we could look back with contentment upon what we have practiced and accomplished therein, and enter a new year in the Name of Jesus. Then peace and joy will surely not fail us, and God's blessings never be missing.

It has been a strange Christmas for me. On Christmas Eve we all had rice porridge, roast beef, and Christmas cookies together with Even and a man and his wife and a little child, who are staying here in the house. Afterwards we said our prayers and sang a hymn and thought of our dear ones at home, who already by that time were sound asleep. You will recall that you are six hours ahead of us in time, which is hard on us sometimes, especially on such holidays when I wish so much for our thoughts to meet, but then it has to be worked out by calculation. Oh, how often have I not taken the watch and figured out what you were doing during the joyful Christmas time; at present, for example, it is very likely that you—Father, Mother, Bernt, Nanna, Lagertha, and maybe Oskar—are attending a ball and are dancing in the best manner at this very moment; it is 5 o'clock here, that means 11 over there. Wilhelm is probably this year one of your steady escorts. Oh, if one only could fly over to you for a little while! I have never seen sister Lagertha at a ball, and in all probability I never shall. But do not think that I am sad—no, my God and my Jesus are consoling me many a time. And when my Munch returns from Dodgeville, I am again gay and happy as a bird, thanking God sincerely for all the good things He daily bestows upon me.

On the First Day of Christmas, I was with my dear Munch. He gave a beautiful sermon in his main church, but it was so cold that both words and thoughts were almost frozen away, although we lit a fire in the stove in the church. On the way home I wanted to run to keep myself from freezing but tripped in my black silk dress and tore it, but not too much—uh! You will have to be informed about everything, dear Mother, good and bad. That day, too, I carried a baby to the font; soon I cannot justify doing this any more, but what am I to do? It is hard to say no. There were much too few people in church, and the offerings were accordingly only about 16 dollars.

On the Second Day of Christmas, he went early in the morning to *Jællerston* [Yellowstone] and did not return until the Third Day. On the Fourth Day of Christmas we had supper with our nearest neighbor, Hans Haug. And bright and early on the Fifth Day, my dear Munch went with our good friend Ole Monssen to Dodgeville, from where he will not return until tomorrow evening. I wanted to go with him, but the weather turned too bad and cold. At present the roads are good, and the weather has been nice the last two days. For the winter Munch has rented an old bearskin coat from a man here, and I put on him everything I possibly can, but it certainly takes a lot to protect yourself from the cold here. Only those who have traveled in these parts can have any idea about the cold wind that blows over the prairie. Munch did a foolish thing when he sold his big sheepskin coat, because an ordinary overcoat is of no use here, but who would have thought of that; however, he will be better off next winter as Holfeldt has promised to get him one from Quebec.

Long interval until January 21, 1856.

The 19th, the day before yesterday, I received your letters, dearest Mother mine; oh, what a joy! When I say thousands and thousands of thanks for every word, I am still not capable of thanking you enough for them. Yes, I can hardly believe that anybody would be so delighted in *our* letters or devour every word with such greed as we do over here with yours. Sophie, isn't that just like her, I dare say she would not forget me, so thank you from the bottom of my heart, my Sophie, for your beautiful pleasant letter!—and please make me happy more often with similar ones. You can not possibly imagine what great pleasure you give me, even the most insignificant news from home is of the greatest interest to us. Write, please write, all of you! big and small, young and old! Yes, I impose on everyone who loves me to write, otherwise I will strike them off my friendship list! Tell that to all my friends.

You, my Mother, are my constant consolement. I know you sacrifice many hours of your sleep to write to me, and although you have a tenfold gratitude therefore, I cannot and will not but very seriously forbid you to do this. You have to take a little more care of yourself here in this life, Mother dear, and not put your health in jeopardy; there are those who will still need you for many, many years to come! Furthermore, it would be nice if you could enjoy some good days in your life; it can not possibly be God's good will that a person should not even have one single Sunday free from housework. No, Mother, once in a while let somebody else act your part, and you follow your own inclinations, then I am sure I know what you will prefer to do. In the past it has been my neglect so, my dear sisters, realize before it is too late what is only your duty to do. I have much to blame myself for, I could have got up earlier in the morning and helped you, my sweet Mother, making sandwiches, dressing the children, and insisting I wanted to prepare the meals alone now and then on Sundays, so that you could go to church. But the regret is here too late, and now it is hard to suffer, because only now do I comprehend what an indolent state I was in. It is strange how you wake up when you leave home and see and hear so much of both good and bad, then you start searching your own self and your relationship to your God and Savior. Dear sisters, Nanna and Lagertha, both of you write that you would wish to hear Munch's good sermons, but be assured that for a true Christian, who goes to church with the right attitude, for him it makes no difference whether the Word of God is announced to him by a good or by a poor preacher, it is after all God's Word, and never let this keep you away from seeking

God's House. From there alone, and from no other place, comes true happiness and joy in this world. Remember why we have been placed upon this earth! and you will find that we are wanting in much for salvation.

The 22nd [January 1856]

We did indeed receive the letters, and they were seized fervently after such a long wait. You must never again let a month pass without writing. The three of us grabbed some pages each and read and talked and hushed each other down. Munch got hold of the part where you told about Lina's engagement, and after having teased my curiosity for a while, he finally told me, so you got a very long nose, Mutter, for your cunning idea. I was very glad to have this bit of news, though; may God make her happy. In a way I had already matched them, for he praised her very highly to me last time I was in Christiania. In any case, greet and congratulate them from me should anybody write or talk to them, it is going to be fun some time to see Lina as a stately mistress in the Capital. What is the name of Emilie's husband? and how is Modesta? is she going to be married soon?

From *Aftenbladet,* which we keep, we had already found out that you and Father had been to Christiania, and you can imagine my great longing to hear more about it. Oh, how well I thought you deserved that trip. Do it more often.

It was impertinent of our good doctor in New York to make you wait so long for the letters, especially since he knew we were anxious to get them to you. Indeed, one day I started thinking maybe the strange address had caused you to worry. I mentioned it to Munch right away, and he had thought so, too. But God be praised, now all this anxiety is over for you, my dear ones!

You must not think that I am in the least afraid to make this journey once again, far from it, I have already forgotten about the seasickness and should be more than willing to venture out on the big ocean at once to reach my dear home; for we will never willingly make this our home as we are much too fond of our dear Norway. But I do not regret this journey at all if God will keep His protecting hand over us.

Everything considered, we do not really miss anything ex-

cept the company of cultured people instead of these silly peasants, who for the most part cannot comprehend at all that we are
a step above them and have more requirements. No, they regard
themselves maybe fully as high and always say *Du,* and many
such things, which sometimes really are highly ridicuolus.
([Added in the margin:] With this remark, Munch believes that
I mean to make a fuss over the *Du* of the peasant; however, I am
not referring to the *Du* of the mountain peasant but to those
who know better) . For example, many will simply call me Caja.⁹
Here are not even any cultured Americans as we are too far
inland where only [land] speculators and such rubbish are rov-
ing.

However, theft is rare here, all of us can go out and leave
the house open, nothing will be missing unless perhaps an American may enter and start a fire in the stove to warm himself or
find some food and drink if he is hungry. This is a custom in this
country, no one feels embarrassment here. Many have come to
our house, I have understood what they were saying and made
gestures to them, but I will hardly be able to learn to talk the
language since there is so little opportunity for that here. Emil
has started in the English school and is learning to spell.

But I trust you would like to hear a little more about our
Christmas. Before the holidays, we were just as busy as everybody at home (here they pay no attention to Christmas, and
many even work right through the whole holiday season. Naturally, even in this respect, the Norwegians are just copycats) .
Munch was studying his many sermons, and Emil and I were
busy with butchering, baking and preparing, don't think we
would not live up to the occasion! Munch bought a hindquarter
of a cow which weighed 200 pounds; the whole cow was 60
Bismerpund [about 700 pounds] after skinning and cleaning.
Munch saw it alive; it was a real monster, he said. We were
joking at home, if you remember, with Emil that he would be
shooting the animals we wanted butchered, but that is common
here; they let them out in the field and just about go on a hunt
for them. Blood and intestines and things of that sort are
seldom used. Some of this meat [from the hindquarter that
Munch bought] I scraped for meatballs, Emil pounded it with
the small Norwegian wooden mortar in a trough, and I got the
best and finest meatballs one could possibly make; today we had
the last leftovers from them, and Munch sighed when he learned

we had no more. I also made quenelles, beef olives, collared beef, and I salted down a barrelful. I hardly know how we shall be able to eat it all. We also had two wonderful hams given to us, which I have salted. Munch came driving home one day with a fairly large pig, I would think a year old (he did not put it to the wagon, though). I am going to pickle these small hams, the head I cooked into headcheese along with a bigger one and quite a few pig's feet, which were given to us by another man. I believe I can get some guts, and then I plan to make Lübecker sausage, I have saved up pork and beef for that. I baked flead-cakes, crullers, and gingerbread cookies or the so-called "Father's cooky," everything very good. But my big Christmas bread came out best of all. Munch bestowed quite a bit of praise on me for all this. Citrus, raisins, and almonds I bought in Beloit; Ole Monssen has given me pailsful of eggs, and I have still many left; we pick up a quart of milk every day from a woman close by, but pretty soon now we will have our own cow. It has not been necessary for us yet to buy butter, it has been given to us from several sources. In other words, Munch has been let off very cheaply so far with the groceries, he has not yet had to buy anything but the meat I mentioned.

We have so many rabbits we will hardly be able to eat them all. Emil has also caught some of these; his gun does not work any more, but he has taken them with his hands after they have been chased down into some small holes for him by a little dog, which I can almost say has sense like a human. This dog is completely devoted to Emil and does not leave him for one minute all day. I don't think Even will manage to keep it when we move from here some day. Just now these good friends are playing outside the window. Emil has also caught a few thrush in some kind of a trap commonly used here, which he put together himself.

I have seen several live deer right outside the house. One was shot the other day by our neighbor, we were given a piece of it. Maybe quite a few of those at home would have liked to participate in this meal with us; first we had that marvelous venison, and afterwards there was soup made from dried peaches. Otherwise I have to use syrup and vinegar for fruit soup this year instead of fruit juice, which I have not been able to obtain.

Believe me, my sweet Mother, the bottles of raspberries and

cherries which I brought with me, have come to good use (the gooseberries, Lagertha, had completely disappeared). First I used the juice, then I filled the bottles with water and shook them, and now I am going to crush all of it and boil it up with sugar and water. Next year I will be sure to have jam, juice, and wine because there are lots of raspberries, blackberries, plums, and grapes in the woods here; furthermore, one of our farmers has a big orchard with currants and apples from which I will benefit until we have our own. There is a Norwegian gardener in the congregation, and he will help us with the yard next spring, although all that can be done is to plant trees as the ground will have to stay ploughed up through the summer. The wild apples are no good, but at a Norwegian shoemaker's I have tasted wine made from wild grapes, and it was extremely good; however, it takes a lot of sugar as the grapes are small and sour. There is supposed to be quite a lot of them around here; I can now see the dried vines twine themselves among the trees, sometimes the trunk is much thicker than an arm.

I hope that next year we shall not be so completely out of beverages as we are now. Our standby is milk and water, because it is not supposed to be healthy to drink only water. The water is very hard, although deliciously fresh and tasty. One can never wash in it without first having given it a good boil with soap, and then a hard crust forms on top which has to be removed. In the bottom of the teakettle an insoluble scale accumulates that becomes harder and harder, in the end I don't think it will hold more than half of what it used to.

You should never any more buy the expensive green soap, Mother. Boil your own according to *Fru Winsnes*.[10] So do I and everybody else here as it is not to be had for money, and our clothes become just as white as at home. I have already twice had a small great-wash, but from now I am going to follow the custom in this country and have the maid wash every Monday what we have soiled during the week. It is not too difficult to find help in these parts, here are quite a few for whom it is hard to manage; three widows have already offered me their services. I had one of them a day and a half, and for this she asked half a dollar, which I can not call unreasonable. I got a maid shortly after Christmas, one of the confirmants, just 14 years old; but she is able and willing and takes fully care of what is to be done. It is up to us to determine her wages, and I believe it will be one and a half dollar per month; she has previously had a dollar a week. I have been busy arranging for her bedding, although this is very simple in this country and consists only of a mattress filled with straw or corn-leaves, a similar one under the head, and also a pillow as big as the children's pillows at home; she got one of the ones we brought with us, and then a cover stitched with wadding.[11]

Believe me, dear Mother, I regret we made our bedding for single beds, because here is only one type of bed, all double, and for these our bedding is both too narrow and too wide. At the moment we occupy Master Even's bed, which is so narrow that it is sufficient with one of our eiderdowns, but it certainly is not comfortable because when one of us turns over it is absolutely necessary for the other to do likewise in order to have room enough. Munch has bought two beds in Beloit, but we would rather not put them up before we get into the parsonage; Emil will have one of them and shall then be in a bed just as wide as ours, but that is the way it is here. In case we wanted to have them made to order, they would be more like we are used to but much more expensive. The ones we bought are factory made.

We have not yet bought chairs and tables. Here they use nothing but wooden chairs, be it at the farmer's or at the minister's, all of them alike, cost half a dollar. However, one can get rockers for children and adults, for rocking is a must for every American woman.

Yeast, Mutter mine, is one thing you never need to miss from now on if you only will do as I am going to tell you. One takes two handfuls of hop to every quart of water; let this come to a full boil and then leave it well covered to soak for a few hours, whereafter the hop is strained out; when this is more than lukewarm, wheat flour is whipped into it until it becomes a thick gruel. Herein you pour a teacup of yeast and stir it well, it is then covered and stays overnight in a warm spot. The whole matter can then be used as yeast; it should be covered tightly and kept in a cool place, and it will keep for more than three weeks. When all of it is used but for one teacup, one makes up a new supply in the same fashion. I have done this and found it most effective, but don't be afraid to put a generous amount of the yeast in the dough, it becomes twice as good. For the Christ-

mas bread I put in according to *Fru Winsnes;* you can't believe
how it raised and how well it turned out.

Our good, healthy coarse ryebread we miss beyond measure.
Rye is hardly to be had, furthermore it is not as nourishing as in
Norway, and we cannot get it ground the same way either. We
are still saving the rye we brought with us in the tins and shall
plant it in the fall, although I am greatly tempted to have it
ground, made into bread, and eat that instead of the dry wheat
loaves. We can not have barley ground either except far away
from here and then with great difficulties, that is another thing
we miss, so rice will have to do.—I write a lot about household
affairs, but I know that Mother is interested in hearing about it,
and it is not intended for others to read.

The forests here look horrible. Here and there you can see
a huge oak, but the greater part of them are burnt black from
prairie fires, or they are torn and broken by storms. In between
is an impenetrable brush consisting of small oaks and other leaf
trees, but mostly of blackberry and raspberry bushes, grapes and
other wild growing fruit trees so densely entwined that it is
almost impossible to get through. All this you may visualize as
beautiful, and it is in certain parts. But then again, in other
places, it is so torn and so covered with dead trees and branches
that it looks like the most horrible wilderness.

There is said to be quite a few snakes here. Indeed, a
woman living in a *Loghus* [log house] in the vicinity even found
a rattlesnake in her cellar when she went for potatoes; but she
was brave, and it did not get to bite her. Another day she found
a snake on a shelf in the drawing room. But please note that they
live in houses where you can put your whole hand through both
walls and floors. People are seldom bitten by snakes; however,
the men will tuck their trousers into their boots when they tend
to their fields in the summer so that the snakes cannot crawl up
their trouser legs, or they use woolen hose and shoes. One morning another woman found a snake in the bed next to her child.
Ugh—isn't that frightening! I may not dare go out of my door in
the summer, for they can hardly come into our house except
maybe in the kitchen that I am going to get now.

We actually heard some small remarks that the congregation found it difficult to afford a kitchen just now when there are
so many other things to be taken care of. Whereupon we reason-

ably suggested to delay the building of the kitchen until next
year, which was approved. In the meantime, they will put some
boards together outside the door from the parlor, where I can
have my cooking stove during the summer, and as long as it is
cold I will keep it in the study. The door from the bedroom to
the outside will be bricked up in the meantime. I imagine that
with the previous letters you must now have received the drawing of our living quarters, so you understand what I am talking
about.

Indeed, I should have no objection to moving into our
house pretty soon, although it is satisfactory here in many respects, then in others it is uncomfortable. Master Even did not
turn out to be as we first thought but is a suspicious, grumpy old
miser of a bachelor; he has taken out of the room all sorts of
things, and now he is sneaking around us like a cat spying,
looking at walls and ceiling. Besides, it is such a low ceiling here
that Munch cannot stand up, which annoys him no end, and he
certainly gets many a hard blow, although I believe his head is so
hardened by now that a few more knocks will not even hurt it.
What is bothering me the most is a constant smell of fried pork
coming up from Even, who stays downstairs; this is the first thing
I notice when I open my eyes in the morning and the last in the
evening; indeed, I am sorry to say I have developed a dislike for
pork.

There are many things you have to get used to in this world,
and our wants and troubles can of course not be counted among
the most severe. You must not at all believe, beloved Parents,
that I am hiding anything from you, to the contrary, I write you
exactly the way we live, I am not in favor of these exaggerations
which have fooled even us in several respects. It is strange now to
remember all those false ideas we had about our future life
here, where we actually can live like in the country at home and
get anything we want for money but for a few exceptions, such
as chocolate, incense, medicines which you can trust; we regret
we did not bring a larger supply of the latter, because doctors as
well as medicines are only rubbish. There are two doctors here,
of whom the best one used to be a grocer, but all of a sudden he
sold the whole lot, disappeared for three months, and returned
as a doctor, has now a large practice and earns money. A Norwegian doctor should be able to do good business here and

would be very welcome, but his life would be a constant journey as people live so far apart. Tell Mrs. Paulsen this, but inform her also that I by no means will urge her to go unless pity for her many sick Norwegian brothers and sisters should make her feel so inclined; because all the poetry, which I and probably others like me believed we would find in such a journey, disappears without a trace as soon as you arrive in this highly prosaic America. I cannot imagine that any poet would be inspired or find any kind of spiritual nourishment here.

                                             Friday, February 15 [1856]
My dearly beloved Parents!

I am so sorry that this letter has not been sent off to you a long time ago, but we have spent a week with the Dietrichsons and had an exceptionally nice visit. There was a meeting concerning the widows' pension [funds], into which also Munch put his first share, a total of 13 *Spd.;* he was, moreover, elected treasurer for this association. On this occasion both Pastors Preus were present, and also Brandt. We were all happy and gay, nothing at all to cause any awkwardness. Of course, I regard the Dietrichsons and the Holfeldts as my own family and feel free to joke with them and they with us. One should think we were silly children and not old grown-ups when we were running around splashing water, throwing snowballs, pulling the comb out of my hair and many similar sports, just like we used to behave at home in the old days. I am going to tell you more about it some other time. Dietrichson and Holfeldt spent a few days here with us later, they left today. Oh, what a wonderful time this has been.

Tomorrow I am going with Munch to Dodgeville, where a nice, cultured Norwegian family, Holmen, is living. I shall stay with them while Munch officiates at two other places in addition to this one. He is also having confirmants and two congregation meetings up there, so we will not return for another week. But before we leave, I want to send you this unfinished letter so that you, my many dear ones, shall not be waiting in vain any longer. Munch had decided to write to Father this time, but he will have to be excused because every day has been filled with duties, excepting the time we have been visiting and receiving visitors.

But as soon as we return from Dodgeville, both of us will write again. Until then, may you, my beloved Father and Mother, truly keep well. May God's blessing and peace be with you always! Give my love to all my dear brothers and sisters, Sophie Pehrson, the Ellegers, the Munchs, my dear Grandmother and everybody there, including all friends and acquaintances who remember me. You will probably receive a letter from Emil at the same time; he has started it. We are doing very well, are hale and hearty.

Munch asks you to get Maus's stories on his account at Preutz and send it with Brodahl, who is married to Consul Hauff's daughter from Sandefjord; he has been appointed minister at *Bleu-Mont* [Blue Mounds], his address is Rakkestad Præstegjeld, Smaalenene. Likewise, there is a man named Ole Glesne who is coming to our congregation from Norway this summer, his address is Rytterager, Ringerige; he will be pleased, I am sure, to bring us anything in case you have something to send. We are casting about in our minds whether to ask you to buy a good warm fur coat for Munch or else ask Father for his wolfskin coat, which I know he would be happy to send Munch if only his black one is not soon too worn for himself; for here a piece of clothing like that is extremely expensive and hardly obtainable. I know your good heart and that you would gladly do all you can for us, that is why I speak straight forward. However, more some other time. Farewell, beloved Father and Mother, may God bless you! My love to *all, all* from your deeply affectionate

Caja

We are waiting for letters again. Ask many to write. I have to iron, otherwise I would have written more today. Good-bye!!!

Mrs. Caja Munch to her Parents, Mr. and Mrs. F. W. S. Falch

Wiota, March 1, 1856

Beloved Parents!

Here I am with my scrawl again, but since Munch is writing I cannot fail to send a small greeting also; besides, I promised to do so in my last letter, which I finished in a hurry. That one, and also one from Emil, I hope are now already well on their way to you. But we are waiting intensely for letters. You must definitely write to us at least once a month. Imagine that no one in Munch's family has yet written us one single letter! I hope it is not so unfortunate that there were letters for us on the railroad that had a collision on the 7th of February, whereby the mail bags burned up.

Father, you ought to subscribe to *Emigranten,* a Norwegian newspaper which is printed by Fleischer and published once a week, and where you then would get information about this and that concerning the Norwegians in America. Munch will also soon write a piece in *Emigranten,* a plan that intends to fortify and preserve our religious faith, and how one best can procure ministers over here in the future. You and Hysing could subscribe to this paper together, then it should not be too expensive to have a copy sent directly to you. I shall inquire about this next time I visit the Dietrichsons and supply you with more exact information. I think this should be interesting to you, maybe the Munchs also would participate.

For quite a while now we have passed a very pleasant time. First, as mentioned, we spent a week down at Dietrichson's. Here were then the two Preuses and also Brandt present; but they left after a few days when all the serious business was taken care of, although they frequently took to joviality. Brandt is a small man, unmarried, and looking so youthful that had I been a stranger I would most certainly have taken him for a boy of fourteen, he really has a pleasant childish face. Dietrichson and I have conspired that Brandt should come to us [at Hovland] and look for a wife among my girl friends, so they should shortly be prepared to receive letters of proposal; surely, I can almost tell who the lucky one would be, but for now they may all live in hope.

The Preuses are both very nice people. We are most urgently asked to come there for Easter, they will meet us halfway with their own horses and buggy if we only would come. I would very much like to do this, but the distance between us is great and the roads terrible to travel, so hardly anything will come of it. It would have been nice to learn to know these ministers' wives also; besides, Adolph Preus, or the "Bishop," as he is called, has an old pianoforte, which he would have tuned in case I came. No one in his family can play it; he acquired it at an auction for thirty-some dollars and really bought it for his sister, Mrs. Dietrichson, who is very musical and had given lessons both in singing and in playing for a long time before she came out here. But when Preus got the piano in the house, he did not like to part with it again. Do you know who is tuning the pianos over here? None but our old acquaintance Jakob Seeman, he takes 5 dollars for each. Indeed, this gentleman almost moved right into our midst as they considered employing him in the printing house, but he was too arrogant for them and demanded too much pay. I don't know how many languages he bragged about being able to speak as well as write.

I received a particularly fine hymnary as a present from Bishop Preus. Now, when these ministers had left the party, we really started to frolic about and had fun just like children. One day, a huge English newspaper had been left in the window and had become completely soaked with water; Munch grabbed it and held it in front of my face, but when I very strictly forbade him to come near me, Dietrichson took it with a very solemn face and said he would dry it, but instead he threw it on top of my head. With no hesitation I bundled it up and gave it back to him right in his face, and that started a war between everybody in the parlor, and handkerchiefs and all kinds of missiles were thrown right and left. In this manner, one day passed after the other with pranks from morning till night. Early in the mornings we were usually woken up by Dietrichson, who came to our door and sounded his Norwegian [harness] bells, of which he is very proud, because the American bells make a noise as if someone was clanking with iron chains, and they are no bigger than a dove's egg; they often use more than fifty of them on each horse.

We were at Dietrichson's for Lent, heard a fine sermon on Sunday by this adorable preacher. We had marvelous wheat cakes on Monday and finished the day by emptying a bottle of champagne which Holfeldt had saved so that we could enjoy it together with them. I had made wheat cakes and a rib roast and prepared everything as well as possible beforehand for Emil, who stayed at home; he had also celebrated after a fashion, for Even had two nice parties while we were away.

When Dietrichson and Holfeldt came to visit us, we were indeed busy trying to make it as cozy in our nest as possible; it was in fact the first time that we entertained company. We cleaned away as best we could, polished and scrubbed all over, so at least it was clean. They slept in our bedroom, and we in Emil's bunk which can be pulled out, and then Emil with Even. They did not suffer for want of food. The first dinner, fried prairie chickens—Emil had caught about thirty of them during our absence—then soup with meatballs, which I made up in a hurry, but they were good. Second dinner, dried cod, of which we can buy a very good quality in Wiota, roast veal, which I received along with a goodly piece of butter from a widow I don't even know, and finally whipped cream with what was left of the jam I brought with me, and *Krumkager* fried in an iron belonging to Kristen Rud. For our third dinner I cooked a delicious brown soup from prairie chickens with breadballs in it. In addition I had ragout of hare and other such small warm courses for them evenings and mornings. We managed to buy six bushels of rye down at Rock Prairie, which I had ground, and from it I made the best loaves of rye bread just like at home, so now we do not need to eat wheat bread any more.

Dietrichson had two vigorous horses here under Emil's protection, and believe me, he took good care of them; he was with the horses constantly, made trips with them, indeed all of us did that, in wonderful weather, a comfortable sleigh, and the Norwegian bells, which everybody stared at like mad. Otherwise we went for walks and had fun from morning till night; if only I could draw, you would have seen a funny picture; you see, Dietrichson got hold of Munch's old shaving brush, which he soaked in water and soap and then washed us all around the ears. But we were quick to find a solution, Holfeldt and I took each a pair of iron tongs, heated them in the stove, and pointed them at him so he could not touch us; Emil jumped over chairs and tables but even so got quite a few doses in his mouth, likewise Munch; however, he soon found a way out, he took the shoe brush and polish down from the chimney shelf and then smeared Dietrichson delightfully in with this; they both approached each other very solemnly, and each warned the other austerely to keep calm, but before they knew it they started another treatment of one another, each with his brush. You can imagine it was an hilarious comedy to watch; at last they went inside and cleaned up.

I don't know what to believe concerning the rumors we

have heard earlier about Holfeldt, because at present he most
certainly is an honest and pleasant man in all respects, helpful in
every day, with a very soft heart, and he does a great deal of good
with his money, in fact more, I believe, than many others would
do. He is well liked and highly regarded among the ministers
here; maybe his constant stay with the Dietrichsons every winter
has had this beneficial influence on him, or maybe one was in
error before about his true character? Not to mention his wife,
she truly is an example of a wife, so Christian-minded, righteous,
and kind as anybody could possibly be. Oh, how often have not
people been misjudged in this sinful world!

Dear Sophie, how are things with Marie Holfeldt? Poor girl,
she really deserved a better fate. You know, she was engaged to a
person who at the same time was engaged to another. We were
talking about her, that she ought to take a trip over here for a
recreation, and then she should stay with me; couldn't you and
she do it together? Isn't Robert soon leaving for Quebec? In that
case you would be all right, for Holfeldt would certainly get you
here from there, maybe for nothing. If we had gone via England
to Quebec, not only would we have arrived here without cost,
but we also would have had the rest of the passage paid for; this
is the way Holfeldt has arranged it for many Norwegians who
wished to get the services of a minister. The Holfeldts had been
looking for us for a long time, the bed had been made, and we
could have traveled with them directly to Dietrichson's. But that
is the way it goes. Now he has promised to take care of anything
for us from Quebec, one only has to address it to Holfeldt, Peter
Street No. 16, Quebec. Nanna, he would be happy to help you
get here should you have the courage to travel alone. You will
have to learn English then, otherwise you won't get very far, but
perhaps Fritz could come with you, that would be so much
better.

How is Nikoline? Ask her if she won't write to me. Give my
regards to all the Ellegers, Pehrsons, and Preutzes. Is Nilsinda
well? Give my love to her, too. Does Emilie talk? Is she forgetting
"Dea"? Has Oskar returned home? Have you had a cold winter?
Have you been freezing much? Have you, my Father, been in
good health? God grant you that! Mother is strong as a little
mountain, I hope! But please be careful. Did you have many
apples and nuts this year? Are all my dear brothers and sisters all

right? Oh, there are so many, many things I should like to know
about. Tell me about everything when you write, I would like so
very much to be with you in your everyday life and not become
a stranger to my own home, which I shall surely see again some
time with the help of God.

It will be a great temptation for us four years from next
midsummer [June 24], because that is when the Dietrichsons
and the Holfeldts are returning to Norway, God willing, and
that is exactly when Munch's designated time runs out here. So
if everything is as usual at home, and you, my Father, will be
able to harbor us for a while, I don't think any power could keep
us here! What a joyous time it would be! I am always living in
this precious hope, and you do likewise, my beloved Parents.

Isn't there really anybody at Grandmother's who would
write a few lines to me? Caroline, you are usually so brave, you
start out on a big, long, long letter to me, and then you make all
the others add a little or rather a lot each, I know you are not
easily discouraged, Caroline; and my little Momsa would surely
like to write to me, wouldn't she? Ditlev also. Mrs. Hageman
must write some, too; the Captain must not forget the "cat's
paw," tell him so.[12] I so often think about all my good friends in
Norway and wish them God's peace and good fortune. Remember me to Ida Spørck.

Emil presumably wrote that he drove us up to Dodgeville
with a team of horses borrowed from a man in the neighborhood
who needed to have them returned to him the next day. Because
of this, Emil had to find his way home alone. Indeed, I was
anxious for him, but already before I returned I was told by a
man who had been down here that he was safe and sound at
home; however, the last seven English miles he had completely
lost his way, but then his meager knowledge of English came to
his rescue. Indeed, he knows so much now that he can go to the
Post Office and buy one thing or another. Frequently he happens
to run into Americans who ask him for directions, and he often
carries on long conversations with them and makes himself understood one way or another.

We drove directly to a small town called Linden, where a
Norwegian office clerk from Drammen lives. His name is Holmen, and I stayed with him the whole time while Munch was
out on business every day. These were cultured people, and

believe me, we do appreciate meeting people like that in this country; besides, they were extremely obliging, had two well behaved and clever children, a girl of eleven and a boy of nine, who talked better English than Norwegian. They entertained themselves by writing the names of all my brothers and sisters over and over again, and also little songs and whatever I could think of for them.

Dear Nanna, send me my guitar music, which I forgot, and if you can get me some more, it would be nice. Munch is not going to pay for this letter, I tell him, because I want the money to buy eggs—you know, Mother, how well I like them.

Wiota, April 13, 1856

My dear Parents!

On the 26th of March we received your latest and most welcome letters of February, for which I thank you a thousand times; they had been awaited for a long, long time with great impatience; we almost believed that somehow they had been lost on the way, but fortunately that was not so. However, you must promise me to write more often, the time between each letter becomes much too long. I believe I am more industrious in sending letters to you, I have done like Aunt Mina and shall try not to let a month pass without writing to you; beloved Parents, you do likewise! There are so many of you who can write. From sister Nanna I have not yet seen one word; you are probably busy getting ready for your wedding, dear sister, but you should not on that account forget me living so far away from all of you, and to whom every word from home means more than the wretched balls to you. My Father also needs a little talking to, I was really disappointed last time not seeing a few lines from your hand, it would do me so good to see a little from you, my dear Father.

[April 23, 1856]

Beloved Parents, time runs so fast I hardly know what becomes of it. Today we write the 23rd of April, and I have not yet managed to send you a letter. It is mean of me, and it has rested on me as a heavy burden for quite a while. But great changes have occurred here since the last communication. We have moved into our parsonage, although it is not yet quite finished. One can barely make it to the house for stones and gravel; on the inside, the walls are not plastered, and many other small matters are still left to be done, so it looks less than good. But we are happy to be on our own, and now the weather is so warm already, we won't suffer any by staying here.

Even sold his farm to a Norwegian shoemaker for an enormous price, which Emil could not possibly procure. This man immediately moved into a bedroom next to ours with his wife and two children. Even departed to some good friends, and in his place we now had the man and the wife and the most awful screamer of an urchin you can imagine in the basement just below us. Moreover, the weather turned milder, and everything that was to be cooked had to be done in our room, so it was hardly bearable. By now they should and could have rough-cast (or plastered, as it is called here, I presume it is the same) in the parsonage a long time ago, but their own affairs had to go before everything, and they claimed not to have time for us at all until they were through with their ploughs and harrows. We then preferred to move in as it was. Now it will certainly be unpleasant when the workers arrive, but they will have to adjust themselves to our comfort, and in the summer it is easy, we will move upstairs while they are downstairs and vice versa. In the meantime, I am getting the curtains ready; last time we were at Dietrichson's I bought some kind of dark red molton for the drawing room, because white curtains will not do here in the summer as they would become dirty in one single day thanks to the flies.

May 2 [1856]
I am very downhearted over the fact that I have not yet finished my letter to you, beloved Parents. Night before last— that was the last day of April—Emil arrived from Wiota [Post Office] with your second letter, dear Mother, it did not take long on the way, so you can see we are not really too far apart. At the same time we received the first letters from Munch's family— Jette indeed mentions a letter she had sent previously, which we, however, have not seen.

You probably think, my Father, that we have completely forgotten your birthday—far from it! You were certainly much more in our thoughts this time. God bless you and make you well and contented again till we meet in joy and love. God's will be done, my Father, in this rests an enormously great consolation for His truly faithful souls, then this pitiful earthly existence with its longings and sorrows can not depress our hearts, then we go bravely forward on the path of faith and accept everything as a gift from the Almighty, who steadily promotes our welfare. I am always in good spirits because I look upon this journey as being very beneficial to me, and because I know that four years will pass rapidly, and if by that time we can get another minister to replace us here and the calculations should not miss completely, then I believe no power on earth will be able to retain us; for Munch's longing to see his fatherland again I think is even greater than mine, almost every night he dreams about it. My own yearnings will surely double when I first realize the possibility of returning.

By all means, do not believe anything but that we are ["heartily" deleted] contented with our position and that we thank God from the bottom of our hearts for His grace toward us. You cannot imagine how good it is to be removed from all kinds of diversions and temptations that pull us poor humans along, and to think only of one's God and of the betterment of one's soul; only now do we realize our great incapacities and many, many shortcomings, indeed, we have much to fight against. But every day we read the Word of God and work on ourselves to become His true children. Oh, that this situation would be the lot of many, how happy they would feel then, even if they encounter the greatest misery and sorrow.

We would have raised the flag on your birthday, Father, but I think it is more difficult here to find a straight flagpole than a lump of gold as here is nothing but rugged oak trees with torn and scorched branches. At first I decided to write so it would reach you on or near the day, but there was no peace here at that time. As Even had sold his farm, he had two auctions. Moreover, strangers moved in and out, and we were in the midst of it all. At one of the auctions, which was conducted in English, we bought a watering can, a table, some stoneware plates, sacks, and several household items. But everything was very expensive,

cattle in particular. The other auction was executed by a Norwegian; Munch and Emil were then in Dodgeville, nevertheless
I bought two small pillows for 1 dollar and 55 cents.

Even is now ready to go to Norway. Think how nice it
would be for you if you could get to talk to him; but, unfortunately, he will go directly up to Christiania, where I will ask him
to call on Grandmother as well as the Bishopess. He has promised to take letters, indeed, he has been putting his best foot
forward the last few days, will pay Munch [his part of] his
minister's salary for 5 years according to what he signed in the
letter of presentation, will not accept anything from the congregation for our stay with him, and has in many ways shown his
willingness to help and assist, so should he call on you, please
show him the greatest friendliness.

I don't think I have written since the last time we were at
Dietrichson's; they were as usual friendly and obliging. Munch
drove with Dietrichson to one of his annex parishes, where he
bought a beautiful dark reddish-brown mare with a white blaze
from a wealthy, genuine Norwegian farmer for 100 dollars in
cash and 35 dollars within half a year. She is 5 years old, used
very little; because of this, Dietrichson exchanged with us for a
while and let Munch use one of his older horses. With this one
we left the Dietrichsons Wednesday before Easter.

We had a fairly nice Easter; Munch made only a few day-
trips. By the way, Easter Day Emil and I decorated the altar here
in the church; this congregation had received as a present from
Dietrichson's congregation a simple altar set which had been
used by them until they now procured a more elegant one. This
Emil and I polished, put large wax candles in the candlesticks,
used my large tablecloth to cover the whole altar, which immediately looked somewhat more ceremonious. Furthermore, that
day Munch gave, as so often before, a very beautiful sermon. I
wish time and time again that you could hear him, my beloved
Parents, brothers and sisters. Sometimes he writes his sermons
out, sometimes he speaks extempore; I have asked him many
times to allow me to send home with Even the sermons he has,
but he says no.

Soon after Easter both Emil and Munch went to Dodgeville,
an unpleasant time for me; for it started in with lightning,
thunder, rain, and heavy winds, and I must admit that I was

scared, although I was surrounded by people in all directions. My gentlemen had had a foreboding of this; therefore, Emil returned alone after a few days with horse and buggy. You can imagine the shock I had before I learned the reason for his arrival, and then my great delight in having him with me; he is certainly a great comfort to both us. Munch was in fact safe and sound with his friend Holmen, ate oysters and had a small glass of toddy in the evening. But due to the weather, he was not able to finish his business until a few days later than planned; therefore he arranged with a man up there to give him a ride down, and Emil came trotting home to me. He was very lucky with the weather that day, but the mud had so messed up him, the horse, and the buggy that I could hardly take care of them, and Munch was not much better when he arrived.

On the way, Emil had bought from an American two turkey hens and a tom (they are about like the ones at home, somewhat lighter in color and bigger maybe) besides a goose and a gander, just like ours. For the turkeys he paid 6 shillings apiece (one American shilling is 12 cents) and for the geese one dollar altogether. Isn't he clever? To be sure, Munch and he had talked it over on the trip up, but even so you understand, dear Father, that he can manage fairly well with his English already, yes, he surely surpasses our expectations, if he is only left alone he is not restrained in any way at all.

Some time after the trip to Dodgeville Emil drove alone to Dietrichson's with his horse to have it exchanged with ours as it [Dietrichson's horse?] would not at all put up with going in harness alone; indeed, it is bad here that the horses so seldom will tug along alone, one rarely sees anybody drive except with two horses. This is the reason why all vehicles are made for this arrangement. Obviously, Munch will also have to get another horse, especially since this one is rather too slender to pull Munch around alone on all his many travels. When Emil brought it, it had a bad leg but is now doing rather well. The shoemaker who bought Even's farm also has only one horse, and now Munch and he have got together so that he ploughs with our "Polly" (her name) and Munch uses his for exchange. Polly, moreover, is very sprighty and not trustworthy except next to another horse. Polly is having a foal next year; you see, our intention is to raise foals and calves for sale, bull calves bring

good money; however, we will not keep more than three or four
cows and two horses. We have abundant pasture since we here
simply let the cattle out on the prairie or in the forest or other
places where it is not fenced in, and on our land there will still
be plenty of hay to sell. Because hired help is so expensive and
hard to find, we will not take on too much but leave the fields in
pastures except for a small piece, where we can plant some
potatoes, rye, and maize. (You ought to get some of this, Father,
it is used here to fatten up pigs, and it is found to be excellent; it
surely would grow if you plant it on the sunny side, it yields
quite a bit, the cattle will eat the leaves, which are also well
suited for filling in mattresses. I have had a good deal picked,
but every leaf must be ripped into narrow strips, which is a
slow process. You may be able to get seeds at Schübler's in
Christiania, have Wilhelm buy you some, Bernt, and have something done about it, you will not regret it. It has to be planted
and hilled about like potatoes.) Besides, we will plant something
they call *Ponkins* [pumpkins]; they grow like gourds but are
bigger, and are fed to cattle and pigs, but they must not freeze in
the winter, and they give the milk an unpleasant taste. It is true
that in certain places here the milk tastes of onion, because in
the spring some type of onion grows in places with deep soil and
moisture near brooks, and this they eat; but this lasts only for a
short while. We have not noticed it yet, but we have it coming,
for here is just the place for it.

I did not get that cow last winter, it was too expensive, and
we had neither space nor fodder for it. But now, two weeks ago,
Munch bought one for 27 dollars, including a kitchen table in
the bargain. She is not so big, but should give plenty of milk; I
have not yet had more than four quarts in each milking, although she had calved eight days before we got her. But she will
hardly eat hay because she had the taste of grass that grows in
spots in the pasture; when there will be more of this, she will
certainly do better. The calf came along, and it must have some
also, so there will hardly be anything for butter the way Munch
wants it. The cow is called "Cate"; Laurvig's beauties by the
same name should not be insulted by this, although I can not
offer any better information than that this is a very common
name here for horses, cats, cows, and dogs. My cow is very
affectionate; if she discovers me outside the door, she comes over

right away and follows me all over, only because I have given her some potatoes and flour-drink. If it was Nikoline she would probably take her along into the living room. . . .[13]

Mrs. Caja Munch to her Mother, Mrs. Thalie Falch, née Staffeldt

Luther Valley Parsonage, August 6, 1856

My dearest Mother!

Already a long time ago, I received your long, lovely, and most welcome letter, where you describe my sister Nanna's wedding, and thank you cordially for it. May God bless both you and Father for your untold affection, concern, and self-denials. Some time you will certainly have your well-deserved reward for all this, our dear heavenly Father will surely be with you and give you many happy days in your old age!

It has worried me for a long time that I have not answered this letter of yours earlier, Mother dear, but just listen to this: Munch and I went down to Dietrichson's as I told you in my last letter. Munch preached there and conducted Communion service for the Dietrichsons, and we stayed with them for three weeks. Then it was decided that Munch should go alone to Wiota to give the service and also look after everything up there. He was received by Emil only, who was at home all by himself, poor boy, as our maid, seduced by a Yankee, had run away and left the whole house. The man himself came and picked her up with horses and carriage, and she left everything as it was, some things clean, others dirty, some things outside, others indoors; indeed, Munch had never seen such a house, the way ours was when he arrived. Workers had been there also, and they can turn everything upside down when they are left to run things by themselves. Emil had not suffered any wants, though, for a nice, kind widow had brought him food, and the neighbors had also sent him some bread. Munch then got hold of some people to scrub and clean all over and returned here as soon as he could, bringing Emil along.

Two days later, we started on our way up to Wiota accompanied by all the Dietrichsons as had already been decided beforehand. We left early in the morning, had a very pleasant day, and arrived happily in Wiota, where everything was nicely

put in order. During the day we hung curtains, the daguerreotypes, Munch's map of Norway, I brought down my sofa cush-
ion, although I have no sofa to put it on, besides Aunt Louise's
footstool; Munch and Dietrichson put up roller blinds decorated
with landscapes painted on canvas, so believe me, in a hurry our
house became neat and cozy. I did not lack any food as it came
to us from all directions; I did not miss help either, the widow
prepared the meals, and one of Munch's confirmants was hired
as a maid. Furthermore, the Dietrichsons and we are now just
like one family; indeed, Mrs. Dietrichson really takes the place
both of mother and sister to me. Oh, how wonderful it is to meet
such a person over here in America, we are so closely united that
hardly any friendship could be tied any stronger between two
families.

After having enjoyed ourselves delightfully up there for a
fortnight and Munch, Emil, and I had received the holy Sacrament of the Altar from Dietrichson, which particularly gave me
strength before the great crisis in my life, we were now supposed
to separate for a long time. The Dietrichsons were to leave us,
which was very hard on all of us, especially when they thought of
what I had in store, at which occasion they wished so very dearly
to offer me assistance, consolation, and comfort. It was decided,
therefore, that we should again go down with them and stay
there until all was well over by the help and grace of God. Are
they not some blessed people we have met here! Think what a
great sacrifice on their part, and what a comfort for us, especially
for my dear Munch. Here they have a good doctor, whom I hope
by God's help that I will not use, besides a certified midwife, and
imagine, best of all, my dear Mrs. Dietrichson to watch over me
and nurse me. Would God that I could send this very comforting information to you by telegraph, my beloved Parents. I sus-
pect that you are worried about me during this time, but you
certainly have had, and still have, little reason for that. I am,
God be praised, perfectly healthy, although heavy and big; they
laugh at me, follow me around, and claim that it must be either
a *big* boy or else two. I find it, of course, a bit uncomfortable to
walk around like this, especially when I forget myself and want
to run to fetch something, or take a fling. The heat has not at all
been bad lately; in fact, we have actually had a good summer by
American standards. The toothache finally disappeared after I

had applied many remedies; Dietrichson even burned me with a wire, and since then I have felt exceptionally good, although I cannot doubt that the time is soon drawing near, for I am growing considerably bigger every day and getting heavier in all my movements. It never occurs to me, however, to be afraid as I am surrounded by too much Christian love for that; indeed, they are trying in every way to take care of me and make me comfortable.

The box with clothing that you sent us can be expected any day now; I am sure I will find some baby clothes in that one, and many thanks for it, beloved Parents, they will be most welcome and doubly appreciated; nevertheless, I have had to prepare myself with a little of everything. Most of it has been cut without measuring and will surely not be too small, you know my weakness already; they have been having good laughs at me and asked me if I really expect to get a one-year-old lad right away, for all of them predict a boy because I am so heavy, but I tell them that I am of good stock.

What is going to be the name of the child? I have no idea of it, but there is plenty of time to think of that when the Lord has granted us this treasure, to which I look forward with such joy that it may compensate for the absence of all my dear little brothers and sisters. Dietrichson's children are certainly nice, but they are still strangers. I have made two woolen swaddling clothes, but they will not at all allow me to use swathe; here they mostly use little woolen skirts [shirts?], of which I have made three; and a thing they use much here is a small woolen bodice directly on the body, later on they wear woolen undershirts, which are used regularly both by women and by children; I will also do likewise, although not for my own person, but for the little one in case God is gracious enough to grant me a child.

Munch has bought a beautiful cradle for 4 dollars; for this I have been given a mattress and a pillow by Mrs. Dietrichson. For myself I have made a very practical dress without a lining, buttoned down front, with no seam over the shoulder and only with a running cord around the waist, and yet it fits nicely; the material is small checkered white and brown, confirming the taste of Munch and Dietrichson, who bought it in Beloit. All cotton material is inexpensive, but everything else is exceedingly dear, and also of very poor quality; it is probably merchandise which they cannot dispose of in the larger places that is sent up here and sold at the highest prices. Havana sugar, so dark and moist as I have ever seen it, costs 10, even 12 cents per pound; Mrs. Dietrichson had once had some in an earthenware jar, but after a few days she discovered a big puddle on the floor of dark, ugly syrup that had seeped from the sugar right through the jar. Indeed, that is how nearly everything is adulterated.

The 11th [August, 1856]

I have deliberately waited to finish my letter as I had hoped that Emil also would have sent you a few words; but, unfortunately, he was here yesterday and claimed that he had not at all had the time to write. Indeed, it was hard on me when he was leaving us, but what could we do? I recalled what you said to me, Father dear, when you asked me not to let Emil continue in his usual sloppiness like at home, and that would certainly have been the case. There was not enough for him to do at our place, and Munch could not give him as much money as he could earn at his age. Now he was set on staying with an American, although they would have liked very much to have him in the printing shop at Fleischer's establishment, where he could have had a more bookish education, learned the printing trade, and been well off in several respects, but he would hardly have made as much money right from the beginning as he now can by working in the field from morning till night; besides, he was afraid it would be too quiet and monotonous in the long run. I wished so hard that he would accept this position. He would then have been pulled along into the world through all the different newspapers, would have developed more interest in reading, be associating with cultured people, who surely would have become fond of him, and would on his return home had a choice between two alternatives, either stay in the printing trade or buy himself a small farm with the money he could save. But now his mind was set on farming, probably influenced in part by Even Kronborg and others who likely have not got their money in an honest way; and I would not by any means persuade him but let him try. And so Fleischer was kind enough to travel with him to an American farmer near here, who is a well-bred man. He went there last week after having got himself a new summer

coat and one pair of light and one pair of black trousers bought
for the money Munch had given him. Saturday night he returned here, believe me I had missed him. He was well satisfied,
was always treated politely, but complained that the work was
hard, he had no rest all day except just for meals; besides, he
found it so lonely going by himself mowing and, in fact, doing
everything alone, for the farm is small and does not need any
more help. But Dietrichson, who really is fond of Emil and has
taken an interest in him, will speak to another American, who is
a very decent man, lives close to the parsonage, and works with
his men himself, besides has a large farm.

I am expecting Munch any minute from Wiota, where he
went Saturday accompanied by a nice young man, Solberg, who
is at the printing shop and who joined him just for pleasure; you
see, it was the first time that Munch drove quite alone with his
own two horses. He has bought another mare from Dietrichson,
whom he will pay some time in February when he gets rich. I
have packed away and closed up the whole house while we are
gone. A Norwegian peasant family, who live close by, have
promised to milk the cow, churn butter, and look after the small
animals. We have eleven big young turkeys and four goslings
left; they live in luxury from what has sprouted in our American
garden without a fence, surely not much, but cucumbers and
melons we had in abundance, besides peas and beans, but what
can we do about it, something had to be neglected. I shall be
poorly supplied for the winter; however, there will surely be a
way.

The 13th [August 1856]
Yesterday I remembered well my dear little Olga's birthday,
God bless you! Let me see you become a good and clever girl. I
suppose you don't ever cry any more now, but read and sew and
will soon write a little letter to your sister in America, who is
happy to receive every word that my brothers and sisters would
send me. You, my Tinka, are such a clever girl, and the next
time Mother writes, you must send me a few lines. We are surely
often in each other's thought these days. Oh, God, how one's
longings for the dear ones grow beyond description on occasions
like these. Indeed, a year ago tomorrow we were trying hard to

be happy and gay, but it was mingled with sorrow. Thank God that this year has been so good, not one day do I wish I were back.

Imagine if little Emilie could become an aunt on her birthday, it is not at all impossible. What fun it would be—my first one and, by God's help, your last one, dear Mother, on the same day! You must not at all let anybody else read this letter; it amuses me to talk to you about one thing or another which would seem peculiar to strangers.

God be praised that this summer is a wholesome one. There are no reports of illness from any part of the country; all of us are quite healthy, and I am remarkably well all day long, day after day. We enjoy a lot of [water]melons these days, believe me; I got many of them from my good friends in Wiota when Munch returned. Here you just put the seed into the ground anywhere and get a lot; they are a wonderful thirst-quencher and have a good flavor.

Please give my dear Sophie Pehrson a thousand thanks for the many friendly letters she sent me, I am really ashamed that I have not yet written her a single letter; yesterday I received both hers and one from Mathilde Allum, which they had sent with Robert. Until further notice from us you must put the enclosed address on our letters, and please inform the Munchs about the same. The most heartfelt wishes, beloved Father and Mother, rejoice and always remain in the good hope that by God's help we shall again be united in four years, we are getting more and more determined on this. Give my love to all dear ones

from your own Caja

Please give a thousand greetings to Nanna and Fritz for the time being, our Lord be with them!

The Second Year, 1856–1857

Mrs. Caja Munch to her Mother, Mrs. Thalie Falch, née Staffeldt

Wiota Parsonage, December 21, 1856

My dearest Mother!

I have received your letter of November 8th, and I cannot express how it hurts me to hear that you are so worried about us, and it is my fault for not having written more often. Oh, Mother mine, don't be angry with me! I must be excused a little, however, as I hope you now have seen from my letter to Nanna, which I finished late in October.[1] I should wish it has arrived safely in your hands, so that you would not remain in this terrible uncertainty. I can well imagine how you feel, and I blame myself terribly for not having put everything aside to write.

Indeed, it is your little granddaughter who is to blame, and you will have to scold her; for she occupied my time so much that in the end I had to get myself a little nursemaid. Now, then, we have three servants, a boy of the confirmation class (whom we only furnish with clothing) to tend to the horses, and then I have been so exceedingly lucky as to get a childless young widow, the likes of whom hardly is to be found even in Norway with respect to being orderly, thrifty, clever, and decent in every way. I only wish I could keep her, but she is not very healthy. For a nursemaid I have so far only borrowed the neighbors' daughters, but I don't think I shall have any difficulty in getting a young girl of twelve to thirteen years for the food and some clothes; for there are several poor families in the settlement.

I have furthermore received two other letters from you, Mother dear, one with Brandt, but the package I will not get until later as he lives far from us; likewise, I received a letter from you in the same mail where the one from my dear Nanna arrived. A thousand thanks for it all, my beloved friends, I am never more happy than when someone brings me letters from home.

Christmas is drawing near. God bless you during this Holiday Season, and may you feel the true peace and joy which our heavenly Father has wanted to bestow upon us poor human beings by sending us this lovable little Christ child! Oh, let us well remember Him and pray from our hearts that He will receive us in His heavenly dwelling when by the will of the Lord the time comes that we must depart from here! May God open the eyes of all my big and little brothers and sisters so that they rightly may rejoice in this great and solemn children's festival!

This, then, is the first Christmas that I have a little child. Oh, how I thank God from my heart for this treasure, who is healthy all the time and getting along very well, indeed, dearest Parents, I wish you could see her! She is really as sweet as any child could be, never ill, God be praised, and living only on her milk, of which she can get more than enough at all times; yes, I must say there is such a lot of it that it almost bothers both her and myself. But then she is getting along well, growing bigger and more beautiful every day. I have of course never seen anything so delightful, but speaking impartially, I must certainly say she is lovely, and this came as a big surprise to me, for truly, I never thought that I would get such a beautiful child. And Munch is totally enthused by her, he can walk up and down the floor babbling with her for hours until he gets tired; because it takes some strength to keep going for any length of time with her on your arm. I often carry her until I get a pain in my chest. She already recognizes both Munch and me and does not like to go to anybody else. She laughs and chatters so you can hear her all over the house. Yes, she is very lively in the daytime, but she sleeps all through the night and has not yet disturbed Munch's sleep; I should wish she would continue that way, but that is probably not to be expected.

January 2, 1857

Beloved Parents, we have entered a new year. Oh, how strange it is to think of. Have we improved during the past year? Have we come nearer to our Jesus? God in Heaven grant that this were so, because for each day we are getting closer to Eternity, and without loving Jesus right from our hearts we could never be received by our heavenly Father.

Believe me, it feels strange to be sitting here in peace and quiet thinking of all the people at home running madly around in the streets wishing a happy New Year. Only few put the proper, true meaning into it, they are more attracted by vain nonsense and the desire for a good glass of wine, and in the end they turn into great sinners, because they lose their good sense and become more like animals than human beings. What a horrible way to start a new year! Maybe some people imagine that we celebrate this day just because it is the first of January and in order to drink and be merry. Oh, how much sin is being committed, even among the cultured class of people who call themselves Christians and really believe they are; indeed, for the latter it is worse, because it is extremely difficult for them to see and realize what great sins they commit daily by their indolence and indifference. Yes, God the Father have mercy upon all of us and grant us a living faith in our Lord Jesus Christ!

Oh, how wonderful it is to be a minister's wife, my beloved Parents! It is like being drawn nearer to Christ, and God forgive the one who still will not listen. I hardly hear talk of anything else from morning till night, as one can reasonably expect, because a minister must always work in his calling. Maybe everybody appreciates his own, but I think that Munch is a good minister and a worthy follower of Christ. His life is a constant struggle against the old Adam, to exorcise him both from his own mind and from that of his fellow man. He lets no sin pass unaccosted; the one who swears, he reproves; the one who is lazy in visiting God's house, he admonishes; and all manifest sins he punishes. No one is admitted to the Lord's table without first talking to him, and when Munch knows them to live openly in vice, they must first truly regret it and really improve themselves or they are entirely refused the Sacrament of the Altar. Sometimes Munch writes his sermons word for word, but he never reads them out from the pulpit; there he cannot tie himself to the paper, indeed, it is as if every word was given to him as it is spoken. May God grant that you could hear him, it comforts me so, and I am sure it would also strengthen you. One cannot help but give him full attention, whether one wants to or not. His strong voice is also of good effect. All who want rightness and truth are very fond of him, but the sinners find him too strict, and so he certainly has enemies who try to give him trouble here, but God be praised, he always proceeds in a sensible righteous way, so their complaints are always turned to naught by their own wickedness.

I was certainly quite sure, dear Mother, that I should have been able to finish this letter Sunday before Christmas; it was so quiet here, Munch had gone to Dodgeville, and I had settled down peacefully to write. But then suddenly Munch entered, the sleigh he was driving had fallen into a hundred pieces some distance from here. This was not unexpected as our neighbor, a shoemaker, had manufactured it the preceding afternoon in the American manner.[2] But Munch in his big, magnificent Lapp fur coat was too heavy to be carried in this kind of vehicle. A little later in the day, the Englishman who had supervised the repairs of the house came for a visit; he had dinner with us and enjoyed my beef broth with meatballs and stayed until the next day. I had given Ingeborg (my maid, you understand) leave to go, so it was impossible to think of any more writing that day, and, as you will see from the following, I was unable to continue until now after New Year.

The Holmens, who are living in the little town of Linden, and whom I think I have described to you before, had promised to come and see us during Christmas, but since Munch did not get up there because of the mishap with the sleigh, we were afraid they would not come; partly for this reason and partly to announce the next divine service for New Year's Day, we got two boys to drive up there with Munch's horses and a borrowed sleigh. They were to return the next day, the day before Christmas Eve, but they did not arrive. Christmas Eve went by, and still they did not come. By this time we were almost certain they had frozen to death on the prairies, and we had a very dismal Christmas Eve. Munch and all three of our servants went to church Christmas Day, I stayed at home alone with my little

Ellen, I thought no one was more entitled to that than I was. Munch was not very happy and could not at all get into the proper solemn mood because he was thinking of the boys; one of them was one of his confirmants and had twice before gone with him the same road. Their parents came here and were very downhearted. But just as I was sitting here in peace and quiet, in came not only the boys but also Madam Holmen with her two children. Her husband was unable to come until a few days later as he could not leave the store, which was kept open both Christmas Day and Boxing Day; there you see how the Americans observe the great Christmas Holidays. They had had much trouble on the way and had to stay overnight because of impassable roads, but God be praised that they returned safely, and you can imagine here was joy.

Indeed, we have a hard winter again this year, a lot of snow, storms, and freezing weather, and under such conditions it is almost impossible to go anywhere. Boxing Day, as Munch was going to one of his annex parishes, his horses went off the road and waded in snow to their ears. Snowplows are unheard of in this country, and to get into a blizzard on the prairies is attended with danger of life. The roads are then drifted over so completely that there is no trace of them, and it may happen that one drives around in a circle without knowing where he will arrive. It is not uncommon that people freeze to death in their sleigh, and the horses arrive in town with dead bodies sitting frozen stiff in the sleigh, holding the reins. Last year it happened that a carriage stopped outside an inn, where the horses regularly used to rest, but as nobody came inside, the innkeeper went out, and lo! there were five persons sitting inside the carriage, and the driver in his box holding the reins, completely frozen and dead. However, this is due to their own carelessness, and I don't feel nearly as sorry for them as for the poor cows, pigs, sheep, and other small animals; what these poor creatures suffer when the weather is that cold cannot be described, for they seldom have as much as a bush under which to seek shelter. Although we have a stable to put them in, they still suffer from cold because it is so open that the snow drifts right in at them. Munch covered the horses with two pieces of white cloth on which I had stitched some wadding for the purpose of covering two windows by our bed; as they came unstitched, the wadding dropped over their sides so they looked like gypsy women, or circus horses with fringes. In this one room reside the horses, the cow, the calf, the geese, the chickens, and during the night the cat, so it makes me think of Noah's ark. Soon another cow will be accommodated there, for Cate does not give us more than one quart of milk a day any more.

I now have two pigs also, which were practically given to us as a present, they are kept in the former chicken house, where we cannot keep any small animals because the mink will take them there. Indeed, this mean animal has destroyed many a fowl for us. Nevertheless, we have quite a few, thanks to the kindness of people. The other day I was even given two guinea fowls.

We have killed many of the turkeys, and I think we will destroy them all because they are so bad in the summer in case I should get a garden. But we plan to apply ourselves to quite a few geese; all the ones we raised last year are alive. One goose was given to us as a present, and that one we ate on Boxing Day. We have also been given turkeys and a lot of chickens. Indeed, there are many who are exceptionally good to us; there are about thirty people who have been presenting us with gifts, such as meat, pork, potatoes as many as we need for the winter, butter, cheese, eggs, and several things like that.

But in spite of this, Munch has had to buy a heifer and paid about 5 *Spd.* for it, and a sheep for 2 *Spd.*, besides a pig for 5 *Spd.* to be salted down. Candles, coffee, sugar, and such things are very expensive. I had a man salt some butter for me last summer, which cost me only 12 cents per *Skippund* [about 350 pounds].

Indeed, we live as thriftily as possible in every respect, but even so there is never more than from hand to mouth as it is called. There is no one, I think, except the one who has tried it, who will believe how expensive it is to live here in America; they have no regard at all for money, a dollar goes faster than a *Mark* [about 20¢] at home. I shouldn't even think of this if we only had no debts. How do you manage, my dear Father? We are letting you down for the whole lot. Oh, we think of it more often than you would believe. If only Munch could get what they have promised him, but the prospects for that are dark; so far he has hardly received more than the half amount for last year. In order to pay Cappelen [bookstore] in Christiania, he had to

borrow from the Widows' Fund. . . . You must write to us, dear
Father, and tell us how it is with this nasty money, I would hate
to see you suffer any want for our sake, and it should be possible
to find a way.

Are you not well enough, dear Father, to write a few lines to
me? I would equally well like to hear about your worries as
about your joys, for the one who leads a Christian life and yet
meets sorrow and hardship, he will have his reward with his
heavenly Father. It is exactly because He loves us and does not
want us to perish that He sends us afflictions. Oh, must we not
be grateful in our hearts for this! Oh, let us be joyful, beloved
Parents! Has not Christ been a human being like us? And should
not we be as happy as He? Why then worry about the miseries of
this short life? Let us rather sing: "Let come what will, I belong
to Jesus still!"

I was very happy to hear that you had been to Christiania,
dearest Parents; God grant that your health will continue to
improve, Father dear! But you must promise me that you will
strictly follow the doctor's instructions and not lose your patience if it does not help immediately; I am sure God will also
add His blessing, I am always praying for that from the depth of
my heart. And you will be healthy and sound when we return
home, and you can run around and dance with your grandchildren, I almost said.

Believe me, my *big* Ellen is sweet these days, I must really
sometimes look at her with amazement; imagine, she is truly
beautiful! Should anybody have believed a thing like that? She
has a high forehead, the point has disappeared, big shining dark
eyes, long dark eyelashes, the eyelashes [meaning "eyebrows"]
are as thick as though she were a yearling. I believe she will
chin, besides her cheeks are not at all too fat but have a white
soft skin, striking color, and she looks so very healthy and content, smiles as soon as we look at her, is very lively and loves to
be part of fun and dance. But she is almost too heavy, her legs
are as thick as though she were a yearling. I believe she will
soon cut her teeth, for she scratches her mouth badly and likes to
bite everything. Paper she is rather fond of, crams, tears, and
bites it to pieces, and she can already sit up and be quiet for a
long time when we play for her with something that rattles or
gleams, I still keep her in her swaddling clothes, but she kicks

her way out of them many times a day, besides she has managed to tear all five of them, so I will soon have to knit her some stockings and set her free. Green silk shoes she has got from Aunt Jette, and a pair of crocheted shoes from Ida Spørck, but the latter she has grown out of long ago. If she continues to grow this way, she will become a giant woman. The Holmens think a lot of her, especially the children; I put her down on the floor between them, and they enjoyed themselves very much with her and laughed heartily all three of them. She makes so many funny faces, to the great amusement of all.

Now I think I have exhausted the subject of my little treasure, whom I love rather well, sometimes I squeeze her so hard that she cries; however, I must still add that she is remarkably good, the Holmens, too, praised her for this; I think she would smile from morning till night if we would play with her. She had not yet had any solid food. She will soon grow out of all the clothes she has got, dresses, vests, jackets, shirts. I won't say anything about the color of her hair, there is still hope.

Munch is extremely fond of her, he says he never thought it possible to grow so fond of such a little creature. I often must laugh at him, for even if he is ever so deep in his serious studies and I enter with her, he drops everything. Sometimes he wants to pull her out of her good sleep to look at her; but in the mornings it is worst of all, she usually wakes up before it is light and immediately starts chattering, then I have to hurry out of bed, roll up the shades so he can see her, and then the two of them will be lying there and keep up a conversation so he quite forgets to get dressed. I can well remember that Father, too, used to do the same at home while Mother prepared breakfast.

Rest assured that both Munch and I have exerted ourselves to keep her from catching a cold during this hard winter in such an airy house. She has completely worn out the scarf I got for my confirmation, who would have imagined that it would be used for this purpose? Likewise, I am sure that Aunt Emilie had no idea that her sheets would get over to America and be used as rags around my child, her name is still clearly visible on a navel belt, I deliberately made it that way to save it as long as possible, but Ellen will soon find a way to destroy it.

To sew for Ellen and dress her up is the greatest fun I know. She has three red dresses about the same cut as the baptism robe that my dear Nanna sent her, one of them is a present from one of the confirmants. The largest one of Lagertha's capes now serves for dress-up occasions, likewise one she got from Jette with a frizz around, which becomes her extremely well. I have made a few small bibs for her and put on some borders in chrochet work which Sophie Pehrson once gave me. She is so good when I dress her, and she likes to be washed. I am sure you remember, dear Mother, how I loved to dress up my little sisters and brothers, and that I love her even more must be permitted, I dare say? The fact that this letter is incoherent and poorly written must also be put on Ellen's account, for I cannot stand to hear her cry ([added as a footnote in the margin:] besides she jumps with joy when she sees me and stretches out her little arms, and then I must pick her up), and the little girl I have to look after her at the moment is too weakly, as the peasant says, to carry her. It is your own fault, dear Mother, that this letter is so overloaded with praise for my little Ellen, for you have asked me to write about her. You will have to come here and judge for yourself to find out if I am blind with love for her and looking at her through double glasses; I only wish you could do that, I am sure you would be surprised.

[January 5, 1857]
Well, let us change the subject lest you should make too much fun of me. You have not heard about my preparations for Christmas. I even made sausage this year, fine meat sausage, hash sausage, and—best of all—Lübecker sausage. I myself scraped, minced in a trough, and made delicious meatballs and soup, to the great wonder of Madam Holmen as neither she nor Mrs. Dietrichson thought that this was possible here in America. I had good success with my Christmas bread, but I had so little sweet stuff to put into it. Flead-cakes and crullers were the only kinds of cookies I made, and some of this I sent around to the neighbors' children and to other good friends; it is so nice to have something to give away. We have also sent out a little meat, pork, turkey, besides some old clothes. There are poor ones here in America, too, you see, and no one knows it better than the minister, who goes around in their homes. I should have brewed some beer for Christmas, all preparations were made; but a keg

is very difficult to get hold of here. We had finally been promised one from a man, but when this same man wanted a christening a couple of months after Munch had conducted his marriage and was accosted for this, he got angry, and we lost the keg. I had been afraid this would happen, and I asked Munch to consider that we were to borrow this keg, but he would not even listen to me, although he dearly wanted that beer. Thus we had trouble for our pains instead of Christmas brew.

Emil, unfortunately, did not come to us for Christmas, the roads were so bad, and the weather cold; Munch's horses had to go to Dodgeville, and to hire another team was much too expensive. Besides, we had a very nice letter from him a few days ago, telling us that he was so busy with two newspapers to be printed between Christmas and New Year that it was impossible for him to come, otherwise he would have walked, which I now in a long letter to him strictly advised against for another time. I also used this occasion to send him both his and my own letters from home, so now he gets enough to read all at once. God be praised, he lives well and is content. At first he boarded with an English family in order to learn the language, but the woman of the house took ill, and they could no longer keep him there. He then went to Fleischer's, where he shares a bed with a very nice young man named Solberg, whose father was among those who were tricked to Ohio by Ole Bull.[3] I should hope that Emil has written to you, I begged of him to do so before he left. Now I probably will not see Emil until Munch goes down to Dietrichson's end of this month for the meeting of the Ecclesiastical Widows' Fund and then, I hope, brings him back up here. I miss him considerably, but on the other hand I am so very happy and calm about him now in contrast to the time he was with those nasty Americans; now he is among cultured people and is himself treated as such, and I can take care of and mend his clothes and be assured that he has everything in order.

Our Yuletide entertainments are soon recounted. They consisted of reading and hearing the Word of God, all possible peace and comfort at home, thinking of Norway and all our beloved friends there, besides singing Norwegian patriotic songs, our wedding song, and other snatches that we would think of.[4] On the Sixth Day of Christmas, the Holmens left, and the following day Munch went away also. I was now left alone and was going to delight myself by writing to the many whom I owe letters; but today, the 5th of January, Munch is coming home, and I have gotten no further than having written to Emil and so far to you, my very dear Parents. And whose fault is it? Nobody's but Ellen's and Hofacker's, because I started to read in Hofacker's biography, and there I found so much that was good and beautiful that I did not want to stop reading. If you have not acquired Hofacker's *Sermons,* you ought to do so, it is a treasure worth more than any money.[5]

Last time I wrote to you, we were probably at Kristen Rud's?[6] Thank God, we got away from there all right, because there was a terrible draught right down upon us from the ceiling. My dear Munch suffered from the effects (now he is well again, and that is why I say thank God), he contracted a bad laryngitis that lasted for several weeks and annoyed him tremendously, he could neither sleep nor even lie down, nor eat, and could hardly swallow liquid food. We managed as well as we could, read in the medical handbooks, and used everything suggested there that we could get hold of, warm applications, gargle, sweet bag with spices, and I don't remember what, but nothing helped. There was no doctor whom we dared ask. Finally we also made some brandy-and-salt,[7] and after having gargled this several times, he improved, I suppose something in his throat broke, and in the course of one day he was relieved of pain, but the swelling did not go down until a long time after. This you must tell to Aunt Louise.

Now I hope that we shall not have to move any more until sometime, by God's help, we shall be allowed to go back to our dear Norway. We are now farily comfortably established, I shall try to describe it as clearly as possible to you so that you would be looking in upon us, as it were.

As you drive along the road approaching the house, you will see a very nice fence of stone, about in the middle of it is a stately double gate, through which you turn in, and then you hobble along across a field on an unimproved road until you get to a very rickety narrow bridge across a brook. Here you will probably wonder if you dare drive across, but there is no other road to our house in case you want to visit us. After that, you turn onto a sloping ascent, it looks fairly as though horse and carriage would slide into the brook; but don't let that bother

you, heart up and all will be well, just drive on until you get to a
very nice level lawn laid out in a circle with a small stone edge
surrounded by plum trees and in the middle a small flight of
steps that are supposed to lead down to a beautiful garden
which, however, is still in its natural state and probably will stay
that way as long as we are here. On the lawn you stop by another
flight of steps that certainly looks as if it would lead you into a
pig's house, but then you must remember that you are in America, and here the pigs have no houses at all. If the path is not
glazed with ice, you should be able to climb the steps in an
upright position, otherwise you would have to crawl on all fours,
for there is no railing, and the steps are narrow, and open in all
directions.

Now you open a front door, which is not too sturdy and
with three small jiggling windowpanes—you see, they are only
fastened with small nails as long as it is so cold that we can't get
them puttied; they are better, however, than the old straw hat
that Munch and I nailed up one evening so the cat should not
jump through. You then enter a small hallway, from where you
immediately have a view of part of the loft through an open
staircase. There are two doors in the hallway, one to the right
and one to the left. You must enter by the one to the right, for
the other, which leads to the bedroom, is locked during the
winter and nailed over with pasteboard, which Munch has put
up to cover all the cracks. Here you come into the parlor, where
you will see Munch sitting in my rocker (you see, he thinks it's
his) in front of a brown painted desk with books and papers up
to his ears. In front of him you will see one half of his map of
Norway, on the other side of the window is the other half, over
which he often runs his longing eye and sighs, and what he is
thinking I often get to hear, believe me. Beside him on the wall
he has all his pipes hanging rather nicely on an embroidered
pillow, opposite these is a portrait of A. Munch.

There are three doors and four windows in this little room,
in other words no walls, you can imagine. Between the two
windows to the west is the stove, a little monster with a long,
rusty pipe stuck through an open hole in the wall, from where
you sometimes will have sand and gravel coming down over your
head. To make it give more heat, we have put it on top of a
turned-over unpainted crate, of which Emil has knocked out one
end, so we can rather cleverly put the firewood there. You must

not step too heavily on the floor lest the whole display should come down; this already happened once, but have no fear, we have now secured it with big nails.

The floor is anything but white, for this was our kitchen while the house was being finished. The ceiling used to be so open that I could put my big scissors down between the cracks, and when we had lights downstairs, we could see by the same lights upstairs as well; but now they have nailed lists between each board, so the ceiling looks striped and rather stylish. The floor is almost the same way, but that will have to stay as it is for this year, because the congregation is poor, and so is the minister.

As you enter, you had better keep your travel boots on, otherwise you will get cold as the basement is rather chilly. On the largest wall, our daguerreotypes are hanging, in the middle all my girl friends, with a family piece on each side, below this the Bishop and the cousins, and at the bottom Cecilie so beautiful and delicate. Under this stands our fanciest table. Two of the Norwegian chairs, our most elegant pieces of furniture, you will see here, besides maybe a couple of wooden chairs, although we only have six of them, and they have to be distributed among our four rooms, so we may have to do without these in here. On the southern wall you will see a new large bookcase filled with many good and richly gilded books, for we have picked out the nicest ones so they should strike the eye in the "estate." The drapes are bright red, and oil-painted shades with landscape pieces on them. Indeed, it is not so bad after all at Pastor Munch's! But please keep as far away from the windows as possible, because there is a considerable draught from them, likewise from the door that leads directly to the outside, and when the wind is from that direction it never gets warm here, and you had better go with me into the bedroom.

First, however, you enter another little mystic hallway, which is lighted from an opening above the kitchen door—there is going to be a window. Here is the passage down to the cellar under the stairway leading to the loft. First you crawl through a small door, then you open a trapdoor and descend into the cellar, it is big and roomy. While they were fixing the garden wall, I got a window there, otherwise it was quite dark. I have also got some shelves there, and I am very happy to have them.

The little hallway is also my pantry. This consists of a large shelfcase which Emil nailed together for me and which stands in the corner between the staircase and the wall, there is not enough room left for me to turn around, so I have to leave the same way I entered; in time I hope to get a window from here out into the front hallway.

We will now go into the bedroom. It is just like the parlor except that there are only two doors and no door to the outside. Here you will find drapes with all kinds of flowers, squares, and figures. The dust ruffles around the bed and the spread on top are of the same material. The bed stands in one corner with a window at the head and one on the side, but we have tightened them by pasting painted linen cloth over all cracks and stuffed them with cotton, cloth, paper, frames [casements?], and I don't know what, so I think we are safe against draught. The other windows in here we have also managed to tighten fairly well. Here we have green roller blinds made of paper; one of them is tied up with two green tassels, and the other one is pulled up with rowels, in America it doesn't matter so much. The bed is standing a bit out on the floor, for the walls are cold and damp. In front of the bed stands the cradle, which is big and takes a lot of space, it is covered with blue molton as it was rather open on the sides, and then I have put a hood over it for the draught. The ceiling is like the one in the parlor, but here Munch had to go to the expense of a carpet over the whole floor, it is very nice; we got it from a Norwegian for about 40 cents per yard; underneath we have filled in richly with straw, which helps a good deal. Here, too, the stove is between the windows to the west, and as this one is a little bigger than the one in the parlor, I had to shorten half of the drapes for each window. Your priceless bureau, Mother dear, is standing at the center of the partition, with Grandmother's tablecloth and the mirror on top; in it we keep our trifles, and in the top drawer Munch has his money and papers. All the rest of our clothes which we use daily I keep in Munch's big trunk, which has been put in here in one corner and is very useful, for wardrobes and, in short, everything that is made by human hand is unreasonably expensive. The packing cases we brought with us serve as containers for flour, grain, and many other things. In the one that was sent to us last summer I keep my sheets and table linen; Ellen has to be content to have her clothes in a basket.

I think I have told about everything in our bedroom except a crude table, at which we usually eat (in fact, we spend most of our time here), and a very nice washstand with a drawer, and a white basin and jug on top; next to it I have hammered up three nails on the doorcase, one above the other, to hang our towels, for on the walls, all of which are masonry, I have great difficulty making a nail stick.

The kitchen has been built onto the center of the side of the building to the south. It is nice and large, with two doors in order to have thorough draught during the summer, and a window. Here the maid sleeps, and the boy in a drawer that is pushed under the bed in the daytime. The cooking stove is standing in a corner, and the pipe leads up through the ceiling. You will see a shelf on one wall with a curtain in front; you will also find a small white-scoured table and a couple of wooden chairs, besides a variety of kitchen tools hanging around the walls, everything shiny and in the best order. The kitchen is always clean and just as nice and snug as a living room.

Upstairs you first enter a loft, where I keep flour, clothes that are not used daily, and several other things; there is a designated place for everything, you may be sure. From here you enter a small room with low ceiling and two windows. Here is a bed with Emil's bedding, a white dust ruffle below, and a spread on top, made of the same varicolored print as in the bedroom; the white curtains that I brought are hanging before the windows (Madam Holmen saw at once that they were Norwegian curtains). The roller blinds are about the same as the ones in the parlor. Here is no furniture at all except when somebody is visiting with us. The stove is ridiculous, an ell long and half an ell wide and tall.

Have I not now given you an accurate description of everything we have? Maybe you even found it tiring to read. The enclosed little drawing of the house will make it even clearer to you.

Munch returned home safe and sound in moonlight Monday night and had had a comfortable trip.

My dear Nanna! Cordial thanks to you for your letter, it was just what I wished to hear from your own hand. You will see from my letter, which I hope you have received, that I have been thinking of you; you will hear from me again soon. May God give you the courage and health to make a serious matter of coming over here to see us. You would be *heartily* welcome! I don't think you can imagine how pleasant this would be for me and Munch, and both of us wish it intensely. Give it some serious thought, Nanna dear! [8]

I am longing greatly to hear from Sophie Pehrson, but I dare not mention it; imagine, I have not yet once written her in answer to all her letters. Tomorrow is my dear Lagertha's birthday, you can be sure I remember you, my friend, God bless you and make you happy! Give comfort and joy to your fond parents, and never forget your Savior!

God grant you health and joy in the new year, dear Father, good luck with the ship, and much money in the coffer, I know you have many holes to put it in! . . .

I would have loved to see Bernt as a Spanish knight. I dare say you deemed yourself pretty handsome that time? How many times did you look in the mirror? Please write and tell me, you have been silent for rather a long time. Should I not wish you a *new* sweetheart for the new year? Or do you already have one?

My sweet little Emilie you must enclose in your next letter to me, I am sure she would love to come and play with Ellen, won't you, Milli dear? For you, my dear Mother, I wish all the best, a little less to do, and more peace and quiet. Friendly greetings to all the other brothers and sisters; Cathinka must be a big, clever girl by now, I wouldn't mind if you wrote me a few lines telling me about all your friends, the school, and the singing.

I have waited too long getting this letter sent off, I am sure you are waiting sorely. Best wishes, and give my love to all good friends!

from your affectionate daughter Caja Munch

Your letter via Emil I have also received; thank you for all of them, I am going to write more frequently hereafter.

Two of my brooches and my golden clasp I have forgotten at home; I believe Reiman, the goldsmith, has them. It was Aunt Emilie's with the red stones and the small pin with a chain.

Mrs. Caja Munch to her Grandmother, Mrs. Karen Birgitte Staffeldt, née Herfordt

Wiota, February 13, 1857

My dear Grandmother!

Finally I bring you my warm thanks for the dear communication that I received by Even Kronborg upon his return to America. I should of course have written a long time ago and sent you my thanks when my kind old Grandmother would deign me such a nice long letter, but the fault is really little Else's [Ellen] and the fact that America is so poorly supplied with help. Imagine, now I have a young girl, who was confirmed by Munch last year, and who knows nothing, and yet she is supposed to get more than 1 *Spd.* per week. Moreover, one has to beg and plead with her to stay; indeed, she regards it as a favor on her part that she serves with us and not with a Yankee.

We can soon expect another spring over here. God give that the time will come when we can be looking forward to spring in our dear old Norway. Here we can certainly not look forward to the summer; indeed, as far as I am concerned, it could stay winter all the time here in America, for I can never get used to the strong thunder and lightning that we have here, and these violent wind storms, it is so frightening, although one knows that there is a God who governs it all. Considering in addition the intense heat, much illness, and these dark, sultry nights when it is impossible to sleep, I find it should be sufficient motivation to bring us back to our healthy and comfortable fatherland, if it is God's will.

But in spite of all, I would not have missed this journey. Even though the body is not so comfortable over here, I think our souls have had great benefit from the tour, and that we by mere grace have come closer to our God and Savior. But I cannot comprehend the statement I have heard from several of the ministers over here, that they intend to stay here for years, maybe even forever. They cannot have any strong longings for their fatherland, although I wonder if there isn't some speculation at work here; for if you want to buy land, like many have already done, and get involved in business and trade, you can surely make some money over here, and that is certainly a dangerous temptation for the good ministers. Dietrichson and

Munch, I believe, are the only ones who are quite determined to
go back to Norway as soon as possible. There, too, is a wide field
to work in for the one who wishes to serve his Lord faithfully.

21st [February, 1857]
Today Munch has left me to go to Dodgeville. This is one of
my worst hardships; I am then the oldest one in the whole house,
I have no one to talk to and no one to give me advice if
something should happen. Last year, I had my dear Emil, but
this year I am quite alone. Oh, then it is so good to have one's
Bible to read in; indeed, there we find more consolation and
encouragement than we are able to comprehend.

Sunday [February 22, 1857]
My oldest maid and the boy are away, so my only company
is the little neat of a nursemaid. After having read a beautiful
sermon for the day, I went down to look after my animals. We
have got another cow, named "Diana," and a dog, three months
old, named "Juno," which looks like he is going to be clever and
big. They get more use out of their dogs here than they do at
home, there is a different breed in them; they know not only all
the people who belong to the house but also the animals, and
they keep all others at a proper distance.

On my excursion I found an egg, one of the first ones this
year, and I boiled it for my dinner along with a little porridge
and beer that I have brewed recently, and enjoyed a fairly tasty
meal in the kitchen. I then took care of my little Else while the
maid had her meal; but if I may say so myself, she was so
beautiful just then that I sat there wishing that you and all my
aunts could have seen her; she smiled and chattered and looked
so sensible, as if she really were talking to me. God be thanked
for this wonderful gift! I am so happy with her, if I only could
squeeze her as hard as I want to, but she is too little yet. She is
certainly strong; she tears, claws, and pinches until I cry out
loud, there are marks in the table from her fingers, and yesterday
she scratched my hand to make me bleed. Hageman will probably find it reasonable to assume that there is some of a cat's nature in my child, but tell him to watch out that she doesn't come

and take revenge on him herself (with each mail I wait for letters from good friends). Little Else looks like her namesake, and may she continue to do so, then she will not be ugly.[9] She has already had three proposals, both of Pastor Duus's sons and the youngest of Messrs. Dietrichson, so she is already giving her father something to think about.

Uncle won't get off so easily, I must ask him once more if it wouldn't be possible to get me some sheet music for the accordion. Dietrichson has now acquired a small pianoforte, and he has borrowed all my song music; I am now longing even more to go down there, but Else says *no*.

On the 25th of March we are going to have a total eclipse of the sun at *8—eight* o'clock at night. Surely, it is quite dark here by then, but never mind that a bit. Everything is the wrong way here in America, and this is no exception; it really says so in the almanac. Indeed, many things are upside down here. Thus a woman is much better on horseback than a man; in many families the men milk the cows and take care of the house, while the wife sits in her rocking chair with the children and reads or usually just drones. The Yankee ladies are terribly lazy, if I can call them ladies; indeed, I hardly think there is a single cultured family to be found here until you get to the larger cities. Although they dress like court ladies, it is still obvious from their conduct and manners that they are of the crudest rabble. They show up in church here; one Sunday Munch had to pause in his sermon and ask the congregation to show two such ladies to the door as they sat and laughed straight to his face; however, they immediately took the hint and retired to the outside across the pews as fast as they could. What do you think of that? And this was unfortunately neither the first nor the last time it happened.

Please give my love to Ida Spørck and thank her for the letter and for the things she sent. I shall write to her some other time. Munch sends his cordial greetings. God be with you and your whole house, my dear Grandmother! Give my love to everybody

from your Caja Munch

Mrs. Caja Munch to her Sisters-in-Law, Henriette and
Caroline Munch

Wiota, Shrove Monday [February 23,] 1857
Dear Jette and Caroline!

Will you permit me to write to the two of you at the same
time? You have both been kind enough to write to me, and I am
truly sorry that I have not before been able to give you evidence
of my intense gratitude for every one of your dear words; but
time, time, my good friends, is short in America. Out here one is
spared from getting any work hired. I often have to prepare the
food if I want a decent meal; most of the time I even have to
bake my own bread and similar chores, and our clothes I have to
sew and keep in order.

But what occupies most of my time is of course little Else. It
is impossible for me to get her a little nursemaid with whom she
will stay, and I am free only a short while during the morning
when she sleeps, and then I have to rush away as if I were
stealing the time. I just now brought her inside. She has been
out for a walk for the second time this winter; so far it has been
too cold for her, indeed, so cold that I have had trouble keeping
her warm in our airy bedroom. She fell asleep during the walk
and is now lying in her lovely cradle so nice and soundly asleep
that it is a real delight to me. Oh, how intensely grateful I must
be, and really am, to my God for this dear child which He has
given me, so big and strong and healthy and beautiful and sweet,
indeed, she looks like her grandmother to a dot, she has the same
kind, *irresistible* eyes, and if she continues to grow up looking so
much like her namesake, she will surely become a dangerous
lady for the young gentlemen who will drop in on the village
pastor from their hikes to get some food and rest—in Norway, of
course! As soon as she saw the light of day, all those who had
seen your daguerrotype, dear Mother-in-Law, cried out, "It is
the very picture of Bishopess Munch!" So it was impossible to
have a moment's doubt about the name she should be given.

We used to call her Ellen, but I have decided to abandon
that completely, for I despise all Yankee manners and have often
laughed and made fun of the Norwegians who christen their
children with Yankee names; indeed, we ourselves would not
have been much better, then. A girl asked Dietrichson to look

for letters for her at the post office; if it was from Norway, she said, the address would be "To Maiden Guri Astersdatter," but if it was from some Norwegians in America, it would be "To Miss Charlotte Jansen." Ugh! Yes, it is dreadful to hear how terrible some of these Norwegian-Americans are. It almost gives you an aversion to everything English.

Little Else has no teeth yet. I am a little worried about that since she is so fat and wonderful, but by the help of God everything will be all right, I am sure. A little girl in the congregation who was born the day before, already has two. May our Lord hold His hand over our little treasure! Should something happen, we would have no help at all here, it is frightening to think how we are absolutely devoid of a physician's aid. "Mangor's Country Pharmacy" stands us in good stead, but then again we are often short of medicines; to be sure, you can buy some that are called by the same names here, but one certainly had better not take most of them, for they are not at all trustworthy.

Believe me, it is a frightful, often sinful business that is carried on here with the medical arts. A man may one day be a farmer, the next day he has bought himself an American drugstore, where liquor actually is the most important article; and after having carried on this for about a month, he sets himself up as a doctor and takes some of his medicines in a satchel on his back and drives around to the poor sick ones, who in their distress take what help is offered.[10] You can imagine what knowledge they have, and I believe, although it is almost horrible to say so, that these physicians, in order to make money, never give a thought to the fact that they may become manslayers. I know several people whose health they have completely ruined for life with their strong medicines. This is how medical service is in the country and in the small miserable towns around here, where the most prominent article is liquor; in the larger cities there is certainly a little better service available, although it is in a bad way even there. There is hardly a doctor here who can be compared with our skillful Norwegian physicians; if some of them would like to come over, they would quite certainly make good business, because here you pay an extraordinary amount of money *to have your life ruined;* and think what a labor of mercy an able physician would do for us poor creatures who live here. You, who live in Christiania and meet so many people, tell them this and ask them to think it over; I can assure you that he would have an income, we have talked to several people who dearly wish for a Norwegian physician; we will give him free lodging as long as he wishes.

All the liquor that is for sale around here has also caused Munch great vexation, for many are tempted by it ([added between the lines:] this must not be understood as if I were tempted! J. S. M.) , and there is, unfortunately, much drinking among the Norwegians in the congregation. Here is a whole settlement where I could possibly except two men, otherwise they all drink. You can imagine that it is unpleasant to be their minister, but one cannot exclude them entirely from the congregation. Munch is hoping that the conditions will improve in time; besides, the congregation is too weak to carry all the burdens that rest upon it without these drunkards. Of course they think Munch is strict, and at a congregation meeting they even stood up and abused him; they reproached him for not having conducted a service that time he had such a bad throat, and when Munch told them he was sick, one of them said, "You could have come anyway!" Isn't it horrible? But then Munch stood up and gave them a very serious speech, whereby several even broke into tears. And since then they have been quiet and have even shown some signs of repentance. Had not this congregation had a minister so serious, determined, and zealous as I dare say Munch really is, it would surely go to its death, for here prevails the highest measure of discord, disunion, and fatuity to the Word of God. It is not, as we thought before we left Norway, an intense longing to hear the Word of the Lord and a craving to partake of His holy gifts that has moved these people to join together in a Christian congregation, but it was just to get their children baptized, to take Communion once in the fall and once in the spring, like they "done at home," as they say, and now and then to go to church and hear a sermon. But to live according to the Word of God, that is a thing they don't want, so you may be sure my dear Munch has a struggle on his hands.

One day a drunken man came into the parlor and would not leave, insisting that it was his house since the congregation had paid for it and not the minister. Munch is having many similar annoyances, but then the Lord strengthens him in his prayers and gives him good hope. Besides, he has a few genuine stalwart men in the congregation, who are a big help and support to him.

Munch is now, as usual when I write, in Dodgeville, I only wish he were safely back home, for last night and today we have had an incessant rain so that our little brook is far overflowing its banks, and the greater part of the field is under water. I expect any minute that our bridge will take off, for it is rickety and not at all fit to withstand a flood. That would be very bad, then even the minister could not get up to his own house. Believe me, it is dreary to me when Munch is away. Last year I could accompany him, but now I jolly well must stay at home with my little Else, who surely fills up many a lonely hour for me; but then, at the same time, I am so worried for her when Munch is away. I know very well that this is wrong, our Lord will surely protect us just as well then as always, but my character is too weak, I do not have enough faith. Oh, indeed, I am sad to say that I have not yet gone far on the narrow path!

Next year we have to start all over again planting trees and laying out a garden, if we will take that much trouble. I hardly think anything serious will come of it, for it is too hot here to do any work ourselves, and help is not to be had; besides, there is so much that is needed if we should think of bringing it to any completion. It would be expensive, and Munch has no money. "Promising is honest, but keeping is hard," I must say, for he is not at all getting from the congregation what they promised him in the letter of presentation. They come and tell us that they are so poor and that they do not have anything, so what can the minister do? All the trees, grapevines, and honeysuckles that we planted around the house last year have been completely ruined by the repair work that had to be done on the house last fall, and in their place we now have big heaps of clay, gravel, and stones, into which we sink over our shoes as soon as we set foot outside the door. My little flower bed outside the parlor windows is also destroyed. Indeed, one could easily lose the inclination to start over again trying to make it pretty, especially when you take into consideration the violent climate of America, which in a flash may break down both flowers and trees with its torrential rain and strong wind and wash away the seeds. But I must have something to look at over here, otherwise I cannot feel comfortable. I shall therefore do what I can to get it restored somewhat.

The 24th [February, 1857]

Tomorrow I am first going to make Shrovetide crossbuns. On the Monday I certainly wished that I had some of Lisabet's course[?], although I enjoyed admirably my coarse rye bread, and I surely could have had some, but I wanted to wait until Munch returned home so I would have fresh ones that we can enjoy together in pleasant quiet. Then he is always so happy to be back in his own home, and I always have to make something extra for him to really make it as pleasant as possible. Last Friday I brewed and got a very good beer, although it is a poor substitute for the Bavarian; Munch often wishes for a glass of that.

I think Munch wants to write to Herman himself and ask him to buy him a good tobacco pipe and some bowls and mouthpieces; all the ones he brought with him Dietrichson and he have completely ruined, and here in America they usually smoke only clay pipes so short that I should think they would burn their noses. They gape and stare at Munch's pipe as something quite strange. Besides, the tobacco is so strong that I am unable to stand the smoke from it.

I hardly know myself what I am writing, for Else whimpers and frets and wants me to pick her up; besides, I really have nothing more to say, I have just finished a long letter home, and one to Grandmother.

Many thanks for what you sent me, dear Jette. Believe me, it is enjoyable to smarten up little Else with the things she has gotten from Norway. The cape she used for the first time on Munch's birthday, and since then it has been washed and pressed many times; the little frizz becomes her extremely well. Munch has retrieved the box from her to put his clergyman's ruffs in it when he is traveling. You can imagine, it is a laborious task to set up these ruffs for Munch; last time, I was at it for almost two days to get one of them fluted for him, but then it did turn out rather nice except for a little burn here and there. If it is possible to get some sent to him next spring with one of the *seven* ministers for whom there are vacant charges here, you would do us a great favor.

I should have written a special letter to little Johan and thanked him heartily for the lovely lock of his hair that he would allow us; it has been put away safely and will probably cross the Atlantic Ocean once more with me. I dare say you are a clever boy now, Johan, and will soon be able to write a letter to cousin Else; maybe you could become her "Knight Aage" if you are not too grand. Is Aunt Jette a strict tutor, you think? Or are you her master? You must write to me, Johan, and tell me, then I shall write you a letter, too. You might ask Grandmother Juul if she would have you daguerreotyped and send it to me, I would love to see all of your curly head. Is he still your pupil, Jette?

I really have some big school children to look at these days, for there is an English schoolhouse a little ways from the church, where there are big and small boys and girls all mixed together, but what they learn I don't comprehend, for I see them outside and hear their horrible screams all day; they used to go sleigh riding down the hill to the church on the school benches and on big boards which they practically tore from the walls of the house, using their red woolen jackets as flags. When you see this youth, you can get an idea of what caliber the people are in this country; the children do not know what it is to respect their parents, they live in a free country, and they are supposed to have freedom to do as they please. No wonder, then, that they are more like animals than people; however, there are exceptions.

Best wishes to you, dear Mother-in-Law and sisters-in-law, God bless you and let you enjoy many happy days in your lovely home! Give my love to all in the family and to other good friends and acquaintances who would be interested in receiving a cordial greeting from your affectionate

                                                Caja Munch

I am longing greatly for letters, we have heard nothing from Norway for a long, long time.

Mrs. Caja Munch to her Parents, Mr. and Mrs. F. W. S. Falch
                                    Wiota, March 31, 1857

Dear Parents!

Again a long time has passed during which I have not managed to write to you. Your last letter to me, dear Mother, was received about two weeks ago, and I thank you a thousand times for it. Believe me, there is joy when letters arrive from

Norway; even when I have no reason to expect a letter, it is the first thing I ask Peer about when he comes from town; so you must please write, all of you. Bernt, honestly, what are you about? I never see a jot from you. And you, Oskar, who have become such a dab at writing! And Axel, and Fredrich Wilhelm, and Cathinka dear, indeed, I have many who can write to me, but see if they do! Lagertha, I have been naughty to you, likewise to Sophie Pehrson, but what can I do? I never get beyond *one* letter, and in it I lump everybody together; I know that all of you read it, and when I write, I am thinking of all.

Next Friday is Sophie Pehrson's birthday, I remember it well although she probably thinks I have forgotten her. I have all the time had in mind writing to her, but I never get beyond thinking of it. Give her my love and all good wishes; we shall raise the flag for her.

With luck, this letter may perhaps reach you on your birthday, dear Father; would God grant that I could do something to gladden you, dear Father mine! But I am too far away. Dear brothers and sisters, do not grieve your Parents! Be obedient and diligent children! Some time when you must leave your home, only then will you fully realize what your parents have meant to you, and then you will regret that you have not behaved toward them as you ought to, but then it is too late. However, if but by God's help I shall return to Norway some time, then I know for certain what I will do as sure as there is a spark of chance. Then Father and Mother are coming to stay with me, and I shall care for them just like they have done for me. This is the crowning feature of my joy in this world. Oh, may God hear my prayer that this may come to pass! Think of all the happiness we would have in glorious *NORWAY!!!*

Munch is at Dietrichson's for a few days, I expect him back today although it is raining steadily, but tomorrow he has a confirmation class and cannot stay away any longer. He had to drive down there head over heels with the money and the records of the Widows' Fund, although the roads are almost impassable. He had to hire conveyance as both of his mares are going to foal and therefore cannot be used. Believe me, I would have loved to accompany him, but my little Else would not go while the roads were that bad, she said, and so I jolly well had to stay at home with her.

It is lively at Dietrichson's now as they have acquired a small pianoforte, and several cultured young people who can both play and sing, have arrived at the printing press, so you can imagine that I would have liked to join them and participate in it all. I am also longing indescribably to see my dear Emil. I recently received a remarkably nice letter from him; he is, praise God, content in his position, and everybody is still pleased with him. To be sure, the pay is small in the beginning, but I have no doubts at all but that his diligence will be rewarded. Have no worries for him, beloved Parents! He has such a kind disposition that our Lord surely will help him through this world to a better life. Wherever he goes, you know people must become fond of him, and as he himself is content and suffers no wants, I think we ought to give thanks to God for that and leave his future weal and woe to Him.

What shall I write about now? I encounter so very little these days, my only excursion is to the church now and then, otherwise I exist only for my little Else, who by God's help is doing well under my care. Constantly I have to sew new clothes for her as she grows out of them as fast as I can make them, although I never make them too small. Indeed, it is a great joy to us seeing this lovable little creature, how she daily gains in sense and size; she already gives Munch and myself great enjoyment. When she hears me talking in the attic or in the other room, she becomes a menace and wants to join me, and when I enter, she stretches out her fat little arms and throws herself toward me, and then you can imagine how very, very happy I am. I certainly have been very fond of my brothers and sisters, but not like this. I often think of myself when I was a little girl, then you and Father were surely just as fond of me; and to think how little I appreciated such love later on, and for that reason you probably do not love me as much now, do you? When Munch and I play with Else, the thought often comes to me that Father and Mother surely played the same way with me one time.

Else does not want to eat anything. I have made crackers for her and prepared them like I did for the children at home, but when I come with the spoon, she gets both hands and feet in motion and hits the spoon so it flies out of my hand; or if I get as far as her mouth, she pouts her lips and sputters the food high in the air, and then what can I do? She has no teeth yet.

One day, I let her loose with her little stockings on, which Munch had bought; you know I am not too clever at knitting. But then she caught such a cold that I tied the fat little legs in again and would rather wait until the weather gets warmer. I take her out for a little while in the middle of the day when the weather is nice, but she is so frightfully heavy to carry when she is in her outdoor apparel, and if I want to sit down with her, she cries. We have ordered a small baby carriage for her from a Norwegian joiner; I am going to put a top on it, for the sun is so strong here.

There are signs of spring already, we have had some beautiful days for a while now. This is no doubt the most comfortable time of the year in this country; later on we get the heat and those frightful thunderstorms. May God hold His hand over us and keep us from illness.

It is almost evening, and I am steadily looking for Munch; but I cannot see any sign of him yet. I have made him a herring salad, I wish he would come. The herring is a present from one of the neighbors, whose children Munch teaches. This school really brings many good things into the house; each time, they bring something of milk, cream, butter, eggs, or whatever else they may have. We have told them not to bring us so much, but the parents are so glad that Munch will teach their children that they surely would rather give him much more. Munch himself gets pleasure from prompting them ahead, although several of them know absolutely nothing. But they are willing, and it may certainly stand them in good service in the future; he speaks to them a lot and urges many good principles upon them. One day, as these children came walking along the road together and saw Munch in the window, one of the little boys hurriedly folded his hands and walked along that way right up to the door, which of course gave us a good laugh.

The new cow that we bought and paid 23 dollars for was supposed to calve in the month of July but dropped her calf the other day. It has probably starved and suffered too much last winter. We have no milk as yet, my own cow "Kate" is not supposed to calve for another week, but then I think surely we will have a lot of milk, it looks like it. I personally give her some meal-drink twice a day, she comes quite punctually to the door waiting for it. Yesterday I set a goose on twelve eggs; I have only two geese and one gander, the others have been killed.

No, I cannot write any more tonight, I am thinking and waiting too much for Munch; he probably won't come after this hour. You are already asleep now. God grant you a sweet and pleasant sleep, and let you wake up tomorrow with peace in your hearts and thanks to God for all good things.

April 6 [1857]

Munch came home that night after all and had been driving in the rain all day but has, God be praised, felt well after it. At Dietrichson's they were all well, and they were very happy to see Munch. It was also good for Emil's sake that he went down there. The printing press is going to be moved to Madison, and now Munch wants Emil's contract canceled so he will only commit himself for half a year at a time. His pay will of course be raised since board and room will be more expensive for him in Madison; and if Emil does not wish to go with the printing press to this city, which is said to be full of temptations for a young person, then Dietrichson, who used to be its director and who does a lot for Emil, thinks that he could get Emil 100 dollars in compensation. But Emil, who is quite able in the printing press and who likes his position well, prefers to go along, I think. Besides, I believe that, with God's help, we have nothing to fear for Emil in that respect, for he is too steady and worthy a boy to allow himself to be seduced. I expect him here this week, he is going to spend Easter with us, for which I am extremely glad, for Munch will leave Saturday for Dodgeville. I have brewed beer for him, and I shall bake a wort-cake of the genuine kind. For the rest I don't know what we are going to eat as we are very short of food at this time. Eggs are our principal food; we have twelve chickens, and they provide us daily with what we need of that item.

On the third Sunday after Easter, Munch is going to preach at Rock Prairie for Dietrichson as they wish to partake of Communion. We will then leave here the preceding week on the first nice day, for I and little Else are going along. Dietrichson himself will meet us in Monroe with two carriages, these people are so kind to us and would dearly like to have us come. Brandt and his wife have been there, but they did not like her so well, she talked so much and was so informed and bragged about her many trips in Europe.

Little Else has a tooth, and I expect any day to see another. Believe me, dear Mother, we both were glad as I must admit that we were terribly worried because she took so long getting any; but this one came very easily, may it go just as well with all the others, then we could not thank God enough for it. It is difficult for babies here when they cut their teeth. I have, however, a remedy that I intend to use in case it should become necessary. That is to make a cut in the comb of a rooster so it bleeds, and this blood is to be rubbed on the gums and is supposed to be excellent, a simple measure which can't do any harm.

When we get to Dietrichson's, I am going to have Else vaccinated as the Norwegian Dr. Hanssen, who came over here last summer, is going to visit Dietrichson with his wife at the same time as we are. Hanssen complains that his income has been so meager this winter, which I cannot understand; maybe he is still too little known. This winter he stayed with Pastor Herman Preus who, although he is a rich man, has been very particular with the doctor. Preus has considerable property besides his parsonage, a lot of cows and horses, and an abundance of everything. Nevertheless, Hanssen had to keep his horse with a farmer, and all winter long both he and his wife had to go over there carrying hay on their backs for the horse. He had to keep himself with firewood and probably had to buy a lot of other things as the good man Preus carries it rather far with his avarice. You can imagine what kind of man this is who could treat Hanssen that way, while at the same time, by the help of God, Hanssen saved his wife from death. She had the misfortune of falling down into the cellar about a month before she was due to be delivered, but she did not notice anything until her time came; then she had a frightful hemorrhage and gave birth to a dead baby boy.[11] Even Preus was quite certain that if she had not had the aid of an able physician, she would have lost her life. But in what way does he show this man his gratitude? Oh, no, unfortunately, there is much frailness among some of the Norwegian ministers here! The ample opportunity they have had before to acquire money has made them rich and has interfered with the peace of their souls. Add to this the fact that one of these young ministers over here is even supposed to be chairman for the others and to travel about and inspect those who are perhaps far superior to him in many respects; this makes them arrogant so they forget their position as ministers and do not even suffer the others to have an opinion.

Even Kronborg has returned and has bought back his property. We have no sexton for the time being, so you can imagine the singing in the church is rather poor.

Two gold dollars should have been enclosed in this letter, but we don't have any now; however, I shall see if we can send them next time. The package you sent with Brandt I have now received, many thanks for its contents, I appreciate everything and shall make use of it next summer if I only will be able to arrange for a little piece of ground to sow in, but both a fence around it and a helper are very expensive, and Munch is as poor as a church rat; but there may be a way.

Best wishes for now, beloved Parents, God bless you and grant that all of you be sound and happy! Write to me as often as you can. Give my fondest love to brothers and sisters, friends and acquaintances from

your daughter Caja Munch

Do not ask to read Nanna's letter, but let her do as she pleases; it contains only some well-meaning advice from a sister.

Please send Munch's letter to his mother as soon as possible. Munch and Else send their cordial greetings to you.

Mrs. Caja Munch to her Parents, Mr. and Mrs. F. W. S. Falch

Wiota Parsonage, May 3, 1857

My beloved Parents!

Now I must break my long silence as I long ago really both wanted and ought to have done; lack of time is the only excuse I have, but that is of little significance, ought I not to have put everything aside for writing since I know that my insignificant words can so intensely gladden my Father who is ill? But to tell the truth, I have not at all had the strength to do it until now when your second dear letter arrived, Mother mine, and I learned from it that my dearest Father continues to improve; a thousand thanks for every word, my dear Mother, God bless you and give you strength in every one of your good and tender deeds! You will surely some time reap a rich reward, only stay sincerely near your Savior.

Indeed, it was sad news for me to learn about my dear

Father's illness. May God strengthen all of you, and especially
you who suffer, Father dear! We know full well that him whom
God loveth, He chasteneth; only give Him your sinful heart with
sincere repentance, and He will prepare you an Eternity filled
with such joy as we in our human body are unable to grasp or
comprehend! Let us not have worries about the future and what
sorrows and joys it has in store, but let us love our Savior with all
our heart and daily reprove ourselves and humbly ask forgiveness for our great sins, then He will repay our zeal and love for
Him many, many, many times. Think always of what it says in
one of David's Psalms: "I have been young and now am old; yet
have I not seen the righteous forsaken, nor his seed begging
bread." Would to God that you had a serious curator of souls
among you, to whom you could have recourse under such circumstances, and who could admonish you and give you strength
in your faith, such as Munch so often does here, administering
the Sacrament of the Altar to the sick provided he finds him
worthy and prepared for it.

From the accounts we have given you before, you have
probably gathered already that only after the stipulated five
years will we return to our dear fatherland if it is God's will.
May God hold His protecting hand over all of you until then so
we may be reunited in joy and happiness. We are going to spend
the last year at Rock Prairie where Dietrichson now resides, and
Munch is concurrently going to serve four congregations here, so
his time will certainly be occupied; may God only grant him
that he will continue in the good health that he has enjoyed so
far here in America, then the duties of the holy office go before
everything. The plan is that Dietrichson after his arrival in
Norway will provide ministers for both charges at once, who
then, if all goes well, will release Munch in the spring of 1860.
Then we could leave America with a good conscience and hope
that our God would bless Munch's labors also in the fatherland,
whether it be in one or the other direction.

I am not much in favor of this moving to Rock Prairie. I
like it best where I am, our parsonage is arranged better, although it is much smaller. At Dietrichson's they have the kitchen
in the basement and thus a long flight of stairs to run up and
down, besides all the smoke and steam comes right up into the
parlor. I have just got it quite cozy around here. The two rooms
downstairs I have just recently whitewashed. At first I did not

know quite how to go about it, but I was not disheartened. An Englishman lives close by, whom I knew to be a master mason; I sent for him, and he came immediately and showed me, you can imagine I strained all my knowledge of English to make myself understood. And after that the wash went on quite briskly; Anne helped me. Munch got quite a surprise when he got home.

Emil, who after a short stay in Madison returned to us again, helped me whitewashing the bedroom. Besides he has papered the kitchen with the wallpaper that we had brought from Norway, for housebugs had started to show up between the boards, and I did not know anything better to do. Now it is almost the nicest room in the house, and we will eat there from now on. I have had the cooking stove moved to a small room on the side, where Emil has put down a floor and something that they here call *Schingel* [shingles] on the roof, which keeps the rain out completely. We have got hold of a newly arrived joiner, who will make me a cupboard with two drawers at the bottom as the mice are about to ruin everything for me in the rickety Norwegian boxes, besides a table, some stools, a buggy and a bed for Else as she has grown out of both her cradle and the little buggy that Munch finally got hold of for her. So you see, little by little we too will be living like cultured people.

Emil is now working on getting a small garden laid out on the other side of the house; he has planted a close row of plum trees for a fence, and between them I shall lay out climbers. Let me not forget this time to send you a few seeds, but it can't be many for they are rather big and heavy, you will get some more when I get home myself—oh, how cheerful we will be together that first summer if everything goes according to our wishes. Lagertha, you must plant these seeds by a wall where they can climb, I suggest a couple on each side of the stairs from the garden room so they can twine themselves up between the two pretty rose trees. Around Father's garden house at the Works they would look pretty if you could bring in some good soil for them; they grow very willingly.

Munch has spaded the other little garden and fixed up the fence around it, but I have not yet got a seed of any kind in the ground with the exception of a few potatoes that Emil planted for me. I still have some kinds of the Norwegian seeds, which I shall put out.

Now it is very cold again after a few days that were nearly

hot; it has been raining almost continuously for a long, long time. My old cow has borne, so now we get good milk again; however, I cannot say that we have gone without, my good old friends have seen to that. We have drawn my wine into bottles, it is exquisite, but I hope to get it even better next year with a little less sugar.

The other day Munch had to go by oxen, which a man in the congregation had used to haul firewood for us, they were 4 ells long, 1½ ell between the horns, and 2½ ells tall. Isn't that a considerable size? Such animals have strength, you can imagine.

Well, I have really waited long enough to tell you something about our little jewel, whom Munch and I love more for every day that passes. Indeed, I wish intensely that you could see and hear her, she can now say almost anything she wants to say, and remarkably clearly; she mostly calls me "Caja," as distinctly as none of my brothers and sisters has ever been able to pronounce it. She is the funniest child you can imagine, Munch says it is all brains with a dress on. Today Munch asked her for a kiss; no, no, she said very seriously and shook her head. If we do something to her that she doesn't like, she says very reproachingly: But Daddy! But Mummy! She goes from one daguerreotype to the other, points and calls Grandma or Grandpa quite correctly, with such a lovely little voice that it would be a joy to your hearts to see and hear her. She is still so cheerful and friendly and affectionate that it is really remarkable; a little neighbor girl is her playmate, and she loves her so dearly, she fondles and pats her continuously and wants so very much to be with her. Recently, she was very ill; one time when Munch was away, a number of children here took sick almost on the very same day, and among them also Else; they had a high fever and threw up everything they got to eat. Oh, what a dreary day for me, and even worse for Munch who had left her so sound and smart. But God be thanked, He had mercy upon us and gave her back to us; I used nothing but oil and brandy-and-salt. Later on, when Munch was away again, she had a high fever, but that was for the nasty eyeteeth, and even now she is ailing off and on as she only now is getting all her awful teeth. Today she is as healthy and cheerful as I have not seen her for a long time; she has grown a little pale and sharp-nosed, but that doesn't matter, otherwise the heat should have bothered her tremendously. Last time Munch came home and found Else ill, he almost got even more depressed, for he came directly from a house of mourning. The Holmens from Drammen just lost their eldest son, a healthy boy of 11, from a severe cold. This had also delayed Munch for a day, so my anxiety was great until I had him back. But now we are, God be praised, all of us together again, sound and quick, and we have our dear Emil with us.

Every moment I am being interrupted by Else, who insists on getting up on my lap and write. Munch just asked her if she wanted to go to Norway, and she answered with great joy: Yes— Grandpa!

Early in June, Emil will go with a very worthy man from this congregation up to Minnesota to *klemme Land* [claim land]. This man has been informed by good friends that there is some quite excellent land up there; he is taking his own horses, and Emil will have free conveyance, both out and back if he so wishes. He will probably tell you more about this himself. He is not able to get into any printing press for the time being, but I for one am happy about that; I love to have him with me, I am so fond of him, and it is true, as Father says, God will not forsake such a good and affectionate soul who is so devoted and faithful to his Savior. At a book auction in Madison he bought a deluxe copy of an English Bible for 5 dollars and presented it to Munch, who appreciated it immensely, and to him it will always be a dear memory of Emil. It is enormously big, with several fine steel engravings in it, and gilded clasps; the actual value was estimated at 14 to 15 dollars. Likewise he has bought a number of copies of *Fridtjof's Saga* for 10 dollars, only to help a wretched poor man who did not even have the money to pay his lodging. Emil is getting on quite well, is healthy and sound, and contented with the prospects which now are open to him to acquire land.

This year I have again had poor luck with my geese. My whole collection consists of two geese, one gander, and five small, newly hatched goslings. They have laid very little, and in this cold weather they die as fast as they come. I set as many hens as I can, Emil has made some small coops for me to set them in.

Emilie must really be quite a sweet little girl, but watch out so you don't spoil her; Nanna, do you hear! . . .

The Dietrichsons are quite determined to leave next spring, and they have definitely promised to pay a visit to Hovland when they get to Norway. They are such kind and straightfor-

ward people, for whom you have no need to feel embarrassed in
any way, on the contrary, I am sure you will enjoy very much
talking to them.

Goodbye for now, dear beloved Parents, brothers, and sisters, our Lord keep all of you strong and healthy. My cordial
greetings to the Munchs and to Grandmother. Munch, Emil, and
Else send their love and warmest wishes. May this letter find you
in better health, my dear Father! Greetings from

your affectionate daughter Caja Munch

Mrs. Caja Munch to her Parents, Mr. and Mrs. F. W. S. Falch

Wiota Parsonage, Whitsunday, May 31, 1857

My dear beloved Parents!

I have just received a long loving letter from you, my dear
sweet Mother, and one from my dear kind Sophie; be you
thanked a thousand times for them. I have already repeatedly
told you what a joy it is for us to get letters from home, but a
good thing is never said too often. I see from your letters that
another box is on its way to us; oh, how kind you are! Would
that it not involve too much sacrifice on your part, beloved
Parents, because then I will not ask for anything at all from now
on. The most insignificant things that you might send are of
great value to me just because I know that you have held them
in your hands; believe me, sweet Mother, it often gives me a
strange feeling.

I always try to avoid thinking of the bygone days, for then
my longing for all my dear ones becomes so much stronger, and
that does not help anything. However, I am often thinking of
the future, and I always have, God be praised, the happy hope of
being again united with you at Hovland. Yes, may God hear my
prayer and keep all of you healthy and sound in spirit and body!
You are being tried hard, beloved Parents, but be of good cheer,
the Lord will surely send you help when His time comes and you
have humbled yourselves completely under His will and acknowledge how very little we humans afford without Him. Indeed, have we but Jesus for our true friend, then we could be
deprived of both house and home, and we should be just as
happy and with patience and gentleness bear the cross that God
in His wisdom will lay upon us.

You probably think it is peculiar that I am writing on a holy Whitsunday instead of working on the salvation of my soul, for which all the holy days are designed, but I hope God will forgive me for this, I had such a strong inclination to write just now; besides, you should know that first I have read aloud for my servants the sermon for the festival by my very good friend Hofacker. Otherwise, I never take anything in hand on Sundays except to read in devotional books. Sunday is not at all a day of rest, you know; to the contrary, on that day we should work on our souls, but how many times do we not offend against this commandment. Alas, we are so sleepy and lazy and allow one hour to run out after another and forget that it concerns the salvation of our souls. And yet, our heavenly Father will forgive us if we only pray with a sincere, repentant heart.

I scarcely need to tell you that Munch is away on a trip, for he is hardly ever at home when I write. This time he has several long trips to make and will be crossing Wisconsin River on a ferry, but it could never occur to me to be afraid, I have so many times seen proof that God is with him on his trips, so I have no doubts this time either that He will keep him safe, so that we can be happily reunited on Tuesday or Wednesday, when he should be back. He left Saturday before last, and between then and now he was supposed to conduct six services. It certainly is desolate and quiet for me during that time, but let me tell you what excitements I have had.

Right after Munch had left, I wrote to ten of the nearest farmers and asked them to come here and clean up around the house, where a lot of gravel and sand is still lying around since the repair work. But only one came, and with him I was outside all day picking stones and raking with all our might; the others promised me that they would come after Pentecost as they had not yet finished planting. Later I had six women and girls here, who helped me stitch two cotton spreads for our beds. These spreads are very common in this country; they first sew the material out of quite small, cut-up pieces, from which they shape stars, flowers, and I don't know what they might think of; in fact, they put fully as much work into their spreads in this country as they do with sofa cushions at home. But then they are sometimes really beautiful and show well on the bed, especially here where they never use bed curtains. My spreads were quite simple, made from some varicolored material; I did not seem to have the patience to be that neat, and I did not have the time either. After that I planted corn and potatoes and a good deal of melons, which I hope we shall enjoy; next year I shall send you some seeds in a letter, they should grow at home in good soil exposed to the sun. This year I have a little garden arranged in regular seedbeds, and I already have cabbage in boxes outside the kitchen window. But everything is unfenced so I have had great trouble trying to protect it all from our animals. The peas are already quite tall, carrots, turnips, and several other things have come up, but we have had such an unusually late and cold spring, so I am sure you have advanced further at home. Now it is raining rather hard, and it has been raining for several days; I wish I knew how Munch is getting along in this damp weather.

We have had some vines planted again, besides a number of plum trees, blackberry and raspberry canes; moreover, we have begged some wild gooseberry bushes and one currant bush, but we have planted a good many small currant twigs all over, and they are getting along and have green leaves already. Outside the two parlor windows I have had the gravel cleared away and soil brought in, then spaded and sown to make a little flower garden; for a fence around it we have a few hazel sticks, which Munch and I went up into the woods and chopped ourselves, and these we have stuck into the ground rather close, crisscross and thwartways, and planted climbers in between, so I hope it will turn out quite nice in time. The Norwegian rye is sprouting and getting greener every day.

I am almost as short of small animals as you are, my dear Mother, only six goslings. We were at Dietrichson's at the time the geese were hatched, otherwise I think I would have had more. The turkeys we have done away with as they grew too troublesome for us and ruined things not only for us but also for our neighbors. The guinea fowls we will kill off, too, for they are no whit better, their meat also is said to be no good, and their eggs are very small, but they are big eaters. Chickens and geese, however, we will pursue might and main. One hen is sitting, and the others are laying big delicious eggs, which are our best food.

"Polly" is well again, and on Easter Tuesday she had *two* big foals, one of which, however, was dead; that, we now realize, was for the best, for she could not possibly have reared two as there has been a great shortage of both hay and oats during this late spring. Munch helped others until he had nothing himself; indeed, when we returned up here from Dietrichson's, "Polly" was so thin that I almost cried looking at her. We expect "Betsy" to foal any day now.

Emil was with us at Easter time when "Polly" foaled. He has always had such affection for that horse, so you can imagine he was happy to be able to care for her and give her flour-drink. The foal is named "Dik" and looks like it is going to be black. My cow "Kate" has borne a nice big cow calf, which will be called "Elly" after Else. Now I have a lot of milk and could have had more if the nasty "Diana" had not lost her calf; she had probably been starved before she came to us. Over the entire country a whole lot of cattle have perished this last winter for lack of feed and shelter; some have lost as many as twenty head of cattle.

Emil, then, has become a metropolitan. I have written him a long scolding letter and sent him all the letters from Norway, I know he enjoys so much reading them, and the postage is not much. He has not written to me at all since he left here after Easter, but from J. Preus, who lives in Madison and whom I met at Dietrichson's, I heard that he is getting along well, he had spoken to him recently. He complained of Emil being so quiet, but then you may be sure that both Dietrichson and we rose to claim that this was just an indication that he had no taste for all the frivolous goings on that we know take place abundantly in Madison; for when he is with us, he is not quiet. Indeed, may God hold His hand over him in that dangerous city! I hardly think he will stay there beyond the autumn, for neither he nor we want him to commit himself to the printing press for all of two years; and Dietrichson, its former director, claims that Fleischer cannot possibly force him to do so. Emil can then go to whatever printing press he wants and get a much higher pay.

Dietrichson received as an appreciation from the printing press a large case containing 12 pairs of big and 12 pairs of small knives and sterling forks besides 12 dessertspoons and two fruit knives of sterling silver. The whole lot had cost 113 dollars.

Well, now I have to tell you a little about our pleasant visit with the Dietrichsons. Our horses could not be used, so we agreed that we should hire conveyance to Monroe, where Dietrichson was going to meet us. But it was just during the spring

work, so it was quite impossible either to borrow or to rent a
horse, and Dietrichson came all the way up here to get us, stayed
with us for one day, and the following day we took off. Else and I
rode with Dietrichson in his landau, and Munch and Pernille
(the nursemaid) followed in another carriage. Else was really
sweet during the whole journey; when she did not sleep, she
played with the reins and with Dietrichson's cravat, he is so fond
of her and calls her his little daughter-in-law. Yes, we have much
fun watching these two little ones together. Gustav is now about
a year and a half, he had just recovered from a heavy pneumonia
when we got down there, which had taken a lot out of him, so
Else was much bigger and heavier. When we ask him what Else
says, he replies *min Dut* [for *min Gut,* "my boy"]. She will get a
silver spoon from him, inscribed "from Gustav to Else."

One day we had roast goose, I took the wishbone and fixed
it up like you did so often for us, dear Father, and decorated it
with four horns, several inscriptions and streamers and I don't
know all; we gave it to Gustav, and it became a general amusement for big and small alike. Else got many nice little toys down
there, a rattle made of bone with a little bell in it, but as she is
rather rough and strong, she didn't take long to break it; a
beautiful little lamb lying with its mother made of plaster,
which she brought with her home, but unfortunately, through
the carelessness of her little nursemaid, it was dropped to the
floor, and that was the end of it. Else was everybody's toy
down there, and especially Dietrichson was delighted with her.
He fed her, in fact, he was about the first one to get her to eat;
now she accepts her cracker-mush quite well. She is so extremely
good-natured, as she has always been, she will sit on my lap at
the table and play with some empty spools for hours, while I am
sewing fairly undisturbed. She never cries during the night, she
only makes little noises until she gets me awake. It has happened
a couple of mornings now that she has been in bed with me, and
when she woke up and saw me lying there with my eyes closed,
she would calmly poke her little finger in my eye until I woke
up. When I ask her where her Daddy is, she turns to him and
laughs, which of course makes him very happy; and when she
cries for him when he is leaving, he can hardly tear himself away
from her. Indeed, she is a great comfort to me when Munch is
away. I love her, but she also loves me beyond measure, and she

really likes to fondle her Mama. Aunt Louise would surely be
delighted with her, for she can be so relaxed when one fondles
her, she nestles up to me and looks me so placidly in the eyes,
and hugs me with both her little chubby arms. But at other
times she can be very cheerful and frolicsome, laughs and makes
an awful noise. Norwegians, but especially Yankees whom I met
on our journey, seemed to marvel at such a big child. She does
not use a cap any more, and her hair is long and brown.

Mind you, she and Emil have become very good friends, she
would rather stay with him than go to Munch. He is an old hand
at handling small children, and he never stopped marveling at
her dark eyes, brows, and hair. Emil looked after Else for me one
whole afternoon while I went with Munch to see a little child,
two or three years old, who had lost one leg due to her father's
negligence in leaving a loaded gun in the parlor. The shot had
shattered the leg so badly that it had to be amputated above the
knee. This cost the parents, whose only child she is, 108 dollars
besides all the tears and grief. But as if this was not enough, the
man who took it off did not know his trade, so now the flesh is
growing above the bone, and it has to be taken off once more.
Oh, the kind of medical care they have in this country!

I met the Norwegian Doctor Hanssen's wife at Dietrichson's, she is a sister of Lieutenant Ulfers. She knew Vogels and
other people in Laurvig; she was kind and nice and straightforward but a little bombastic in her ideas—it was plain to see that
she had been a governess for several years. The doctor himself
was not present; he had not yet received a good vaccine, but as
soon as he gets it, a message will be sent to us, and we will go
down to Dietrichson's with our little darling to get her vaccinated. As yet Else has only two teeth.

I may have told you before that at Dietrichson's they have
an old pianoforte, and the joy and thrill this gave me is indes-
cribable. All my music is now there. I started to play my old
dances, pieces, melodies, and songs, and forgot completely that I
was in America; in fact, when I heard the first chords from Mrs.
Dietrichson playing, I could barely keep from crying. Oh, I
thought of all the wonderful times we had spent together with
song and play, and music has a strange effect on me. I quickly
picked up what I had forgotten and entertained both myself and
others. Mrs. Dietrichson and I played duet, but with her singing

it did not go so well as it is a little uncomfortable for her to sing right now, she is going to lie in again coming fall. May our Lord keep her! I will of course go down to her and help her all I can, I have found a sincere friend in her, and I believe she can say the same for me.

June 1 [1857]
    Madam Holmen is also having a baby, and that will be very soon, I believe. May God grant that everything will go well with her, she is already along in years and has not had any children for the last nine or ten years. I would like to go up to her, but they have such a small house that there would not even be room for me and my little Else, and we would no doubt be more trouble than help.

    When we visit the Dietrichsons, you cannot imagine all the fun we have; such as when we drove out into the woods one day with horse and wagon to get some wild grape vines and plum trees, which we found in abundance and brought home with us. Mrs. Dietrichson, who is not so light-footed now, was seated on top of the load with her knitting, and this way we traveled safely home. But then we had to get all this planted. You see, we wanted the vines to climb and cover the whole house, but since this was made of stone, it was not an easy task. We tied them to long poles and directed them up toward the attic windows, where some of us were stationed to fasten them under the roof. But this was not enough to keep them safe against America's strong winds; we had to drive ladders [rungs or pegs?] between the stones in the wall itself and tie them to those; and to be able to do this, we figured that the farm hand should climb out of the window and stand on its edge, and while Munch supported his behind (under favor) with a big broom, he could use his arms and thus got the vines fastened—to everybody's amusement and delight. Dietrichson was not at home during this scene, but he got just as fresh and vivid a picture of it from a drawing by Munch portraying us all. In this manner we can frolic like children and have much fun together.

    Next Sunday is confirmation here, and any day of the following week I can expect the Dietrichsons to arrive as he is going to have Communion services for us the following Sunday. During his visit here at that time there will be a big congregation meeting, six persons will be told to come down from Dodgeville and *Otherkrik* [Otter Creek] congregations. It is a question whether they can keep Munch as their pastor or not as they will not at all fulfill their promises in the letter of presentation, and they are holding back such a big portion of his salary that it can not continue this way any longer with empty words and promises. In the Dodgeville and Otter Creek congregations they are completely insane, they do not want to incorporate and join into a regular congregation; they do want to build churches, but it is to be open for any odd tramp who wants to come and preach to them, and of these there are a large number in this country. Law and order are not supposed to rule in their congregations, this is a free country, they say, and everyone can do as he pleases; if he wants to contribute something for his minister, that is fine, but if he does not, he may leave it at that. They will not hear of rules and regulations among themselves. And in this manner it cannot possibly go on any longer, especially since Munch hardly has received half of what he should have had during these two years.

Do not get worried, dear Parents; after all, these are only trifles, and we are sure we will be all right, we have One who will be certain to aid us! In fact, the worst has already occurred, and that is that you, my beloved Father, must spend so much money on us now in this for you so difficult time. Oh, this is very, very hard for me to think about! But it must and shall be otherwise, I am always in good spirits, and the hope that better times will come never fails me. The Lord will surely not forget us—no, on the contrary. First he has punished one of Munch's most eager opponents with insanity. Next he brought to an end another's unworthy wanderings here on earth by a sudden and horrible death. He was a young and vigorous man, he left his home in good health and went into a café to read the newspapers, but as he was reading he grasped his throat, fell from the chair, and was dead instantly, although there were five doctors present. This man, who was wealthy and had great influence among the Norwegians, always tried to harm Munch and opposed him on every occasion; finally he became a Methodist, but even so, out of love for his countrymen, as he explained, he had to attend their congregation meetings to give them guidance so that the minister should not get too much power over them, and he turned many of them completely insane. A third opponent is leaving, and I shouldn't wonder if it would not be possible now to bring about peace and order. Holmen struggles like a hero among them at all hours.

Down here they are a little more peaceful in this respect, but an unfortunate indifference to sin and indolence to the Word of God prevails, besides, in one settlement, an awful drinking. However, Munch has several good, sincere, and fine people as his friends, and for their sake it would hurt him very much to have to give up his charge. Yes, beloved Parents, however happy I would be to be together with you again, I could never wish for that to happen before the determined time; what, then, would become of all these forlorn sinners? They may not have another minister again.

But now I will tell you what Dietrichson has done to come to the aid of Munch and this congregation. He has collected a sum of 100–200 dollars, which will be presented to Munch at the congregation meeting by a representative from all the Rock Prairie congregations. These have by many affiliations a close connection with the congregations here and are so well informed about everything that most of them exclaimed: "We certainly can not comprehend how it has been possible for Munch to bear with their indifference for so long; this is not at all to support the minister," they said, "for we know very well that such a master as he is at preaching would have no difficulty in getting another charge, but it is to assist the congregation; for we really feel sorry for many among them, and had Munch received what was rightly his, he would not have had need for more."—These funds will fill in many holes, believe me. Oh, how much we would have liked to send it all to Father, but unfortunately that is not possible. Ugh, how those nasty dollars can embarrass people! But do as I do, dear Parents, I try as much as I am able to have a good covenant of conscience with God, next I work all I can to fulfill my duties here on earth, then I cannot do any more, and so I leave the Lord to take care of the rest, thank Him for daily bread, am cheerful and content, grow plump and fat, laugh, frolic, and am so happy that many times I ask myself: how long can such happiness last, and if it is really good for me to be so happy? Yes, it is indeed true that I feel happy, and for that I thank God from the bottom of my heart.

My dear Mother, how are things with you? Are you careless these days since you feel so poorly? Maybe I should scold you a little—you must be sure to take care of yourself. Don't you remember you are a grandmother? You must not run around like a young girl any longer then. When I get home, I may appear to be your mother and you my daughter, the way you behave.

At this moment Else is sitting with a big hard cooky in her hand, and she is chewing and gnawing with her two little teeth, it is a pleasure to watch her. Oh, that you, too, could share my delight.

You must give my greetings to Madam Preutz and thank her so much from me, think how we will thrive on jam should it arrive safely. Munch has written to Holfeldt and asked him to handle it in the best possible way, for we concluded it would be quite impossible to guard the crate from being turned upside down and thrown as far as from attic to cellar—we certainly had a good laugh at your expense. If you had only seen an American railroad, you would never have written as you did, they rush along like savages.

Well, what is Wilhelm thinking of? Has his little heart been stolen already? And he who promised me that he would never get married, but would become an old, nice, rich uncle. Give him my love and tell him that I am looking at him and Hanna many times every day, laughing and thinking about how the two of them now are kissing and caressing and having it so snug and cozy in their love for one another. They hang next to each other on my wall—well, Hanna is a little higher up than he is, but that is of course in order—ladies first. Ask him to write and tell me how he is doing as an engaged man, I should surely like to hear a little about that. There has always been a kind of old-womanish love between the two of us. Yes, give them both my affection, wish them all the best, but ask them to wait with the wedding until I get home and can celebrate with them, then Munch will marry them for free.

Father dear, why do you want to sell Faret? [12] Please don't do it. Let Bernt have Faret to run and take care of and let the profit go to him, but he must let us stay in "Runtom" the first summer we are home again. [13] This is the American way, you see.

Has Aunt Stina arrived in Bergen? I have not heard anything about that. And which of the girls does she have with her? Where is Uncle Jacob? Please tell me everything about all the people I know. Have Fog and Prebensen given up keeping store? Whom do you have then? You must let me know about Olga, Elna, Emilie, and all my sisters and brothers. Is Lagertha clever at the piano now? Why doesn't she ever write to me?

Is the old shoemaker still with you? Ask him if he doesn't want to come over here and make me a pair of boots. I can't get any I really like in this country. Yesterday I threw away the last pair I brought from home—no, what am I saying, do you know what I have done, I had a pair of white ones, and I colored them with ink, they look steel gray, and so I have again got myself a pair of good boots. The Charlot bulb you sent me is sprouting and growing, I sowed the caraway seeds up on the hillside, and I hope we will have caraway sprouts from them next year. We got this delicious dish at Dietrichson's. There are still many who are very good to us, and they are sending us butter and eggs and a little bit of everything.

Take care of yourselves, dearly beloved Parents, may God hear my prayer that all of you will stay in good health; then everything else may go as best it can, there will always be a way, you know. God bless you! Greet all and everybody from the bottom of my heart

from your own Caja

Pastor J. St. Munch to his Mother, Mrs. Else Munch, née Hofgaard

Wiota so-called Parsonage, July 16, 1857

Dear Mother!

Yesterday was your 67th birthday, which both Caja and I remembered, although we were not able to give it a festive stamp as we neither have wine nor extra food or companionship which could aid us in giving the day the splendor which would correspond to its importance. In this house, salt meat is course No. 1, milk is course No. 2, and the clear water is our table wine; and these ingredients, I dare say, are too much in disagreement with what is generally known as "eminently festive spirits" to be applied as an expression of our sentiments yesterday. But you may rest assured that we remembered you as warmly as if we had been sitting spruced up at an elegant family dinner, although we were eating salt meat, and that we drank your toast in the clear spring water with the same heartily well-intended wish for your true well-being as if we had been tippling wine. – To speak seriously, may God give you all the blessing in things temporal as well as spiritual which we wish for you, then your old age will surely become gentle and placid! May He hold His hand over you, so that all of us may see each other again! –

It is a long time since I wrote to you, dear Mother, and you probably expect to hear much news and to receive from me a letter rich in contents. But you must excuse me if you are disappointed, for it is not in my power to make something out of nothing or out of an awkward matter, and I shall have to search thoroughly to find one thing or another with which to fill up four large pages without getting insipid or dull.

Well – our domestic life will then have to be brought up first. Caja and Else and I are well-content and happy with each other, and we need no reinforcements from outside to enjoy ourselves. But when such reinforcements arrive, we are nevertheless very happy and would rather not renounce them as long as they have become available. Thus we had no objections at all when one fine day we saw Dietrichson with wife and a couple of children drive up to our door – that was in June – and we had a very pleasant time as long as they stayed with us. Dietrichson conducted Communion service for us and preached in my church. They stayed about a fortnight with us as they were prevented from returning home by several days of insistent bad weather. Yes, we certainly have some potent weather here sometimes. We had rain and thunder and lightning for three days on end, and the flood was so big that a little brook which runs just below the house swelled into a big river while bridges broke into splinters and the roads were impassable for several days. When finally the passage was reopened, not only the guests but also host and hostess and little Else with her Abigail went down to Rock Prairie Parsonage, where we then exchanged our roles as we became the guests and Dietrichson the host. Accordingly, I conducted service down there as D. had done at my church, and everything went as usual, only with the change in the host-guest relationship. I now smoked D.'s pipe as he before had smoked mine, Caja now enjoyed Mrs. D.'s food as Mrs. D. before had been sitting at her table, we now expressed our thanks to them as they before had thanked us, etc.—a turnabout which gave us considerable amusement.

Finally we had to part. But instead of Caja and I with fair Else leaving Dietrichson with his wife and children, Dietrichson and I got together and departed from our wives and children. For we were going to Koshkonong to A. C. Preus, at whose house all the pastors here were to gather for a ministers' meeting and a church dedication. We started out on Monday, the 22nd of June, and arrived Thursday afternoon by railroad at a station called "Stoughton," from where we had about eight English miles to Preus's place. There, at Stoughton, we met Ottesen, Brodahl, Brandt, and Koren, who came each from his direction, but we were presently unable really to enjoy the meeting as Dietrichson and I, who had our clothes together in one suitcase, discovered to our consternation that our luggage was nowhere to be found. *Trainet* [the train] had gone on its way, and we stood there as empty-handed as if we had been looted by robbers. What was there to do? The church dedication was to take place the following day, and we had no clerical garbs nor anything else; and our ministers' meeting, combined with another church dedication at Pine Lake, Brandt's congregation, would be keeping us away from home for about a week. As it is at present, it was then exceedingly hot, and we did not even have a shirt for a change of clothes. How jolly! But never mind, here in America one is not easily intimidated, and we proceeded on our way to Preus's. There I was able to borrow a new clerical garb from Preus, and Dietrichson got an age-old one, for Preus is well equipped with all kinds of goods and chattels. The fat Dietrichson could hardly get the gown around himself, but the surplice helped; and I looked a little outgrown, although A. C. Preus is also a tall man. I borrowed a shirt and a cravat from Brodahl, so it turned out fairly well. The dedication was very solemn, and the considerable number of ministers participating (we were ten all told) contributed especially to make it so. A. C. Preus performed the dedication, and I gave the entrance prayer. The following day, our suitcase arrived—we had telegraphed for it—so we had only the fright.

We had pleasant days. Besides the Norwegian pastors, a Swedish Episcopalian minister, Unonius from Chicago, was also present, and a German-Lutheran pastor, Lochner from Milwaukee. This whole flock of ministers were sleeping upstairs in two rooms, and there was no lack of merriment. The heat was bad, and because of it one could observe airy, ghostly figures in white (though short) draperies move around in the night.

We were treated excellently at Preus's. He lives comfortably and has many rooms, but neither here nor at the two other parsonages I have visited [Rock Prairie and Rock River] is the location as pretty as it is at my place. Mrs. Preus [née Engel Brun] certainly had her hands full waiting on so many guests, but she did very well. Of all the ministers present there, Duus was the one I liked the best. He has grown heavy and fat. But I do not think that he likes America well as he lives so extremely isolated, far from all civilization.

After the ministers' meeting we traveled by railroad to Pastor Brandt, but on the way we stopped in Milwaukee, where we had dinner in a German hotel, completely in European fashion with proper food and Rhine wine; in the American hotels you only get water and miserable food and service. . . .

We arrived at Brandt's on Saturday evening and were received by his very talkative wife. I think she probably regards herself as quite erudite, but she is unable to sustain it. . . .

Finally we came home to Dietrichson's after having had an expensive trip. And a couple of days later, the Munch family departed and arrived safely at this so-called parsonage, where we now stay in all possible peace, that is, as far as the heat permits us to have peace. For we now have American summer, and that is not exactly gentle. Particularly Else seems to suffer as her little plump, fat figure is bothered quite a bit by the heat. She is our pleasure and joy. She is now eleven months old, has four big teeth, crawls around on the floor, shouts Da-da and Mam-mam in proper style, and continues to look like you. It is remarkable how fond one can grow of such a little one. The Yankees who see her, call her "the big baby," and rightfully so, for she is really the biggest child of eleven months that I have ever seen. She can stand up by a chair.

We have now gotten our garden into a little better shape than we did last year. Peas and beans and cabbage, etc., look very good, and both potatoes and maize corn are shaping up well. But, you know, all of it is just a trifle, more for pleasure and diversion than for any real benefit. However, potatoes are an exception, for they are many a time our only dependable food. Indeed, food is difficult here, and help even more so. On the whole, life here is one of renunciation and rich in wants, but just because of that it is a life which may be greatly beneficial to a young minister. If we ever get home to dear Norway, we have at least learned to use the world like those who do not use it, and we will endure a great many things over which we would perhaps have grumbled before. Add to this the experience which is gained over here with regard to everything concerned with the discharge of the holy office, and the greater determination and self-possession which again and again is called for here, where each man is so much on his own, and which exactly for this reason is more and more acquired, then I would say that to a minister, life in America has many advantages. But I repeat: for flesh and blood it has no enticement. Wants, disappointments, and hardships attend us every day—but the Lord also attends.

We are poor in this rich land. The congregations are not fulfilling their obligations and have failed me, everything is exceedingly expensive, and I cannot do anything about my debt at home. For this reason, it is possible that we will be coming home in two years if it is God's will; it is at least quite likely. Because of the breach of promise on the part of my congregations (there are too many people from Land and Hadeland), Dietrichson's congregations have sent me an offering of $188, so that the church here should not have the disgrace of having its minister leaving because of hunger. Thereby I am a little better off this year. But we have no anxiety for our livelihood, for the Lord will surely provide in one way or another, and we are indeed getting our daily bread three times every day. Caja is getting fat and chubby, although she is longing for home. She asks to be remembered most warmly to you and Caroline and Henriette and rejoices in the thought of meeting all of you again.

A large number of emigrants from Norway have arrived here this year—about 10,000 all told, and also in my parish we have received a reinforcement. But land is not to be obtained here, so they have to go on further. It is *madness* that so many emigrate! Thorn and thistle grow as abundantly here as in Norway, and America is the downfall of many a youth. *Aften-*

bladet has been horrible concerning the emigration; you go up to Meidell, Mother, and tell him that he has prostituted himself, and that he is speaking of things that he does not understand.[14]

Dear one! Goodbye! God be with you and all at home

Your son

J. St. Munch

The Third Year, 1857–1858

Mrs. Caja Munch to her Parents, Mr. and Mrs. F. W. S. Falch

Wiota Parsonage, August 12, 1857

My dearly beloved Parents!

With all dispatch I must send you my heartfelt thanks for everything in the crate that we received with joy last week. I am so delighted with every little thing you can hardly believe it; from all the things you sent I realize so clearly your deep concern and love. God bless you for it! I am so happy, so happy! Yes indeed, from the moment I heard the news that a crate was arriving, I have been looking forward to getting it, and although it arrived very late in the evening, we could not think of putting off the unpacking until the next morning, but as not to wake up Else we first carried it out into the yard and broke it open, and then in again, and the unwrapping started. Even the little handful of hay which was there was admired and compared with the coarse hay of America. For every package of tobacco Munch picked up, his smile grew bigger and bigger until he beamed from ear to ear for joy and delight at the considerable quantity. Everything looked wonderful until we got to Emil's shirts and to my great sorrow I discovered spots of juice; four of them had escaped the coloring from their dangerous neighbor, but the rest had got more or less of its contents, although nothing at all in the front, and I hope to get all of it off again. These, and also some of his woolen stockings, were the only items that were spotted from juice, two bottles were unbroken, and nam nam! delightful to taste! one with raspberry and one with gooseberry juice. The one packed in the medicine chest was broken along with a small bottle of camphor essence, but everything else was well preserved and without any damage at all. Of Sophie Pehrson's notes on the bottles we can not see one iota although the labels are still there; however, we know how to make use of it all, except for the "Pimpinille" drops, about which I would like a little more information.

We have already made use of our medicine. In fact, everybody around here turns to us when something is the matter. Oh, how wonderful it is to be able to help one's neighbor! But usually the farmers wait too long before they ask for assistance, and then it is too late. Such was the case recently with our best friends in the neighborhood. One of their two sons (the same one of whom I told you, that clasped his hands every time he saw Munch) had suffered stomach pains for quite some time. Finally they came to see us, and we immediately went over there, employed some harmless remedies as we dare not launch too far afield, but it was too late, he probably already had an infection in his abdomen; a so-called doctor was summoned, who gave him some powder which he could not digest at all, and he had to give up the ghost. Fortunate he was, for he was a pious and gentle child. Give this some thought, dear brothers and sisters, and be good and obedient, you can never know the day the Lord will call you, and if you have been naughty, have disobeyed your parents, quarreled and hit each other, have lost your temper and have been nasty to the servants, then you will not by any means be received by your Father in Heaven, and you will be in such misery that I cannot bear to think of it! Oh, I pray to God for you very often, so now you must help me so that you may be *saved* and go to your Savior Jesus Christ, who loves small children so very much when they are cheerful and happy. You did not at all behave as you should when I left you, you often hurt your much too kind parents, you did not attend church by far as frequently as you should, and the Bible—the Holy Book—was lying on the shelf gathering dust. Read diligently in it, and you will find out how you must live and behave if you want to be with your Father in Heaven.—You may be amazed that I can write and mix everything together in this manner, but forgive me, it came to my mind! I was just present at this boy's funeral, and I cried like a child thinking of all my dear brothers and sisters.

The chocolate was wonderful. We have already had it a couple of times. And one cake we ate directly, you know my weakness, dear Mother; the jam I have sampled and tasted so often that now I feel the worm is getting lively in my stomach, so I very likely will have to swallow the bitter pill and take some essence of wormwood. Else rejoiced at all the beautiful things she got and was so delighted with them that she wanted to eat everything all at once. She is very busy right now and seems very concerned as she tries to answer and thank all her donors. However, she has left it to me to thank Grandfather and Grandmother as it otherwise would be altogether too much all at once for her young head. She was so fond of her cap I could hardly get it away from her; next winter, God willing, it should be marvelous for her, and you can't imagine how sweet she looks with it on. Did you really think that the cute blue dress would be too big for her? No, not at all! She squalled terribly when I put it on her as it squeezed her plump arms and waist, but that is easily altered, and she will be using it as a Sunday dress for a long time to come. The shoes were too small so I had to give them away to another little girl, but thereby you also gave me a great pleasure; I had just talked Munch into buying some material for a dress for this child, so now I took the boots and added a woolen skirt of Else's, and everything was very gratefully received. They sent us some eggs in return, and a piglet which yesterday stood roasted on all fours on our dining table.

We live very well these days. People are kind, giving us fresh meat, and never a day goes by that we don't enjoy something from our garden. I have so many peas, I hardly know what to do with them, although I give away a lot. The cabbage is already so big I used it for "mutton-and-cabbage" the other day. We eat our own potatoes daily. We think it is very enjoyable to watch all this sprout and bear fruit, which we ourselves have planted.

Yesterday Munch and our boy brought in our rye themselves. We had to store it in the stable loft for the time being until, one way or another, we can get it out of the spikes. Else and I were onlookers, and as we were standing by the loaded wagon while Munch was throwing the rye to the boy in the loft, a snake fell out of one of the sheaves and to my horror landed at our feet. Munch killed it instantly.

Our hay is for the most part put in stack. We have faithfully joined together in trying to make up for the lack of help available here, which only has been a pleasure since we have had such an excellent summer, without too much heat, cool nights, and refreshing rain. Today we have an aggravating, strong, warm wind, as so often happens in these parts.

My dear Munch has gone to Monroe today to have himself daguerrotyped for my birthday. I should not have known about it, but then he did not have a clean clergyman's ruff, and I, who was kept completely in the dark, was foolish enough to tell him that I certainly would not flute one for him until he told me what he needed it for. Afterward, when I had been informed, came the regret, and I promised never again to be nosy. By now I have only a small space left to bid you my heartiest farewell, but you know

your own Caja

I am sorry that this letter is so late in getting off. The two dollars are for the tobacco. Will you make out all these eleven letters? [1]

I must add, when we ask Else what the cuckoo says, she answers: hoho, hoho.

Pastor J. St. Munch to his Brother, Andreas Munch

Wiota Parsonage, November 16, 1857

Dear Brother!

We received some time ago a dearly appreciated letter from you, and since I just now have some time to spare, I shall reply to it. It is, however, in the nature of the circumstances that the letter essentially will be a family letter which will be visiting the ground floor of *Saabygaarden*.[2] For this reason, you must excuse all the prosaisms and dry matters, which I will be regaling. Herein lies, of course, no crack at my dear ones in *Saabygaarden*, as if they would prefer prosaisms, etc., for we know very well that the fragrance of poetry has penetrated every crevice there, as Henriette can relate, although Herman probably will deny it. But as the letter is supposed to be a family letter, which the distance and the infrequent correspondence demand, it will be necessary to touch on a great many things which should not be included in a letter to a poet—besides, I surely have no need to

remark that I am "prosaic from head to toe," and that it therefore should not be entered to the account of the volition if a
selection of "notes of the day" and newspaper palaver is to be
found therein.

I have during the whole summer been leading a rather
agitated and in many respects interesting life as most of my time
has been occupied by journeys to various regions and for various
purposes. It is impossible for me now to give a detailed report of
what I have experienced during that time, although a great
many things certainly deserve to be placed on record. However, I
will, as I know it would interest you, extract as well as I can a
summary of it all and send this to you as an example of what life
entails here, both of good and bad, big and small, earnest and
jest, under circumstances which in *all* respects are fermenting
and unsettled. In particular, I shall dwell on my three main
tours as these will procure material for multifarious reflections.

My first journey took me to Koshkonong Parsonage, whereto
all the [Norwegian Synod] ministers had been summoned for
a conference and a church dedication. I had never before been
gathered with my colleagues, and I was glad, therefore, to have
such a good opportunity to get acquainted with them. Although
we actually do not have an apparent supreme head but consti-
tute a small church republic, we have agreed, nevertheless, to
entrust A. C. Preus with a certain authority *prae ceteris* (*primus
inter pares*) as he is both the oldest and indisputably the ablest
and most resolute in an administrative respect. For this reason,
the conference of ministers was to be gathered at his place and
under his leadership.

We were altogether ten ministers, but during the conference one got a headache, another a stomach ache, and a third a
conference ache (i.e., he always goes upstairs and to bed when
the debate becomes too powerful for him), so the number was
reduced to seven deliberative persons, and this "body" was very
active, especially at night as quite a few of the ministers here are
in the habit of conducting long discourses in their sleep. Although the heat was intense at the time, the sojourn there and
the social gathering with the brethren was very pleasant and in
many respects profitable to me.

It was with a certain apprehension that I went there as I
have all the time been in opposition to A. C. Preus and a few of

the other ministers concerning the question of establishing an academy among ourselves. These have wanted to transfer it to, or rather to unite it with, the German-Lutheran university in St. Louis, Missouri, while Dietrichson and I wished to have it among ourselves. On that subject, both Preus and I had gone rather too far, and an unpleasant relationship had developed. However, the meeting evened everything out, and we made peace.

Otherwise, the discussion was concerned with ecclesiastical and theological matters, which have no place here. None of us are rousing theologians, but neither are many of us utter dunces, while several have acquired an ecclesiastical view, and a firm attitude gained in the struggle, which seldom is found among so young men at home, where the Church slumbers sweetly in the arms of the State. The discussions, therefore, tend to take a more practical direction, even in the domains of theology, and exactly for that reason were they particularly profitable to me, since I—if I have anything—have more theory than practice.

There is a difference between a Norwegian ministers' meeting in America and a corresponding one in Norway. At home, they sit stiff and sedate, row after row, on long benches, while the chairman stands straight on a cathedra, holding the reins of discipline well tight. Here, however, are no differences of station, no archdeacons or bishops, no perpetual or stipendiary curates, and already this does a lot. Besides, one acquires here, without knowing it, an indifference to form, which certainly many a time goes rather too far. Behold for once the Norwegian ministers' meeting at Koshkonong: On the sofa sits the chairman with one leg on the back of a chair, beside him the secretary with both elbows on the table and his head resting on his clenched fists, across from them a minister astride a chair with his arms resting on the chair back, over there another enveloped in clouds of tobacco smoke, over here still another with his knee pulled clear up to his mouth and with his hands clasped over his leg as if he were afraid of losing it—and so on—but everything congenial and cordial as it must be when we, who otherwise live so far apart and besides are always prepared for a struggle, get the opportunity in brotherly love to speak about the one thing needful, which to us is also the one thing joyful. However, in the midst of this apparent disorder and formlessness, the chief endeavor was directed toward the maintenance and consolidation of order and necessary forms within our church community, and I have the hope that the more such formless meetings we can have, the more will our young church community be strengthened and fortified both inward and outward.

After the ministers' meeting there was a dedication of the largest church which has so far been built among the Norwegians here, namely, West Koshkonong Church, which surely holds 1000 people when it is as crowded as it was that day. I gave the entrance prayer, and Preus was bishop. Besides, an Episcopalian clergyman and a German-Lutheran minister were present, both of them in the clerical garb characteristic of their churches.

After this, we traveled to Rock River Parsonage, where Brandt resides with his consort. But first we made a trip to Milwaukee, which about 30 years ago consisted only of a couple of huts and now is a city that in size is equal to, and in grandeur far surpasses, Christiania. From Milwaukee we then went by railroad to Brandt's place. After having been a bachelor for a long time, he has now got himself a wife (and a month ago also a daughter). You know, perhaps, Diderikke Ottesen and her oratorial endowments. At their house, as a novelty, we had Norwegian whey cheese and spiced cheese (made at Sande Parsonage),[3] as well as Bølling's sirup cookies. It seems strange here in the distant America to see before one's eyes, and to take into one's mouth, provisions from Norway, and therefore one cannot call it childish when we right reverend clergymen stood like children in a circle around her, who fetched from her chest-drawer one bit of cooky after another, which we then very carefully put away, some into our mouths and some into our vest pockets to bring it home to Mother. — Also at Brandt's there was a church dedication.

Well, this in short was my first journey, whose details with regard to conveyance on railroad, etc., I shall pass over. However, it may perhaps interest you to hear that in this new country we traveled almost all the way on railroad and thus covered several hundred miles in a very short time. It is unbelievable how the spirit of speculation reigns here; everything is calculated for trade and commerce, and no means is too formidable when it comes to the attainment of the great purpose: worldly comfort and power. Now and then, therefore, a judgment of God does indeed fall upon this rapacious, mammonite people; thus in the course of the last two months, the most desperate financial crisis has set in, one bank has broken after the other, railroad companies and great commercial firms have tumbled down, from the borders of Minnesota to the Atlantic Ocean, throughout all states and territories. Like a tornado has it torn across the country, and no ever so secure commercial house has been able to withstand its might where it raged at its worst. But the people are not easily bent; only few regard it as a sign from above.

During the months of August and September, I was a missionary, that is to say, I brought the Word and the Sacraments to the hosts of fellow countrymen who have settled west of the Mississippi in Minnesota. I have during those few weeks experienced more than I otherwise have in many years and in a certain sense led a life that will never recur, even if I should happen to make a similar journey, for that would then be the *second* time, and that is, under such conditions, something quite different from the first with regard to the impressions that it leaves. One can surely become familiar with anything whatever as long as it remains within the limits of our capacities; but no matter how deeply and intensely one may enter into the different circumstances, the *first time* still retains its own "loom," as the fashionable dandies at diction would say.

Such a journey is, of course, arduous, yes indeed, many times for flesh and bone quite unbearable. But one thought conquered all the others and thereby made the most difficult task easy, namely: this you endure for the sake of Jesus; and one feeling dominated all others, namely: now you are receiving help and assistance from above—and when I thus after an intense prayer had perceived the power of *Him* who is strong in the weak, then I could rejoice in such a way as I never have known before, and as I now more seldom can do. What benefit for my "belief" this journey has had, I cannot recount here in these lines, but I perceived again and again how now this, now the other of the comforting enunciations of the Lord stood out more and more clearly before my soul, so that I could touch and feel it, as it were, so true was it—indeed, I understood quite well how the "Word" was made "flesh" and dwelt among us, this to be understood not merely in the purely historical sense.

Many a time I experienced the truth of the Words of the

Savior: "In the same hour it will be given to you with what words you shall speak," when exhausted from travels and sleepless nights I was to commence a trying function and hardly had fifteen minutes of quiet to study the communion sermon and the homily; although I was only dimly aware of what I would speak, it became clearer and clearer to me the further I proceeded in my sermon, and in the midst of this successive elucidation appeared the feeling of the Lord's immediate assistance and strength both for soul and for body. Thereby the courage of my faith grew to the point that it had to find expression in the confession, in the testimony to my Savior, which I was just then bearing, wherefore, of course, the sermon became far superior in regard to warmth and force to what I often afford when I have had plenty of time to think everything out. Again and again I had to acknowledge: "What do we have that we have not received!"

Also in another respect did I perceive the nearness of the Lord. I had not made an itinerary for my journey as I was ignorant of the location of the settlements, and I did not have any conveyance of my own as I had to travel the first part of the way by railroad and steamship and therefore could not bring with me horses and carriage. Thus I could not know how I would be making my way in the new country, where the roads still are poor and there is much wilderness. But everything went so easily that I was brought to think of the pillar of cloud by day and the pillar of fire by night, and that He still lives who carried Israel on eagle's wings. To be sure, I had to resign myself to a very simple and uncomfortable conveyance as I always had to ride in a *Lumbervogn* (that is, a work wagon) with a board to sit on, and now with oxen, now with horses—I once even had to use the conveyance of the Apostles—but with all this everything went so easily and well that I surely could understand Who was assisting. Besides, I did not have one sick day on the whole journey, although "board and room" was quite difficult many places.

I shall first give you a little information about the Norwegian settlements there, and then illustrate the descriptions with a couple of sketches.—Minnesota Territory (now "State") is situated west of the Missisippi and extends westward to the possessions of the Indians and northward up to Lake Superior and the Canadian possessions, while it is bounded to the south by Iowa. The Norwegians have settled in the southern part of the country and live much closer to each other there than they do in Wisconsin, besides they have occupied the best land. Many of them are prosperous as they have owned land here in Wisconsin before—but all are poor in one respect, namely, in the Word of God; for, although there must be several thousands of Norwegians living in Minnesota, there is not one Norwegian minister but only itinerant bunglers who call themselves ministers but have only the name. However, two are coming from Norway this fall.[4]

To get there, I first had to go by railroad to Prairie-du-Chien, which is situated in Wisconsin not far from the outfall of the Wisconsin River into the Missisippi, and from there I took the steamship up the Missisippi. What must strike everybody on such a journey is the combination, unknown anywhere else, of the crudest spontaneity and the most refined luxury, of the simple, coarse forms of pioneer life and the whole apparatus of "indispensables" of the European civilization, in short, of ancient and present times, of inception and relative completion, with no interlink, no intermediation, no gradation, just simply juxtaposed and thereby "alright." While the settler on shore splits beams for his log cabin or clears the woods to plant the first potatoes, while here and there (although now seldom) a forlorn Indian, wrapped in his blanket, curiously stares, you sail past the banks of the Missisippi in the most elegant steamship you could desire, where everything is arranged with a splendor and luxury which far surpasses what is usually found on board steamships in Europe. The saloon occupies almost the whole length of the ship as it has been placed *on top* of the deck, above engines, paddlebox, etc., which makes the ship rise rather high above the water. Inside the saloon there are doors on both sides leading to staterooms, and in the saloon itself gilding and white lacquer and carvings and state and splendor are applied in such a way that you would think you were entering a princely hall. Negroes in great numbers serve at tables, where the whole attendance takes place by word of command and with a precision that is quite astonishing. In short, everything inside must make you think that you are directly in the center of civilization, while everything outside gives evidence of the pioneer country, where man by the sweat of his brow extorts from the soil the first meager crop.

Wherever we went, it was really interesting to see this same naïve combination of the forms of a life of nature with those of refined living; I was reminded of what I have read about wild chieftains [in Africa or Polynesia], who adorn themselves with a pair of trousers tailored in London, or with an epaulet, and otherwise present themselves *"in puris naturalibus,"* and I must admit—I found it equally comical. Rousseau would have been fooled here, for if he went out into the woods crawling on all fours, he would perhaps behind his trees be vexed to see a party of Yankees camping on the river bank with their champagne bottles and cigars and oysters, etc., etc., while the railroad whistle dinned his ear.

But another couple of generations, and every trace of the primitive state will have disappeared. Already now, the traveler in Minnesota may find hotels which in comfort and splendor scarcely yield to any hotel in Europe. About this, Lector Voss will have something to tell, for he has visited these regions this summer, you know. But what he cannot tell about, is how a missionary fares on his wanderings through the pioneer country. About this I may perhaps be able to give a little better intelligence.

I shall describe a couple of days of my travels, and these may serve as an example *instar omnium.* After having conducted divine services in the settlements closest to the river, I got a man with horses and wagon to convey me and the clerk, who accompanied me, to the interior of the country. We had a journey of 40 English miles to the nearest Norwegian settlement, and as we got started late in the morning, we could not count on getting there that day. We started out over trackless roads, across brooks and little rivers with no bridges as the wagon heeled over, now to starboard, now to port, so that I had to hold on to the wagon box *all day* with all my might in order not to be thrown overboard. The road went over desolate, wild prairies, and from there into thick, dark woods, where only a couple of years ago hordes of Indians had their home. Now, however, hardly one was to be seen. As it drew on toward evening and darkness closed in, we had to rap at the door of a log cabin, where an English family lived, who were quite willing to harbor us for the night. It is the custom here that a traveler is never denied shelter, be it ever so late at night. We were then shown to the loft, which had an open hole instead of a window, and in a so-called bed I got some rest for my tired limbs.

Early next morning, out again—the same exercise to avoid a tumble, the same wobbling and shaking of the wagon, so that when we arrived in the Norwegian settlement, I had a pretty good idea how a poor gout-peddler must feel on a wet fall day. But then you got a good rest when you arrived, you will probably say. No, my friend, then it just started. The wagon pulled up by the door of a low log house, half as big as the hut in which you lived out at Maschmann's, and this is where I was going to have my headquarters. The people were friendly, and very happy to see a minister, but they could offer nothing save a hearty good will as everything else was lacking.

The log house had only one room, and in it were man, wife, three dirty urchins, one newcomer with wife and a grown son, another newcomer with wife and a small child, besides myself and the clerk. In this narrow room, where the rain was beating through the wall (for it was raining hard), where the floor was a single mud puddle, where the cooking stove radiated a strong heat (although it was early in September) and a not too pleasant smell of pork, I had to spend two nights and two days, and conduct two divine services with baptism, confirmation, and communion!

The nights were the worst, for then the door had to remain closed, so that the stench increased in strength with each breath emitted by the snoring troop, while the clerk and I fought a close battle with bedbugs and fleas. This battle ended, as so often happens, with victory for the superior forces. In the middle of the night, I heard behind me: "Ouch! Oh! This is the limit!" Then it sounded like a sweating iron, the kind they use to curry a horse, and when I looked, there was the clerk working his limbs most energetically with all ten fingernails until he finally surrendered and took flight, not only out of the bed but out of the cabin, whereupon he went to rest in the haystack and did not return until morning.

In the meantime, I continued the fight alone as best I could. But as the whole army of bedbugs, which previously had to deal with the clerk as well, now turned on me, even I had to utter wails of distress and beg for quarter. The wife, who was lying on the floor, heard this and asked directly: "Is the pastor sick?" "No," I said, "but the bedbugs are too healthy." She out of bed, the man likewise, then I, all of us "in light raiments," the mattress out of the door, then the blankets, and there I stood in the middle of the floor, tired, sleepy, with a headache, and unable to find rest as the bed was now almost empty. Then the man came in with a new straw mattress, which he had filled with fresh hay, and on this I lay down, with only a sheet for cover— but I had little or no sleep all night.

In the morning, the parishioners came, I had to conduct a long service with nineteen christenings, and did not get my dinner until five o'clock in the afternoon. What further increased the difficulties was the fact that the rain forced all to gather inside the cabin, so that I had no more than two square feet to myself. But, as I said, the Lord was with us, and everything went well.

The next day, I had another service, and the third day (Sunday) big performance in another house, where there was more room. For the sake of comparison (that is, with the work of Norwegian ministers), I shall tell you what I had to perform that day after two wakeful nights: (*1*) registration for baptism of 21 children, (*2*) sermon for 21 churchings, (*3*) communion sermon for 60 communicants, (*4*) mass, (*5*) main sermon, (*6*) christening of 21 children, (*7*) communion and mass, (*8*) examination for two hours of 8 young people who wished to be confirmed, (*9*) confirmation service for 6 of them, (*10*) communion for the same 6. When I was through, it was six o'clock, and I started at nine o'clock. But the Lord was with me, and it went far better than I would have imagined. This I have stated to demonstrate the truth of what I said above about the assistance of the dear God in time of need, and about the blessings that attend the holy office.

I should have told you about my third journey, the one to the Synod, but I have to put it off till some other occasion as I am running out of time. I shall then describe our Synod and give an overview of the situation here as far as our church is concerned. We have now decided to establish a theological seminary (college). More about this later. But, dear Andreas, in the meantime you must write me a *long* letter about everything that you can imagine would interest me; *I am ignorant about every-thing at home.* If you do that, you will get a letter.

Farewell, dear Brother!

Yours, J. St. Munch

Everything here is as usual. Struggle in all directions is of daily occurrence, but the Lord is strong. We are in good health, have a sufficiency of daily bread—but vicious neighbors. Else is lovely and amuses us very much; she can crow as the cock, grunt as the pig, bark as the dog, etc., etc. How is your Johan?

A blessed Christmas I wish you and all at home. Greetings of love from both of us to Mother and sisters, and little Else asks Grandmama that she be remembered in your good wishes for our welfare. Goodbye to all of you.

Kindly ask Herman if he has received the two dollars from Cappelen, and if he has bought pipes for me. Next spring, many emigrants will come from the district of Land directly here to Wiota. Dean Aabel would surely be of assistance.

Can you get me some news? I would like to pay for it.

Mrs. Caja Munch to her Parents, Mr. and Mrs. F. W. S. Falch *with a Postscript by Pastor J. St. Munch*

Wiota Parsonage, October 28, 1857

My dear Parents!

It has been a long time since I wrote to you, but it is also a long time since you wrote to us, so we won't even talk about that. The reasons are perhaps nonconsequential on both sides, we could have written had we only started it, isn't that so, my dear Mother? Surely, however, the good intentions are not lacking on either side.

My dear Munch returned safely and happy, thank God, from his journey in Minnesota, although he had many burden-some functions there. In fact, even the pastors here in America showed great surprise when he told them about it. I am only going to tell you what he accomplished on one single Sunday: First, after having preached on the preceding Friday and Satur-day with quite a few christenings and communicants, and not having slept the last two nights, he started early Sunday morning to register more than twenty children who were to be christened, and their godparents; then eight children presented themselves as they wished to be confirmed; these were very carefully cate-chized for several hours, and he accepted six of them. Then the service started in the same small parlor crowded with people; first he addressed twenty-three or twenty-four women to be churched, after that he gave communion service for sixty com-municants, next mass and the sermon from the pulpit, then the christening of all those twenty-four children, then to administer bread and wine for sixty communicants, thereafter confirmation of the five [sic] children, and finally communion for them; so when he finished, it was completely dark. But after having slept well the following night, he felt so refreshed on Monday that he could have started the same functions all over again if it had been necessary. However, it is quite clear Who bestowed this strength upon him, oh, none other than our heavenly Father, whose mercy we never appreciate.

You are surprised, maybe, that Munch could confirm these children without having more knowledge of their Christian faith. But it is really the dire need that forces the ministers in America to take this step; as soon as they realize that, due to the great distances, the children do not have the opportunity to benefit from the guidance of a minister, they reluctantly perform this function when it is requested, hoping that the Lord will add His blessing to it for the future; otherwise, these children would grow up without being confirmed, as so many unfortunately do, which certainly would not be any better.

Munch christened 100 children during his journey. Some parents had two children to be baptized at the same time, one of whom was usually capable of walking. He baptized one set of twins, who were named after the Emperor of France and the Queen of England; they were the children of a Norwegian woman married to a Frenchman.

Munch surprised me by coming home from his trip a few days earlier than he had planned, because the steamer in which he traveled down the Missisippi found it convenient to sail into a forest with them, and there they remained for a whole day until finally another steamer arrived and took them in tow; a huge tree had penetrated one of the paddle boxes, and it ap-peared to have received considerable damage. Certainly, they made up a fire in the woods and tried to repair the damage, but they did not succeed. No human dwelling was visible in any direction. The passengers entertained themselves eating wild grapes. By this accident, Munch was delayed and was not able to keep his appointments for the services he had already announced, so he thought the best thing to do was to go directly to his dear home, where his return was anticipated with great longing—yes, I believe the joy was just as great on both sides. It is not easy to be alone for such a long time, but the Lord and His comforting Words helped me to pass the time. Munch was also lonesome for his loved ones at home, in one of his letters he wrote: "Now I understand why your father always was in such a hurry when he was traveling."

He also had to try a little of everything. He had used all different kinds of transportation, railroad, steamship, walking, horseback riding, conveyance by oxen or horses on lumber wagons with Germans, Englishmen, and Norwegians, across small rivers, swamps, and rough trails, so that many times the wagon stood fairly on end, but God was merciful and kept him safe. He thought the worst of all was when he stayed in places that were not clean and he had to be in the same room, very often, with 6–7 adults and a whole bunch of dirty, naughty, screaming children, who sometimes messed with the food that later appeared on the table, and from which he had to eat without a thought. Then, when he had gone to bed at night together with all these people, either up in a loft, where the clear sky was visible in all directions, or else downstairs in the same room, then the bedbugs really went into action so he was unable to get any sleep. But then, on the other hand, he also came to several places where it was very neat and clean, where he had his own room, good and tasty food, so then he made up for what he had had to forego in those other places. And when he came home to me, I could not at all notice that the trip had strained him in the least, and together we thanked from our hearts our God and Father, who had been so merciful and kind to both of us during the separation.

Little Else did not recognize him upon his return, but it didn't last many hours. At first she looked at him very puzzled, but when he gave her an apple, and after he had walked up and down the floor with her a couple of times, then very soon she recognized her Daddy, and she did not know any more where to point when I asked her where Daddy was, because I had taught

her while he was gone to point to his daguerrotype, which hangs
on the wall. Else is, thank God, very healthy and clever and is
each day becoming more and more entertaining and funny. She
can tell me what the cuckoo, the rooster, the cow, the dog, and
the cat say; if we hand her a small whip or a rope, she calls out
"get up," which is what they usually say to the horses here when
they are supposed to run; this she has learned from her faithful
admirer, Gustav Dietrichson. She can not walk yet, her little
nursemaid is a big blockhead when it comes to training her for
that, and I myself have neither the time nor the patience to walk
around with her, so I am sure it is only due to lack of practice;
she walks with great speed along the walls, chairs, and tables, is
very clever pulling down things and doing mischief. She likes
especially getting into Munch's bookshelves, where she managed
to tear down a whole lot of books in one minute, and then she
laughs heartily afterwards as she knows right well she is not
supposed to do it. She has quite a few teeth by now. We have just
moved her cradle upstairs, where my good little newcomer maid
is staying with her as she is being weaned. That is harder on me
than I had anticipated—why, I was really so foolish I had tears
in my eyes the first night I had to sleep without my little treasure
at my side. Munch laughed at me, and later I regretted it as our
Lord could very well punish me therefore and *really* take her
away from me. She is extremely good and sleeps almost all night,
but this girl is also very good at taking care of her, she has been a
nursemaid in Norway and is very fond of children.

Here I had a delightful interruption as my little servant
arrived with letters from my dear home. Thousands and thousands of thanks to all of you, and very ashamed I retract my
words in the beginning of the letter and hurry even more to get
it sent to you, my beloved friends. I understand that Lagertha
has been seriously afflicted with illness. God be praised that you,
my beloved Parents, now have this dreadful fright behind you. I
thank my heavenly Father from my heart both because He sent
my dear sister this illness, and also because He this time so
mercifully spared her life. This may be an awakening for my
very dear Lagertha seriously to continue the Christian life that
already has started to move within her. The Words of the Bible
will clearly tell her and everybody else what they must do to be
saved. At present I am reading in the works of Miss Grace

Kennedy; they are very pleasing and instructive entertainment if one takes to heart all the words and admonitions from God contained therein. Preutz may have this book in the rental library.

My confirmation day is also the 11th of October, Mother dear; this, then, is an important day in our family. Why do you insist on having Munch's birthday on the 22nd instead of on the 21st, precious Mother? If I remember correctly, the very same thing happened last year. It is the 21st, please remember this for next year. On that day we were invited to a wedding, but as Munch's throat was not too good and he was scheduled to start on a long journey again in a couple of days, we found it best to be careful and stayed at home, which we rather wished to do anyway. While he was in Minnesota, I had made him a robe, as nice as I was able to make one in America, and this was his only gift. The weather was beautiful, I raised the flag. Before he went to the church to marry these two people, I treated him to Norwegian chocolate and sponge cake, for dinner we had his favorite dish, mutton-and-cabbage, then currant compot, and after supper I had to put out a tray with treats—nuts, apples, canned plums, and grapes—besides bird cherry liqueur, which I had made myself. He had one of his best friends staying with him almost all day as he brought *"Rettigheta te Præsten"* (the Minister's due) as he expressed it, and this consisted of twice the amount of wheat and oats that we should have had, and in addition to that a couple of bushels of turnips and two pieces of butter. Our good friends are continuously sending us gifts.

The same thing happens this year as last year, namely, that I am still writing on the letter you should have received on your birthday. I know that you treasure my letters, and therefore I should try even harder to give you this pleasure on your day of glory, but you will have to forgive your untrustworthy daughter, your other two grown daughters will surely do better. I see all of you in my thoughts: you, Mutter mine, have no peace to sit in the red parlor and be amiable as it is Saturday, although Nanna and Lagertha, who hopefully has completely recovered, will take care of everything in the house for you; but you will, nevertheless, have to go in and drink coffee with fresh wheat cake which Cathinka has brought with her on her way home from school— oh, could I only be with you! But we will not think of it, the time will surely come, and then the pleasure will be even greater. I will be with you in my thoughts and pray deeply to God for you, my Mother, that He may give you the peace and tranquility, which you surely deserve after your lifelong devotion to your family.

I had also decided to send a letter to my dear Nanna for her birthday, but all my good intentions failed because, right after Munch returned from Minnesota, we had to drive down to Dietrichson's, where I had promised to stay during her confinement, and we arrived in good time. After a long, tiresome journey, which started early in the morning, we arrived at Dietrichson's in the dark late that night. Here we found the lady of the house at home alone. She was very happy to see us, and the very next day in the afternoon she gave birth to a big, beautiful girl. Dietrichson returned home that evening, and there was joy and happiness, first because everything was well over for his wife, and next because he found his dear friend Munch in his home; they had a lot of things to discuss, and I divided my time between Mrs. Dietrichson and Else. She had an excellent and capable certified midwife, who had just arrived from Norway, and it was a pleasure to watch how well and able Mrs. Dietrichson was all the time—to the great joy and comfort of her husband, who had to leave her after a few days to go to the Synod, which this year was to convene at Pastor Koren's in Iowa.

Munch thought it too expensive for him to make this long journey, and besides, his congregations are not affiliated with the Synod, so he felt it would be justified for him to stay away. But as it was Munch's own proposal concerning a separate educational institution that was to come up before the Synod, and since it was very likely that this would be the first as well as the last Synod he would ever attend in America, he decided to go along. Well, with that I got enough to do. He had neither a whole pair of trousers nor a coat. I patched the trousers as best I could, and I got him to buy a new coat in the nearest town, so he left looking fairly decent and respectable.

In the meantime, Else and I were to stay with Mrs. Dietrichson, and whenever I wished to leave, Dietrichson's horses and buggy would be at my disposal to bring me to my home, where I was most strictly ordered to be present before the day Munch had set for his return as he did not at all want to come back to an empty house. This I found perfectly reasonable. Nevertheless, I postponed my return trip until the very last day because the midwife had left Mrs. Dietrichson, and as she was only about ten to eleven days old, she was certainly too weak yet to dress her little one herself; so this task was left to me, and I felt, therefore, that I had to delay the journey as long as I could. But what happens? That very morning the weather turned so bad with wind and sleet that it was quite impossible to travel. You can imagine my desperation. Munch would arrive in Wiota that same evening if the weather had not also changed his travel plans. We consoled each other as best we could, and to forget the terrible weather that roared outside, I started to play with all the children in the evening, carrying Else on my arm. So the day passed, and I went to bed that night with the firm decision that I would leave the following day, no matter what the weather turned out to be.

I got up very early in the morning and made everything ready. The weather was fine, but the roads terrible. The man who was supposed to drive me did not show up, but as he lived by the road we were to take, I decided myself to have the horses put to and to have another man, who lived close by, take me that far. With this in mind, I went out in the yard, and what do I see but Munch and Dietrichson driving down the hill! Now all our worries were over, although I got a scolding before he heard the whole story.

We then stayed another day together with our dear friends, and the following morning we started on our way, trusting our journey in God's hand, for the roads were horrible. However, we traveled safely to within a couple of miles from our home when one of the wheels came off our buggy. It went off easily enough, but we were not able to fasten it on again until they got hold of a blacksmith—you see, here they have a different device from the one used at home. What could we do now? It was getting dark, no house within sight. Else and I were standing on the road, and the man did not know what to do. Finally Munch and the other man arrived, they were a little behind as they had only one horse, and besides, their wagon seat had broken, so I did not dare sit up there with Else. We then decided that the wheel was to be put back on, and that Else and I would sit in the buggy, one driver would walk and lead the horses, while the other was to follow behind and give notice when the wheel would slip out again. Munch was to drive ahead in the other frail *voiture* to lead the way. Our wheel did not even show signs of wanting to leave its position, in fact, we finally thought we might have traveled all the way with a loose wheel, and getting bold by this thought, we continued the rest of the journey in this fashion and arrived happily and safely to our home, thanking God from our hearts that He so mercifully had held His hand over us.

Everything went on very peacefully and in a friendly way at the Synod meeting, even though the ministers were divided into two parties. Some agreed with Munch on the founding of a separate educational institution among the Norwegians, from which they could procure their own ministers in the future. Others, to the contrary, cast their votes for joining the German university over here to have their ministers educated there. Munch's idea was victorious, though, which was also more to the taste of the people. On the one Sunday they were all gathered, Munch had to deliver the sermon, for which he received general praise from all the ministers; even Koren had to break out in eulogies over his brilliant abilities, as he said. It must have been a solemn spectacle when all the ministers participated in the Communion services at the same time; Ottesen officiated first for all the others, and then Preus for him in return.

At the Korens it had been very congenial and comfortable. Leis was very obliging to Munch and was interested in hearing exactly how I was doing in every respect. It was Christiane who had written this about Munch, and she had heard it from a lady in Christiania, so it could not possibly have come from any of our letters; the whole affair is only gossip and slander, as one always finds in this world, and should be paid very little attention. You must attest the truth of my words that if one tries to set bounds to this, it will become increasingly worse. She said, furthermore, that it was supposed to have come from Munch's family; perhaps one of them has expressed himself rashly concerning this matter, but from my letters they certainly could not have drawn such a conclusion. Let us, therefore, forget the whole thing; it could not possibly harm Munch.

The Korens were living in a very beautiful place, yes, even nicer than ours. She had a nice garden with lots of cabbage and carrots. Their two lovely daughters were healthy and clever, but very naughty. Leis looked tired, but was sweet, friendly, pretty, and graceful. It appeared that Koren wants to be the master of his home. They had been able to add to their parsonage, so there was no lack of space, and it was elegant throughout. The food was good and nourishing, she had ample help, but then there were also a lot of people gathered every day.

After we had been together again in peace and quiet for a couple of days, and had celebrated Munch's birthday, my dear friend had to start out on a journey once more. Oh, these constant travels here in America surely make one's life miserable! Now he has been gone for eight days, but I hope that, by God's help, he will return tomorrow. The weather is nice and mild, we have had a beautiful autumn. But if the summer are not any warmer in India, then I surely feel sorry for them, for you should know that here they call this time of the year Indian summer when the autumn is as mild as it has been this year. ([Added with pencil in Pastor Munch's hand:] This explanation of Indian summer is not correct. Indians, that is, America's original inhabitants, whose best time for hunting is in the fall.) But even so we have had a fire going in the stove all day for quite some time, and there are no leaves or flowers left anywhere.

This year Munch bought a bigger and very nice stove for the parlor. The maid and I polished it the other day. She was not familiar with this kind of work, and as I really wanted it shiny, I took it on all by myself. Now it shines fairly like a mirror. I have put our carpet in the parlor this year; it will make our bedroom cold, but Else is now so big that for the most part she will be keeping us company in the sitting room, I believe, especially because Munch is so infatuated with her that he can hardly leave her for a moment when he is at home, yes, she will very likely become just as big a Daddy's darling as her mother was. She is outside riding in her little buggy every day now, dressed in a blue overcoat made over from my old dress, and with little red mittens on her hands, a gift from our newcomer maid Anne. She has also got a very nice piece of woolen material for a dress and a bead necklace from another maid, and from her nursemaid a little doll, which she is very fond of, she holds it in her arms and sits and rocks and sings to it.

Last night the cows ate all my collards. I had gathered from the garden and brought everything safely into the cellar, far more cabbage and carrots than I believe we can eat. I moved the collards out into my little flower garden, where I doubled *Fenset* [the fence] and made it as strong as I possibly could with my small sticks, but even so they had broken through and eaten every last leaf of my collards.

I have French beans, Mother dear, and I have sliced up two whole jars. Such a machine seems to be unknown here.[5] They never bother too much about preparing their food. They do have green beans, but they boil and serve them whole, and at the table they put cold butter on them and eat them that way. I have salted cucumber salad, preserved piccalilli, and quite a few plums and grapes, some raspberry, blackberry, bird cherry juice, the latter actually tastes more like real cherries than bird cherries. The juice from them is excellent. My wine from wild grapes I believe will turn out quite good. The wild grapes are not very good to eat, they are about like blueberries in size and taste, but more sour and somewhat tarter. Lyngonberries and blueberries are not to be found around here.

This year has been an unusually good year for fruit. I have myself picked or been given all my berries. One day while Munch was away, I took Else, both maids, and the boy with me up into the woods to pick berries, but as the woods here are almost impassable, I stayed with my little darling at the house of a Norwegian woman nearby while the others picked an awful lot of berries in a short time. I have also gathered a great quantity of nuts, and I will be able to buy some apples from a Norwegian farmer. This, then, will be the first year I can say that I really stocked the house for the winter, and many a time I catch myself thinking that this year I will maybe not be so happy as the previous ones when we had nothing. However, God alone ordains in this so it is not proper of me [to feel this way], and I really repress such thoughts immediately.

We now have four cows, two of them are not paid for yet. The one that lost her calf we will kill for Christmas, she looks big and fat, so I trust we will get a lot of tallow for candles; I mix it with some lard, and they burn just as good. My two hogs, which we also will slaughter, are not too poorly looking either, especially the one that rubs the other ([with pencil, Munch's hand:] neat pig!) .

Emil has not arrived yet, but I will forward all the letters to him. I have just written to him, but he is so particular that he will not even write to me (but sends several letters to Munch) because I have failed to answer his last communication. I am expecting him here any day, and I am looking forward considerably to his arrival. They seem to have much to do in the press, and by increasing his pay, they have persuaded him to continue there for a short time, although he has not at all agreed to a new contract and will very likely not stay on much longer anyway. I shall be happy the day he leaves Madison. Jakob Seeman is probably doing his part to entice him into temptations, but God be praised, Emil has been firm and will surely never forget his God and Savior, who so mercifully has stood by him. All of us would like so much for him to go to Beloit, a big city of good morals, where the Flekes live. He could easily learn bookbinding there as well, but as far as bookkeeping is concerned, I hardly believe he will be able to learn this thoroughly in America, they are not exactly particular in this respect here. I don't think there should be any difficulty for Emil to go back with us in two years, if he himself would want to do that, at home there is probably lack of help in this field also, I trust, especially if he goes to one of the bigger cities, Christiania or Bergen. As far as his money is concerned, he will certainly get it, even if those in the press will be mean enough to withhold it, for Munch owes the press some money for books, which he purposely has retained in case such a situation should arise.

My dear Mother, we never see Norwegian newspapers. You must definitely report whatever you believe would be of interest to us in them. . . . If I won't be able to write you this time, Nanna dear, please forgive me, I am always thinking of you with happiness and sympathy. You are on the right path, continue this way, and you will soon find consolation. My dear Lagertha must really take good care of herself this winter, do not go to those bad, pernicious balls. Oh, what a nest of sin Laurvig is beccoming when so much vanity and fripperies and fandangles take place there! Oh, how they would benefit from listening to one of Munch's stern sermons! God bless you and be with you, beloved Parents! Until we will be together again by God's help. I doubt that Munch will accept another charge here in America.

My boots fit me perfectly, but they must by no means be any

smaller. Otherwise I don't think that I wish for anything other than a few tobacco pipes and a clergyman's ruff for my dear Munch. Take care of yourselves, dear Parents, brothers and sisters. Greetings to Grandmother's and to Munch's and to all my good friends

From your daughter
Caja Munch

My time does not allow me to send a long letter today. However, I would like to add my friendly greetings and inform you that I am home safe and sound after my many and long travels. I have to excuse the Korens, who only related what they had been told and thought that this information was true. I would probably have said the same things if I had heard a similar story.

J. S. M.

Please send this letter on to Mother.

J. S. M.

Mrs. Caja Munch to her Mother, Mrs. Thalie Falch, née Staffeldt

Wiota Parsonage, January 18, 1858

My dear Mother!

Now I am writing with delight and happiness because, a couple of days ago, I received your and my sister Lagertha's dear, long awaited letters, for which I thank you both from my heart. It seems to turn out the way Mrs. Dietrichson predicted when she heard that we had decided to write each other every month, for she thought that we would not be able to keep this promise. But please, don't be worried. You know, quite unessential reasons could easily occur which would prevent me from writing; you should always imagine the best and not the worst. Emil certainly deserves a scolding because he has put off his writing for so long. From Munch's letter you will see that he is here with us, and I have asked him not once but twenty times to finish his letters and mail them.

The last time I wrote must have been in November, when we were getting ready to drive down to Dietrichson's for the christening but were prevented from going by impassable roads, to the great disappointment of both us and them. Since then I have hardly stepped outside a door.

I had a lot of butchering done for Christmas, which I enjoyed doing—I seemed to live over again the old days in my home. Everything turned out well. I made almost all the things you prepare, dear Mother, although I did make some kind of meat sausage which I marvel that we never thought of cooking at home. I had to make black pudding for Munch, he likes it so well, and I had the pleasure of treating my dear Emil and Munch to delicious things for a long time. My baking for Christmas consisted of wort-cake, Christmas bread, flead-cakes, hartshorn pastry, and apple pie. I finished everything early, and we had a quiet, peaceful, wonderful Christmas Eve and Holiday Season. During this time, Munch visited only the nearest parishes, from where he returned the same day. He married one of his best friends after Christmas, Emil and I went to the wedding. The next day, we had four or five families in for dinner.

I find that this letter has a strange, brief style, but for the moment I am not capable of doing any better. The reason for it may be that for so long now I have been staying within these four walls, without seeing or hearing another well-bred person. A couple of days ago, Munch and Emil drove down to Dietrichson's, but I could not come along as the roads were very bad. Emil has since returned with horses and carriage, and not for a few days yet are we going to go and get Munch a short distance from here, for he went with Dietrichson to Chicago to organize a congregation there.

We are having a strange winter this year, no snow, no frost —may God bring us a healthy summer!

19th [January 1858]

My dear Mother, I am so stupid with my writing this time and don't know with what to fill this sheet of paper, much less two, which I have written before. All of us, God be praised, are healthy and well, my little Else remarkably so—oh, how deeply we must thank our Lord for that! She runs around on the floor just as fast as I do, and is like a toy to all of us, especially to Emil. He tumbles her, squeezes her, lifts her to the ceiling, and the two of them make a terrible noise, just the way he treated his small sisters and brothers. I imagine you recognize his ways. Once in a while Else finds him a little too aggressive, but as a rule they are great chums. Just now she is outside, trundling in her little carriage. I have let her stay in the fresh air as much as possible all this winter (if one can call it that). It goes rather slowly with Else's teeth, she still has only eight, but otherwise she is making a rapid progress in every respect. She understands what I am telling her, and several times, to our surprise, she comprehends what we are talking about [between us]. She also sings in her own fashion, about Mammie, kittie, and the doll, so I hope that she and Emilie in time will be singing duets for us. My guitar has become her toy, and with this she poses in front of the cat and plays and sings. She chuckles and laughs like a grown man, you have never heard such a funny laughter, I don't know if it is pleasant or ugly. She is always sweet and smiling, yes, I must really say she is a good child, but she has nevertheless been spanked quite thoroughly already. When company arrives, she is often the first one to greet them, she is a real busybody, nothing escapes her attention, and she wants to grab hold of everything; if she continues to behave in this manner when she gets bigger, she won't be easy to handle. Munch and I are almost too fond of her, she is everything to us, and we can amuse ourselves so heartily just playing with her. May God continue to keep His protecting hand over her! And may He give us wisdom and strength to bring her up so that she will carry her Christian name to the glory of God.

The 20th [January 1858]
I am writing a little every day, Else detains me more than you believe, she is now at the age where one is most importunate to one's Mama, and I like so well to have her with me. Besides, this year I have put our carpet in the sitting room, so it is best for her to lie down on that and tumble around. Out of Nanna's woolen dress Else has got two good everyday dresses and an apron, which are nice and warm for her, but she looks just as wide as she is tall in those. She has also started to use the long pants, but I have had to let down all hems. Two gray cats are her favorite playmates; however, one of them in particular is a little mean, so she gets quite a few scratches.

I still have my newcomer maid, and I am hoping to keep her until well into the month of June, although our unpleasant neighbors try everything possible to get her out of here. They pity her because she is here and does not learn English, besides, they maintain that I am not any better than they are, and when they can manage without a maid, so should I also manage without a maid; I am big and strong enough to do my own work, they say. Yes, it certainly is a congenial spirit that possesses the Norwegian people when they come over here! When in addition there is a good share of gossip and slander circulating about us, and always ill will and opposition and grumbling and an ungodly way of living everywhere, then I really don't know if they deserve to have a minister among them. Yes, indeed, we have been through many a trying time, but God is merciful, He sends us this for our own good and gives us strength to carry it with patience.

But for a few honorable Christian people, most of Munch's annex congregations have dissolved since New Year, so we are now here completely at loose ends and could be home by spring if we knew how such a hurried return would be received, and if there is hope for Munch to get an ecclesiastical position at home, and also if it would not be more correct for us to go to another charge and stay there for another couple of years to enable us to pay off what we owe my dear Father. Undoubtedly, money is easier here than at home. If we only knew what is God's will with us! He has now in so many ways really disclosed to us that we ought not to stay on in this impious congregation. However, Munch will try them a little longer in case he should succeed in organizing a congregation in Chicago.

Pastor Dietrichson will go back to Norway in the spring of 1859 if it is God's will. He has already resigned his charge, and you can imagine that our desire is great to join him. But then there is so much doubt, and Munch feels that he should perhaps rather take over Dietrichson's large congregation and in addition serve his good friends here as an annex parish. One thing lies heavily on my heart in case we should go home so soon, and that is leaving Emil. But he only laughs at me when I mention it and maintains that he will not return at all for many years, not until he accomplishes something of consequence. It does not seem to affect him in the least that we might leave him. Indeed, I marvel to hear and see our boy Emil now, so big and heavy, brave and bold, gay and smart. I then told him that I was afraid he would run off and get himself married to one of these Nor-

wegian Yankee dolls, but then, you may be sure, he laughed and
answered both Munch and myself that there could be no harm
in that. But Munch suggested that Father might not then receive
him very cordially should he come home dragging along such a
hag. I am certainly happy to have him here with me; in fact, I
have to hug him several times a day. He is so good, and he
putters around tidying up and fixing everything for us. Munch is
very fond of him also, you know. But now, unfortunately, it
appears to drag on for him getting another position. The shortage of money has its effect on this, too, and we would so much
like to have him nearby.

Let me not forget to tell you about a strange party we went
to before Christmas, it will probably give you some idea of the
kind of people we are surrounded by, and whom the Norwegians
describe as *"fine Folk"* [distinguished people]. One day, here
came a little daughter of our nearest Yankee neighbor and
invited us for dinner, and at the same time she asked to borrow
all of our sterling spoons. We accepted, although the inclination
was rather weak, but we did not want to hurt their feelings,
especially since we thought the party was because of us as they
were going to have sterling spoons and, as we then surmised, soup,
a dish that otherwise is never used among the Yankees. So we
dressed up in our best finery, I in black silk with all my trinkets,
Else like a doll in her blue woolen dress and all her embroidered
clothing, and Munch in his black suit with a white cravat, so all
of us looked as elegant as possible, for we had never been out
among Yankees before and wanted to show up in all our glory.
Thus attired, off we went, but—how surprised and amazed, and
utterly disappointed we were! Certainly, we knew beforehand
that they were plain people, but we never imagined they would
be *that* crude. The people of the house received us in the most
slovenly attire you can imagine, dirty, tattered skirts, and shoes
that shuffled around their feet. As we entered, there was nothing
to sit on but a bed, which stood over in a dirty hole where the
woman was cooking the food. It appeared to be some kind of
Doning (bee), an awful lot of ragged, dirty, rough, and dreadful
menfolk who were there to help the man bring in his corn, and
all their matching womenfolk were sitting around a bedspread
sewing—this was so huge that it filled the entire room but for a
small space where the dining table stood. Well, we sat down to

eat with some of this rough rabble around us—ugh! They
laughed and snickered, whispered and buzzed, swore and spat,
and were so noisy it was terrible. Yes, if we had entered the most
awful drunken tavern at home, it could not have been worse.
Naturally, they stared at us as if we were wild animals. The food
was good, meat and pork, cabbage and jellies, and coffee; there
was no sign of soup. But after we were through eating and had
been sitting around for a while, Munch came over to me and
said: "No, put your things on, we will leave, this is no company
for us"—and so we left, wishing them "good-bye altogether."

I am not sending you more than this one sheet this time, for
Emil has written three. To be sure, he claims that I will not be
allowed to put mine in with his because his is so old—you see, he
will attempt to fool you a little with the long distance and make
you believe he has sent it earlier; for the same reason, he does
not want to thank Mother and Lagertha now for their last letters
either. But I told him I would reveal the whole story, thank you
both from him and from myself for the letters, and promise that
we both would write soon again. God bless all of you! Stay well
and healthy! Be happy and content, remember me to friends,
and warm and heartfelt greetings to everyone from
your always affectionate Caja Munch

Mrs. Caja Munch to her Mother, Mrs. Thalie Falch, née Staffeldt *With a Postscript by Pastor J. St. Munch*

[March 1858] [6]

. . . . Since I am talking about newspapers, I must mention
that we now have obtained Norwegian papers again. Holfeldt is
kind enough to let us have *Morgenbladet* free, we pay only the
postage from Rock Prairie. The same Holfeldt is really a kind-
hearted and charitable man, he has even presented Munch
with a nice, good and warm, black fur cap as a Christmas favor.
In the spring of 1860 he is quite determined to return to Norway. If one could just join company with him! But they are of
good means and will very likely travel as real big shots.

On Lady Day [March 25], Munch is again going to Chicago.
He and Dietrichson take turns each month preaching there, the
income at present is not any more than to cover the expenses.
Last time Munch returned from Chicago, he brought me a very
beautiful, big, nice and warm plaid exactly like Nanna's, so I

must think of you, dear sister, every time I use it, and Munch says the same. It was cheap, 7½ dollars, but now during all these bankruptcies such goods are sold for half price at some kind of auction. Here in this country, they seldom use a coat during the winter, indeed, hardly ever, and I am happy to go along with this fashion, especially since this type of shawl is much warmer than any of my coats.

We have had an extraordinary winter, so mild, yes, I can almost say warm, until a few weeks ago, then it turned cold with an insignificant amount of snow, just enough to use a sleigh. One day Munch took me on a drive with an old, reliable, good mare we have and the Norwegian harness bells, but it was of no use, all we did during the whole ride was to talk about how much more pleasant it is to go for a drive in Norway. All the snow is gone already, and Munch had to drive on wheels to Dietrichson's.

On Palm Sunday, Munch is going to preach for Pastor A. C. Preus and have Communion service for him and his wife, and I will then be home alone once again but cannot say a word as for some time now I have been so fortunate in this regard.

Should there be an opportunity this spring, please be so kind and send me a netting needle and some coarse black silk, I would like to make a net for Else as I do not know any other way to keep the hair out of her eyes. She tries by herself, poor thing, to push it away with her plump little hands. The other day I braided her, but it was such a difficult task that I promised it certainly would be the last time, she would not sit still at all.

Hanna and Wilhelm are perhaps married by now? I wish them all the best from the bottom of my heart, tell them that if I were as near to them as I now am far away, I would give them as a wedding present a big, big barrel of extra fine American wheat flour with the wish that *Hvedebrødsdagene* [the honeymoon, literally "the wheatcake days"] will last as long as there is flour in the barrel. I expect a letter from Wilhelm every time; he should not break a given promise.

You must also congratulate Sophie Ellegers. You had lots of news to tell me last time, dear Mother, it is so good of you; see that you continue to tell me anything and everything, I love it all, and I know of no better way to thank you than to report back to you, bag and baggage, all that might happen in my quiet, lonely home.

Do you know what Munch and I do when we really want to enjoy ourselves? We talk about Norway and how we are going to spend the first few months at home. We all know very well that it depends solely on God's will, and that we do not command the future, but neither can such a pleasure of fancy be sinful. Just listen: We will disembark in Fredriksværn, where Father, Mother, all my sisters and brothers will be standing with smiling faces to receive us. We will then drive home to Hovland with *"Storegulen"* ["Big Yellow"], *"Svarta"* ["Blackie"], or whatever horses Father will have, with *"Otello"* running up front. After having stayed at Hovland for a few days and rested and rejoiced out of all good bounds, all of us will go to Christiania—we cannot part company at this moment, so they will have to find room for all of us in there, one way or another; we Americans could very well sleep on straw mattresses in an attic, we are not used to better things.[7] And then, after having visited the whole of our family, we go back with you to Hovland, and if Munch has a few pennies in his pocket, we will rent a small house by the seashore, where we will stay and go swimming and wash off the seared and sun-parched skin of America. And you will then come out and visit us every day, and I shall wait on you American style. We must buy and bring along a cooking stove from here, no matter how poor we may be, and this will be my kitchen standing outside with a few planks serving as a roof so it will not rain into my kettles. Yes, believe you me, I have learned to take things in quite a different manner; even if I had the house full of company and did not have anything to offer them but bread and butter and a hearty welcome, I would not be dispirited, those who would not put up with this, I would obliterate from my list of friends. I don't quite know how we will manage our first winter. Munch will probably not get a permanent position so soon, and it would be uncomfortable to stay at the farm, so you would have to put us up at Hovland. I would take the place of the housekeeper, and you and I, dear Mother, should be doing the chores around the house just as in the olden days—my, oh my, what fun! My cooking stove could be put upstairs in the maid's room, and we would cook some in American and some in Norwegian fashion. Coffee, sugar, and various such trifles I hope we could manage to furnish ourselves. Oh, well, I trust you and I should be able to agree on these things, dear Mother, I don't believe the two of us would "dry up"! Father and Munch would chat, have a game of chess now and then, and play with the children. Munch should probably be able to get some income of his own in Laurvig, maybe he could become a curate there now in case he were present, think how wonderful that would be! I really think he would not object to that. Oh, my dearest Parents! If we only get safely home, then I have no doubts at all that there, too, we will get a sufficient livelihood, and we do not require any more, money and abundance are things that I wish for least of all in this world.

I still have my dependable, clever newcomer girl and will keep her at least through the month of May. We really have had a nice and good time in our house this winter, God be blessed therefore. But my dear, beloved Munch has had many a hard fight with his congregation. However, I believe the worst struggle is over by now, and that little by little it is becoming evident to many that Munch only proceeds upon the Words of the Bible itself, and that this is a necessary, upright, and Christian procedure, which wholly and solely makes for their own true welfare. At the last congregation meeting, he won a considerable victory over all of them, for he had written down a number of things about a minister's labors and duties as a *curator of souls* in his congregation. This met with universal approval and, what is even better, I believe it woke several up from the lethargy into which they had lulled themselves in this respect, partly by their own lax Christian life, partly by lax ministers at home. It is terrible to hear how the ministers in several places in Norway must have a rather flexible conscience.

I have cut eight new shirts for Munch, which I am now trying to sew, but I am afraid it will be a slow process as I have no help with this work except what Anne can do for me, and that, you can imagine, does not amount to much. I have recently finished sixteen collars, eight for Munch and eight for Emil. His new shirts from home made Emil very happy, but he would have liked to have them a little fancier in the front. You ought to know he has become a grand Yankee now and likes to look nice, he is very careful with his clothes, got himself two vests and a pair of elegant trousers, extremely well tailored, besides I have put new frontpieces, collars, and cuffs on several of his old shirts; the nice linen shirt fronts which I once made for Munch have been given to him, Munch never used them, and Emil liked them very much. So you understand, as far as clothes are concerned, he can stand a whole siege. His new woolen hose were very large, the boots fitted perfectly.

Very soon I am going to brew beer—am I not clever that I can brew my own? The wine from the grapes, which I made last summer, turned out very well; it could, maybe, have been a little less sweet, but I will do it better next time, I had neither measure nor weight of anything. I am now going to draw it onto bottles and leave it until next summer, then it will be nice to have with water to quench the thirst. Would you believe that we here on our table in America have genuine *Gammelost* ["old cheese"] from Bergen—a gift from a man in the congregation; furthermore, we have been promised another one because he got a small puppy from us, for which we had no use. Several of our friends continue to give us butter, eggs, chickens, and whatever else they have. I will not write any more in this letter now until Munch returns from his trip so that I can tell you about it directly.

[a later date]

Dear Parents-in-Law!

Caja has left this page for me, and as I would very much like to send you a greeting, I shall not leave this good opportunity unused. I arrived home the other day from my Rock Prairie trip with a scurvy mouth (I have not been bothered with this since that Easter when I visited at Hovland), but since I otherwise find myself in good health, I am not paying much attention to this, as I have already made my good fortune with the ladies.

I am rather embarrassed when I supplement Caja's letters because she usually has covered everything and nosed through every corner, so I find nothing left to write about. However, I can bring you this piece of news that it is now settled on our part, if this is the Lord's will, that we next summer—1859—will move down to Rock Prairie, and that I will administer that charge for one year together with Wiota until Dietrichson at home in Norway finds a successor to become the permanent minister from 1860. We will very likely have a good income that year, and we will also attain our great wish to be able to return to Norway in the previously determined year 1860. All of Diet-

richson's congregations have offered me a position for five years
from 1859, but however much I cherished this offer, I dared not
accept it as I do not find it commendable for Caja's and little
Else's as well as for my own sake to prolong our stay in this
foreign country any longer. I have now a hope that I will be able
to furnish my own congregations with a minister in 1860, although the truth is that a great part of my parishioners rather
wish themselves free of everything but whiskey. The Rock Prairie congregations are the best in America, and I have already
gained their confidence as I have officiated there several times, so
I am sure that, by the help of the Lord, I could spend happier
years there than here, and also save up a little for the household.
But America is America, and since both of us wholeheartedly
long for the quiet peace and beautiful scenery of our home, then
I think that we should not let the matter of money take command. Love for one's fatherland is a *power* that one cannot
reason away, it is completely like love in the days of youth, for
the more one tries to smother it, the more it gains in strength.
However, if during this coming year the pecuniary conditions at
home should become worse, so that we hardly would be able to
meet the storm, then we will still have time to change our
decision. The delegates from Rock Prairie declared that they
hoped I would in the course of this coming year decide for the
five years, and that they would be prepared at any time to make
adjustments in the resolution already agreed upon (namely, that
I administer the charge for one year) if I would only let them
know that I was willing to become their permanent minister.
But when I think of the singing birds and fragrant fields, the
foaming waves and rushing streams, the lovely air, the crisp
winter, the glorious spring, and the sweet summer at home in old
Norway—oh, then I cannot reason any more, then rational
thought falls silent, and the love for our fatherland carries us on
powerful wings over sea and shore to the fair regions of our
home. This is only an echo of what I recall I wrote immediately
after our arrival here, and so it must be. For these silent, desolate prairies and stunted oaks, this hot, feverish air, and these
slow, muddy, and soundlessly gliding rivers that lurk in serpen-
tine meandering through fetid marshes, with much cheerlessness
in both nature and people, make us so *extremely fond* of the
charm of our home.

Otherwise everything is the same. The Lord is with us, and we have peace within. The same Lord be with all of you now and evermore.

Yours affectionately,
J. St. Munch

I should like very much to have a few words from you about your wish concerning our returning home. I believe you will agree with us.

Caja asks me to send all of you her and our beautiful little Else's greetings and good wishes for your well-being.

The Last Year in Wiota, 1858–1859

Mrs Caja Munch to her Parents, **Mr. and Mrs. F. W. S. Falch,**
With a Postscript by Pastor J. St. Munch

Wiota Parsonage, October 24, 1858

Dearly beloved Parents!

Last night I received another long, loving letter from you, my sweet Mother, God bless you for that! I am ashamed as a dog that I have not written more often this summer. When I see and hear what you accomplish every day, I have no excuse at all. However, I did send you a letter in the beginning of August, whch I hope that you now, by God's help, have received, and that it has reassured you.

But why be so worried, beloved Parents? Don't you know that not even a straw can fall to the ground without it being God's will? And what God sends, is for our real welfare, be it sorrow or joy. Put your whole cause in His hand, and do not have so many unnecessary worries for what the future will bring. It consumes your physical strength and, most of all, it prevents Jesus from taking abode in your hearts. Oh, I wish with all my heart for you to have a good life, dearest Parents, and to feel a little of God's abounding blessed peace in and around you. Is it really necessary, my dear Mother, that you must in this manner throughout your whole life be a slave of things temporal? Is it not possible that you could arrange things a little differently? Could you not let your grown children take care of themselves a little more than I imagine they do? Do you still get up in the morning and make breakfast and serve for all of them, bringing it hither and thither? Could you not get a maid dependable enough to set the table in the morning while all of you get dressed, and then first start the day with a prayer to God, with everybody in the house present? One of you could read a part from the Bible, for instance, all of Paul's letters, one chapter each day, and next the morning prayer for the day in the hymn book, or one of Fredrick Arndt's Contemplations. Oh, this would surely, by God's help, bring a great blessing, the servants would go to their work with more happiness and get to understand their duties better, the children would become more thankful for their daily bread, yes, it would bring many, many wonderful fruits if it were performed in the name of Jesus. The first step, I have felt, is difficult to take, but start in the holy name of Jesus, He will give you strength, and never mind what the world will say, but keep firmly in mind that it is not so easy as many imagine to enter the Kingdom of Heaven. Only read the Bible, Hofacker's sermons, and the Word of God in other books, and little by little it will become clear to you as it has to me. But God help me, I am still far, far, far behind! God have mercy on us poor sinners!

Since the last time I wrote, we have had an extra nice time, so there you see how little you have had to worry about. However, it is my fault, I could have written to you. First we went down to Dietrichson's in July with both our little girls, about which I wrote last time.[1] Next we celebrated my birthday alone in peace and quiet. I got a beautiful gold cross from Munch, which I wear every day on a ribbon around my neck as a sign that I am a minister's wife and also a bearer of the Cross—oh, would that I could be that in truth and faithfulness. Our little Else's first birthday was for us a great delight and joy. Munch gave her a cat that could open its mouth and cry; the first few days, she was a little afraid of it, but now I believe she has put the fear aside and has already deprived it of half its head. "Onta will fix it," she always says when her toys need repairs. From me she got doll, from Emil a picture book, from Anne a "shepherd's hat," and from her dauntless knight Gustav a whole box full of cookies and candy, which she was allowed to dispose of as she pleased; first she distributed from her gift, then she had a good taste of it herself and ate so much that she got a stomachache afterward. A small bird made in Norway was also given to her by our little newcomer boy.

Just after the 20th [August, Else's birthday], we were to

accompany Munch to Holmen's in Linden, but Else was not feeling well, and besides I thought it would be too much traveling back and forth with them, so we decided to stay behind. After having returned safe and sound from the trip, Munch stayed at home for a couple of days. Then he went to Chicago, made the return trip via Dietrichson's, and got him, his wife, the three younger children, and a maid to come along with him up here, where he gave Communion service for us. We spent a pleasant time together, had afternoon coffee in our little garden, I had made Christmas bread, flead-cakes, and rye rusks, I had bought and butchered a sheep, so I treated them well to roast and mutton-and-cabbage. Besides, almost a whole sheep was given to me, and several chickens, and eggs and butter. I made liqueur, apples were given to me, and we picked nuts. One day, Munch, Dietrichson, and Emil drove out to go fishing; indeed, they returned with fish, which we were innocent enough to believe they had drawn themselves, but we later learned they had been caught "with a golden hook."

After they had spent a week with us, we went with them to attend the big general meeting of ministers at their place, about which I have much to report. It provided Mrs. Dietrichson and myself with quite a bit of work. Since I arrived from Norway, I have not previously been in need of a proper dress, but now Munch had to let his money roll. I had already made myself two cotton dresses, but of course, those I could not use in such fancy company. So I first got myself a plain, maroon and white, striped woolen dress, almost exactly like one Aunt Constance once had. Then I acquired a solid-colored dark brown dress of fine wool at one dollar per yard—anything of good quality is extremely expensive in this country. Furthermore, I had to cut out a width of the skirt in my black dress to make a new bodice for it as I had completely grown out of the old one. In other words, I have made five dresses for myself this summer, in addition to the clothes for Munch, Emil, and the children. Else got a beautiful pink woolen material for a dress from Gustav, which I trimmed with red cords, you can imagine she looks beautiful in that costume. Thalie had a little green and red woolen dress, also trimmed with red cords. So you can see, I have had quite a bit to do this summer.

When we arrived at Dietrichson's I had to assist with all the preparations, but you must not think that this took place according to Norwegian standards, because then it would never be possible to have so many ministers gathered in an American parsonage. All crates and superfluous pieces of clothing had to be removed from the house, for here you never see a clothes closet or a storage room, this stuff therefore had to be put in the barn. Upstairs at Dietrichson's place are practically three rooms. In one of them were four beds, so eight ministers were to sleep there. In the second room were two beds, where four German professors were to sleep. And in the third—actually a small attic room, through which all of them had to pass because of a mistake [in the building of the house]—was a bench, where three little boys were sleeping. Dietrichson and his wife and the three youngest children were sleeping in a small room downstairs. In addition, the gentlemen had two rooms to stay in. They ate in the kitchen, which is in the basement.

We cooked in a small boarded shack and on a stove placed outside under a big tree. Mrs. Dietrichson and I had tied and secured the pipe to the branches with iron chains—you may be assured, the two of us were rather efficient together and were not easily dispirited.

But now the whole house is occupied, and you will probably ask where did we, the servants, and the eleventh pastor sleep? Fortunately, a few steps from the parsonage is a small house, which belongs to Fleischer, who has moved to Madison, and which now was empty. Here five maids slept in a kitchen, among them my Anne, whom I brought to look after the children; in a room in front of the kitchen were Munch and I and the two little girls; and upstairs Pastor Stub and wife stayed with two children and a little girl confirmant, who is *conditioneret* and boards with the Dietrichsons. Emil was also invited to come, but he absolutely did not want to go. The boy slept in the hayloft.

Mrs. Dietrichson furnished most of the bedding. She borrowed some from us, and also your big tablecloth, which thus for the first time was used on a dining table, all my napkins, sterling silverware, and other such items that we could supply them with. We gave them two geese, some cabbage and other greens, of which I have plenty.

They were eleven Norwegian ministers assembled, the twelfth did not come, besides two German professors, the others

were ill. For eight days the Dietrichsons accommodated and fed
all these people, would you dare to undertake such an assign-
ment, my dear Mother? But listen how everything went, easy and
simple. In the mornings they had bread and butter, cheese
(homemade), meat patties, or eggs, or any other little things
that we might have left over from dinner, and coffee. For dinner
they usually had two kinds of "knife-food," but we did not
change the plates, and never more than one kind of gravy and
hardly any creamed vegetables, and also soup or cake, beer to
drink, which was simply brewed from syrup and hops, very good
and tasty. Afterward, coffee and cake, and in the evening the
same as in the morning, only tea instead of coffee. When the
tableclothes got dirty, we had them washed and ironed them a
little before they were put back on the table, very unconcerned,
don't you think? But that is the way one manages in America.
The formerly so finical Koren even offered to draw water from
the well for me, imagine, so he has also put aside his notions and
has become very agreeable and pleasant.

Everything went along smoothly and quietly, so Mrs. Dietrichson and I had the opportunity to stay upstairs and listen to
the interesting theological discussions as long as they were carried on in Norwegian. But a few days later, the Germans came,
and that was the end of all comfort and ease. Now everything
was to go on in German. Indeed, there are several of the Norwegian ministers who quite childishly look up to the Germans,
and praise and commend them so at every opportunity that the
rest have become rather inclined to be anti-German.

You can imagine it was interesting to see and hear so many
ministers gathered. Sunday there were two services. I went to
church in the morning and listened to a very beautiful sermon
by Pastor Koren, his deportment and appearance in the pulpit
were really attractive, and what he preached was as straightforward and natural as it could be and surpassed all my expectations, I had anticipated something more artificial and affected;
and handsome he is, that is a fact. He likes to be important, but
I can tell you the other ministers brush him off, they call him
the coxcomb of the Synod, he told me so himself. Toward me
as well as to all the others he was exceedingly nice and friendly,
in fact, he was one of the ministers I liked best, although most
of them are really very congenial people.

Sunday morning they all were in their clerical garbs and

proceeded to church two by two while the bells were tolling, a very solemn sight. The church was overcrowded with people, the singing was forceful and lovely, several of the ministers have an ear for music and sing four-part hymns. There were also some visiting precentors, so it was really very beautiful, and then Koren's excellent sermon—yes, everything was so exalting and did a lot of good to a poor, lost, clergyman's wife.

But what happens! While we were singing the final hymn, Dietrichson fell down in the church like dead. They carried him outside, poured cold water over him, tore off his clerical ruff, cravat, collar, and unbuttoned his shirt, but still there was no sign of life. Ugh, I have not been so terrified but twice before, I recalled Pastor Brun and was sure I would never see him alive again. Finally, some twitches appeared around his mouth and in his arms, and little by little he recovered and was taken home. A Norwegian doctor, who is staying in the settlement, was called, and in the afternoon he was again up and around among his colleagues. Poor Mrs. Dietrichson was present during the whole episode but marvelously collected and composed, she has indeed seen him this way several times before.

Pastor Brodahl preached in the afternoon. Anne went to church and I stayed at home with the little ones. This is the least fortunate of the ministers I have met here. I never heard him open his mouth to say either yes or no, or pro or con, about what was discussed, with the exception of one evening when I played the piano and sang a little for them, then I heard Brodahl above all the others, it was strange how he then had become enlivened.

While I played the "Champagne Galop," there had been a very lively scene by Koren, who came forward as if in a ballroom in former days, stiff and trim, very affectedly pulling on his gloves, to the laughter and enjoyment of all the rest. Yes, indeed, they often had such mirth among themselves. One day they were talking about one of the Germans who were due to arrive, that he was so big and fat, "not very unlike a sailor," said one. "He really looks very much like Dietrichson," said another. "Thank you very much," said Dietrichson. Koren was immediately ready to mince the matter and maintained that he looked more like a sea captain. "Oh, yes," said Dietrichson, "if I have a choice, I would rather look like a sea captain than a saloon captain." [2] Universal laughter.

Koren came over to me once and said, "think of it, the two of us have really danced together!" Leis is believed to be very weak, her husband could not give me any other information than that she was tolerably well. In the month of March, she will be lying-in again. Koren asked Munch very fervently if we would come up to their place at that time. Yes, if it is at all possible to get through, we will go, because it is not only my most sincere wish, but it is simply my duty. Their two beautiful girls are supposed to be awful crybabies; the oldest one will place herself across a chair and ask her father to spank her, but he can paddle her as much as he wants, she just goes on screaming. It is believed that she has been frightened. Don't talk about this to any of the Hysings, I am sure the Korens themselves are relating whatever they want them to know.

Pastor Duus, who recently lost his wife, was a very nice man, a better person is hardly to be found, I think. He has three small children, the youngest one completed his first year while his mother was lying in state. He was composed and calm like a true Christian, but his eyes were quite red and swollen, he told me himself it was from weeping. He now has a maid to look after the little ones, but he hopes later to get a German parson's widow to stay with him. We asked him if he could dispense with any of his children; no, was the definite reply, he was so fond of them, he could not think of being away from them. He has changed congregation recently and has moved closer to us, so he has promised to come and visit us during the winter.

It was entertaining to hear him tell about the Indians, he previously lived so close to them and had quite a bit to do with them. Duus is a big, stout man, like Bauman, with completely gray hair, which causes the Yankees to regard him as a strangely youthful old man, and to give him considerable respect. He has stood up to the roughest people and threatened them to do as he told them. The Indians he has met in big bands in the woods, howling like wild animals, but they have never harmed him. His wife was often afraid, especially one time when they came right up to her at the parsonage, but luckily, just at that moment, Duus came home. When the Indians get drunk, they are dangerous. Then they hand over all their weapons to one man, and he is not allowed to taste anything strong until they are all sober again, then he is supposed to get drunk; but in the meantime he must watch closely over the weapons, so that they should not kill each other in their madness.

Now I have wandered from the ministers' meeting all the way to the Indians! You would probably like to hear a little more about the former. Wednesday, Pastor Larsen preached, a young but serious and outspoken man. His sermon was peculiar but really good. He pointed out several great truths from the Catechism and spoke about them, things that we appear to know so well, but which, just because of that, need even more to be revived for us and be refreshed in our memory. However, his delivery was rather too slow to my taste.

What was actually discussed at the meeting will be too involved for me to report, and besides of little interest to you. It concerned mostly the organization of their church body, the schoolteachers, how they should take care of the children, and how they should get ministers and the Word of God to all the misguided and neglected Norwegians who live scattered in all directions here in America. You probably know that the Norwegians here have joined with a German evangelical Lutheran university in St. Louis, to which they will send a Norwegian professor provided they will be able to procure a man who would be qualified to occupy this position.[3] Several Norwegian boys have already been sent down there to be educated as ministers. God alone knows how this will go. There is some fear that these ministers raised in German will not be suitable for the Norwegian people. However, this union with the Germans is only supposed to be temporary until the Norwegians get strong enough to establish their own university and can secure their ministers from there; for it does not look promising with candidates traveling here from home, besides, I hardly believe that any minister who has come from Norway could possibly think of staying here forever, and for that reason there will always be many vacant ministerial positions.

Concerning Dietrichson's travel I still cannot say anything definite, but I believe he will be coming home in the spring, and then he will certainly visit at Hovland and bring with him our daguerreotype. Munch and I brought little Else with us to Beloit one day and had ourselves daguerreotyped. We took four groups; two were to be sent home, one to Hovland and one to the Bishopess; one was given to Dietrichson for his birthday, which occurred right after the ministers' meeting, wherefore the Stubs and we stayed a few days longer than the other ministers; and one group is already hanging on our wall. They must all be called successful, but the best one was spoiled by the daguerreotypist getting a spot on Munch's forehead, and to improve this he smeared some red paint over it; but I don't think it shows any, and I wish that this one should go to Hovland, for Else looks just like herself on it. However, he has promised to take another group for free if we only can make it down to him before spring. It is good of me on all of them except that I am equally wide and tall, but that the man certainly could not help; and the bows on my waistband have made me look rather worse than better. I was dressed in my old black costume from Norway, Munch in clerical garb, and Else in a small checkered green woolen dress, indeed, she is so sweet—well, you will be able to judge that for yourself. She was quiet beyond expectations, but you cannot imagine all the tricks the man performed to hold her attention —to our despair, for we had to laugh at him also. He hooted in bottles, struck matches and lit a piece of paper, whereupon he smoked it, put it up to his face, and made awful noises because he burned himself. He took a big black piece of cloth and stuffed it into his mouth with many ridiculous gestures. The fellow was a real comic, and he talked English, so Else was quite surprised. We thought that Thalie was too small, she would only have shown as a lump and spoiled it all.

The ministers were completely charmed by Else, her brown curly hair (of which I sent you a lock in my last letter), her plump and fat arms and neck, her small and nimble figure, nicely dressed at that. Koren, who is so distinguished, could never lay eyes on her without exclaiming: "How lovely you are, Else." She ran about among them, talked and had fun, and was so gay and red and white as a rose—indeed, I cannot understand how we have gotten such a beautiful child, it must be because I thought she would be so ugly. Little Thalie was also visiting with the ministers, and then they all cried out how big she is. "She is really a model of a child," said Ottesen and lifted her clear to the ceiling.

Indeed, these two little girls of mine give me many a joyous time. When I enter their room and they both stretch out their arms toward me, then I just stand there completely enraptured that our Lord has given me two such lovely little creatures to take care of. A more sweet-natured child than Thalie I hardly think could be found, she is so fond of Else. When Else runs around and acts for her, she laughs excitedly, and Else is so delighted with her, although her caresses sometimes become rather hefty. They are already able to entertain each other. The little one is quite advanced for her age, probably because she was on her own so early. She knows the difference even in the girls who take care of her, and she recognizes Munch very well, not to speak of myself. It is a long time since she cried when I left her. Thalie has such lovely mild eyes and will also perhaps become a beautiful child, she has very little hair yet, so the color is almost uncertain.

Else is talking all day long. Everything she says is clear and distinct, and she certainly can ask many funny questions. We have to laugh at her particularly when she talks just like Anne, who is from Land, where they have a peculiar way of speaking, . . . and in between comes something in English, like "good-bye" and such, so we have a wonderful time listening to her. She is mighty naughty these days, but then she gets a healthy whipping, yes, indeed, so it shows on her little behind for several days. Munch has managed to teach her to come over and kiss the rod and ask for forgiveness. To spank Else is one of the worst duties I have, but the Bible demands, and I obey.

I still have Anne, and I hope she stays through the winter, am I not fortunate? The rest of our housekeeping runs along in its usual manner. A drunken man came in yesterday and scared me terribly. We are at home alone, Munch and Emil are in Dodgeville. He was a Norwegian, but I knew he was horribly rough in that condition, and I had no way of knowing what he would do. But he did not go any further than to lie down on the maid's bed, and as I was afraid he would spend the night, I got a message over to my neighbor man, who cleverly duped him into coming along with him.

For Munch's birthday we were all at home, and we spent a very nice day together, indeed, he claimed that this was the nicest birthday he ever had. All of us were in good health, and I made things as cozy for them as I possibly could. Emil had been to Monroe a few days before, and I wanted [him] to buy a rocking chair for Munch, but none was to be had. Munch scented out this and hinted that I could have arranged to get him something a little ahead of time. Of course, I was very unhappy about this, but what could be done about it? The day arrived, Munch was rather quiet, did not want to dress up, and talked about visiting the Norwegian school that day. But when he entered the parlor, he had to sing a different song. Behold, there were no less than three packages with his name on. First he opened one which contained a big case with several small compartments, in which there were a new razor, shaving brush, soap in a little cup, and several small items for a man's toiletry—a gift from his wife, who had already early in the summer ordered it from a carpenter for her dear husband and had absolutely not forgotten him, no, she had for quite a while cheated him out of many a golden dollar to buy with. In the second package was a golden pen with a gilded holder and an English book from Emil, and in the third a black silk scarf from Anne. Now everybody was joyful, now he had to go and trim himself up and did not take off for any school. After a while, his two daughters, dressed like little dolls, came in to their Daddy, each with a small parcel in her hand. Well, by now he did not know at all what to say, now he understood that I was not unconcerned about him. Else had a nice pocketknife with four blades for him, and Thalie gave him a coin purse accompanied by the wish that it would be so full of gold in 1860 that it would be enough to take Daddy, Mummy, Onta, Else, and her home to Norway. In the morning I made a sugar cake, which I presented to him with a big bouquet of flowers and also a bottle of my homemade wine, which is very good. So then we drank a toast to Munch in company with our three servants. For dinner we had collards (for the first time from what you sent me, dear Mother), roast goose, creamed cabbage, hopped beer to drink, and then apples. Both children were hearty and sweet, we had them with us in the parlor almost all day and had such a pleasant time with them. In the evening we passed the time talking about Norway and all our dear ones, cracking nuts, and eating apples and jam.

May God grant that we can experience your birthday together in the same joy and happiness, my dear Mother. You thought maybe I had forgotten the day since I have written this much without mentioning it. No, but I wanted to save the best for last to be able to talk to you really from the bottom of my heart. You know I wish you all the best, my dearest Mother, but as I can afford nothing, I will pray for you to our dear Father in Heaven that he will bestow upon you some encouragement and consolation in your burdensome lot here in this life. But do not grieve, my dear Mother, this is only a time of trial, and if you endure in the face of God's judgment, then the joy will be so much richer with God the Father in Heaven. You probably think many times that I am writing in a strange manner, and that I am saying things that are not fitting for a daughter. But I must, sweet Mother, I assure you it is done out of the most childly love for both of you. May God command you also to write to me and remind me, I need it so much and would thank you heartily for it.

I have a thousand greetings to you from Munch and Emil on the occasion of the day. They are not due home until Saturday evening, and should the weather be good, the flag will be raised, and a toast will be given in your honor. There will be a service here on Monday, which is All Saints' Day. Else and Thalie are also sending Grandmother many cordial greetings.

Would only that this letter were with you now instead of with me, but I hope you have received, if not mine, at least Emil's letter. He wrote while we were in Rock Prairie, which consoled me. Furthermore, Munch sent his Mother a letter for her birthday, have you not read that? I think of my dear Father every day and pray so fervently to God for him; if only dear Father could get some encouragement and have more joys and less sorrows, that I think would be the best medicine for him, but what can I do to help in this? Write more often? Certainly, but then I would have so little to write about. If only, by God's help, I could get home some time, then we would always have wonderful days together. It is Munch's steadfast decision that he will return in 1860, as far as it is up to us frail creatures to decide on anything.

What you told me about little Emilie was certainly very sad, but with God's help I surely believe it will pass, and if it does not pass, then be of good comfort, beloved Parents, God alone could have inflicted this on her, and what He has done, He has done for her own true benefit; maybe she otherwise would have become a frivolous and fêted young girl, like so many who walk around in Christiania without thinking either about their Sav-

ior or the Everlasting Life. Oh, yes, let us thank God for everything, He has surely His judicious purposes.

All my dear brothers and sisters receive my warmest greetings, I am thinking about all of you so many times, and I often
talk about you. May God be with all of you!

The locust trees you must try to protect against the frost as
long as they are young; here all of them froze the first winter. I
have gathered a lot of seeds of various kinds, which I will send to
you with Dietrichson. I have plenty of cabbage this year, but
every day I fight the cows, who want to eat it up for me, so I can
well understand your great annoyance, dear Mother. Would you
be so sweet and send me some stock seed in a letter? Has Fog
closed his store?

My work these days is to sew rags. A woman is going to
weave me a rug, my old chemises were good for nothing else, but
as they are white, I want to color them yellow with lye and
vitriol.

Farewell, beloved Parents, brothers and sisters, and be
greeted from your affectionate

Caja Munch

[On the margin in Pastor Munch's hand:] I send my dear
Mother-in-Law the friendliest greetings along with my best
wishes on the occasion of the 31st of October! I shall write more
later, but now Caja has occupied all the paper. Have no worries
about us, we are all living very well.

Mrs. Caja Munch, and Pastor J. St. Munch, to Mr. and Mrs.
F. W. S. Falch

Wiota Parsonage, March 1, 1859

My dear Parents!

For a long time now I have been waiting in vain for a letter.
The last one I received from you, my dear Mother, is dated the
12th November, and since then we have heard nothing from any
of you. Give God that everything is well with you and that you
are in good health. May the Lord keep you and give you strength
until we see each other again, with God's gracious help that
should not be too far off.

I should have written a long time ago, but since at the same

time I would like to tell you *definitely* whether we are coming
home in the spring or not, I have put it off until now when I can
bring you the happy news that we will leave Wiota Parsonage on
the 2nd May and will return together with the Dietrichsons to
our dear fatherland, where we, by God's help, hope to join our
dear Parents, brothers and sisters, family, friends, and acquaintances not later than the middle of the month of July. We have
taken this important step in Jesus' Name, hoping that He then
will give His blessing hereto, and that it will come to pass with
God's will and to our true benefit.

The occasion for this is that Munch now has been released
from his letter of presentation in Wiota, and he then preferred
to go home and work for the propagation of the Word of God
rather than once again accept another charge here in this free
America. More about this when we meet and can talk about it, if
only God would grant us this joy. I hardly dare think about it!

After you have received this letter, it will hardly be of any
use for you to write to us as it probably will not reach us. If time
and circumstances permit, I shall send you a few lines from
Quebec, where we are going to stay for a few days. If no steamship is sailing from Quebec to Hamburg, we will take a steamship to Liverpool, from there by railroad to Hull, and then by
steamship directly to Christiania. It will be hard for me to see
my dear home from the sea and have to pass it by, but then I will
come quickly, you may be assured. Oh, how I am looking forward to it! If we go to Hamburg, our arrival will be delayed
somewhat, because then the Dietrichsons absolutely want to see
Copenhagen and all its remarkable things, and we, of course,
will go along. Please don't be waiting for us, and by all means
don't be worried, everything rests in God's hand! If He will
allow us to come home safely and be joined with you in happiness again, then we shall all of us together thank Him deeply for
that. And should it be His will not to bring us back to our
fatherland, then we shall also thank Him deeply, because then
that will be to our best benefit. The time of arrival is impossible
to predict on such a long journey, so you must delay your
anticipation until you see us. Dietrichson wants to do everything
possible to get to Copenhagen, in fact, it has even been considered boarding a sailing ship from Hull to Elsinore and traveling
from there by railroad to Copenhagen. Dear Parents, do not,

therefore, be concerned at all should it take us until some time in the fall.

We are, God be praised, well and healthy. Little Thalie has been weaned, she has grown thin and whimpers now and then, maybe she has more teeth coming. Munch, Else, and I took a short trip down to Rock Prairie to purchase the most important necessities for our journey. In the meantime, Thalie stayed at home with Anne. When she saw me again, she threw herself at me and started to cry.

I have lots to do now, believe me, to get everything taken care of for our long voyage. Furthermore, Anne is having her wedding soon, which delays me considerably, and my nursemaid is going to be confirmed. We now have one of Holmen's daughters in the house, she is going to read with Munch until we leave. The 21st of this month we are having an auction—would that this unpleasant event was over and that the buyers would pay a good price. Here are hard times, and we will be coming home cropped to the skin! If we only could have returned early enough to celebrate my dear Father's birthday together, but since this will not happen, I wish him all the best on this day as well as on all the others that the Lord will grant him to live among his children and grandchildren.

Emil has acquired a farm in Minnesota from Pastor Preus for 200 dollars, the most marvelous land you can imagine, with an advantageous location, close to the prospective parsonage there, in the midst of a nice Norwegian settlement, and this for a dead bargain, so we can not at all blame him for not wanting to return with us now. May our Lord keep him and protect him until the time when he will follow, we must place everything in God's hand. Munch has promised to write to you, I have so little time, therefore I hope you will forgive me when I end the letter here, wishing all of you a hearty good-bye until we see each other!

Your affectionate daughter
Caja Munch

Dear Parents-in-Law!

So what do you say to all this? Because you can not yet completely understand our situation and the present compelling

reasons for our departure, you are probably taken by surprise at
this sudden and unexpected piece of intelligence concerning the
decision we have made. I can imagine that you are even a little
worried that everything is not as it should be, and that this
decision of ours could perhaps be precipitate and not made in
Jesus' Name but in the effervescence of our carnal, impatient
mind. Considering in addition our precarious financial situation, which you are both most keenly aware of and most deeply
involved in, I am prepared to hear from you a reproach that we
so soon are finished with America. But, on the other hand, I am
equally convinced that the joy at getting us back and the longing
for the two little girls are being felt by Grandpapa and Grandmama with such strength that you solely for the sake of our
meeting again will draw a sponge over darker thoughts. And,
verily, you can now be happy with us, for *the Lord* has willed it
so that we should leave this place. Our decision is not a precipitate action but a matter which has been discussed for a long time
very thoroughly, which has been viewed and pondered from all
possible angles, has caused us many a wakeful night, and has
been promoted with many sincere prayers. Dietrichson and I,
and Mrs. Dietrichson and Caja, have had multitudinous deliberations, Pastor Preus (the chairman of the Church Council) has,
together with myself and Dietrichson, looked into the circumstances of the congregation, and all of us agree in this: *In Wiota
can no true servant of the Lord work any longer.*

A predominant part of the congregation have finally revealed the evil which *for several years* has existed in their hearts,
and which at certain times I have perhaps been able to repress,
indeed, some time ago to the extent that I believed I had pulled
the "poison fangs," as I wrote to you. But the fire has smoul-
dered under the ashes, and just before Christmas, the storm
broke loose with American fury as the settlement of people from
Land, where I am located, openly declared to me that they
wanted another minister, who would not keep them in such
constraint. By constraint they mean abstention from vices that
disgrace the life of a Christian. Now the congregation is split,
and my friends will have to patronize Rock Prairie, where they
should get a new minister this coming summer. Both Preus and
Dietrichson recognize now that Wiota should never have been a
separate pastorate, because it has for many, many years been a

hostel of discord and dissension—but too late is forfeited, as the saying goes.

On the whole, the congregations over here are not suited for *strict* ministers—this is, just between us, also the reason why my friend Dietrichson will have to leave, for he and I are of one piece, only that he is fat and I am slim. If one wants to do well over here, one has to walk on stocking feet and wear velvet gloves, as we say, and this art we do not intend to practice toward the supersensitive, Americanized, un-Norwegian countrymen, who mince around on tiptoes and are unbearably impertinent and rude. There are some honorable exceptions, but they are so few. I cannot recount all the rude niceties and coarse abuses which have been applied here against Dietrichson and myself—of that we shall give you an oral account—but you may rest assured that it is an incontestable fact: Here no *sincere* minister can stay any longer.[4]

Consequently, I have only two choices, either to go home or to take a charge somewhere else here in America. But in the latter case I have the choice between a well-organized and a number of still quite unorganized charges. The well-organized one is Rock Prairie, and there *I* would not wish to go. The several unorganized ones would put me many years back in time as there I would have to start from the beginning just like I did here, and once again go through all the spiritual and temporal wants connected with life in a new settlement. But this is too hard and surely not the Lord's will, especially since I hardly would be suited for this after having tried it before. Therefore: home to Norway in *Jesus' Name.* Certainly, we are poor, but rich in hope and of good cheer in the Lord, so we will surely be succored. Also at home, devoted ministers are needed now.

Concerning Emil, he is, by God's help, well off as he has acquired a farm in the *best* Norwegian settlement in Minnesota, close to the parsonage. He is very eager to try this and would like to stay here a few years to save some for his return home. It is much better here for farmers than for ministers.

I am running out of space and will therefore have to finish this my last letter to you from Wiota Parsonage with many greetings to all of you, old and young, with the prayer that the dear God will let us meet again in a happy moment.

Yours affectionately,
J. St. Munch

On the occasion of the 25th of April I forward my heartiest wishes for your spiritual and temporal well-being, dear Falch! Now you must recover and stay healthy for the time when we and the Dietrichsons will arrive at Hovland.

Tell the salmon not to leave Laagen this summer, but to stay there until fall!

An American Adventure

Excerpts from "Vita Mea," an Autobiography Written in 1903 for His Children

by Pastor Johan Storm Munch

JOURNEY TO AMERICA AND ARRIVAL

IN WIOTA

IT HAD BEEN the intention that we would leave immediately after our wedding. But Falch could not raise the money
so soon, so we had to wait—much against our wish. We did not
get off until the first part of September [1855], then to go to
Hamburg by a Norwegian steamship, and from there by sail
packet to New York, as the German steamships were engaged in
transport runs to the Crimea with troops from England. It was
an uncalculated wait, and it is easy to understand that both for
Caja and myself, it was rather trying to stay there as newlyweds
in the old surroundings. The new family life does not go well
with the old, no more than new wine in old wineskins. But we
had no choice and had to try "to make the best of it." Caja had
her twenty-fifth birthday as a married woman on the 14th of
August and had all her girl friends with her. I would not advise
any newlyweds to stay that long with the parents. It sort of spoils
the honeymoon.

Finally, the day of departure arrived, and that was sad and
hard enough. It was nice, however, that Emil came along, that
was decided in the last moment. We drove down to Fredriksværn, and there we went on board the Norwegian steamship
(I believe its name was *Viken*). After having taken a rather
moving leave of relatives and friends, we stood out to sea and
bid farewell to the fatherland. It was a solemn moment as we
watched the country disappear under the horizon; we could not
know whether we would ever see it again. But we were young
and bold and put our trust in God, so we kept up heart.

The crossing to Kiel was a stormy one, and an old woman in
second class was convinced it was Doomsday. From Kiel we took
the railroad to Hamburg, where we—foolishly enough—put up

at an expensive hotel near Jungfrausteig. However, we had an
introduction to a Mr. Wage, who was married to Amalie Rieffel,
a concert pianist who had been in Kristiania, and they received
us with great friendliness and got us a cheaper but very decent
hotel in Hahntrop . . . Wage procured a basket of wine for us,
which came to good use on board as the water was not the best in
the world. Finally, we got on board, and I immediately had the
first foretaste of the conveniences of the trip when the mate
rushed over to me and shouted: *"Die Tonne ist kaput"* [the
barrel is falling apart]. For we had our clothes packed partly in
two boxes, partly in two big barrels, which were supposed to be
easier to handle. We then got the ship's carpenter to fix it and
paid him for it. But in New York, we had the same trouble with
it, so we regretted this packaging.

The ship was an emigrant ship named *Rhein,* and its master was a Captain Haak. It was fairly conveniently arranged.
The cabin was roomy and was divided into two parts, of which
we had the aftmost. Our fellow passengers in the first class were a
German craftsman and his family, who were returning to America, next a German Doctor Neuhaus, who had been in fortress
arrest for several years as he had taken part in the disorders of
1848–49. He was a very cultured and pleasant man. Then there
was an American from the Southern states, Mr. James, who
always went around sucking a lemon. He, too, was friendly and
obliging. He had been in Copenhagen, and knew a little German, and he could never forget what a delicious *"Rothe Grütze"*
[currant porridge] he had gotten there.

The ship *Rhein* was an old vessel and very leaky, so there
was a steady pumping. We heard later that this was her last
voyage. It was during this incessant pumping that a boatswain
sang the verse which I often have repeated for Caja and which
she hated as she was seasick the first couple of weeks (the refrain
was: *"und mit der Eisenbahn"*) . There was also another person
on board whom she didn't like. That was a young German who
steadily went around and puffed at a pipe filled with cherry
leaves, which gave a nauseous smell. We called him "the Pipe."
Caja used to sit on deck to get some fresh air, but when he came
along, she had to go inside again.

The food was good on board at all meals; only the con-
densed milk was bad. I remember well how the steward would
stand by the dinner table next to the captain and balance the

soup tureen while the captain ladled out. He balanced so well
that never a drop was spilled, even if the sea was high. The
captain kept on shouting when we had finished our plates: *"Wer
wünscht?"* And there were always ample supplies.

In the evening, when we had finished our supper and the
captain had left, and the steward was gone for a moment, the
German artisans rushed to the table and emptied the sugar
bowl. That happened regularly. They did not mind at all that
we were watching. Elegant people! But to us they were generally
courteous, and they never bothered us.

We had much fun with the doctor and the American. We
learned quite a bit of German from the doctor and could speak
it rather well. In America I even met a German who asked me
when I talked to him if we speak German in Norway.

Generally, we had rather nice weather, only a couple of
lesser storms which, however, were soon over. But worse was that
we had cholera on board, probably brought from Hamburg.
Many of the emigrants were ill, and eight persons died, including two of the crew. The doctor had his hands full. He had free
passage in return for serving as the physician on board, and he
spared no pains and was steadily down on the *"Zwischendeck"* to
keep an eye on the patients. The dead were quietly dumped over
the side during the night. There was a married couple, both of
whom died and left a little child behind. Toward the end of the
voyage, as we approached land, one of the emigrants came over
to me and said: *"Herr Pastor, Sie haben ja keine Kinder, neh-
men Sie dieses Kind."* We had much compassion for the little
one but could not very well adopt the child, who probably was
left with one of his fellow countrymen.

Week after week passed by. After about a fortnight, Caja
got well from her seasickness and could enjoy the pleasant air,
which became milder and milder as we were getting nearer to
land. The captain and I played chess now and then, but as I
steadily beat him, he got cross, it seems, and did not want to play
any more. One evening as we sat with our game, we heard a
crack as from a canon. There was quite a gale blowing, and it
was dark. Both of us rushed up to find out what was the matter.
It was the jib that had been ripped so the fragments were lashing
about. It was not easy in the dark to get everything in order, but
it went all right.

After a five weeks' voyage we were approaching land. Already we could notice the smell of soil. The pilot came on board, and we set course for Staten Island, an isle in the seaward approach to New York. There we had to remain in quarantine for a few days before we were allowed to go ashore. I remember that on a beautiful Sunday evening, while the church bells were ringing, we were walking on the island, bought peaches (which we had never tasted before), and were having a delightful time. But then the trouble started.

We were put ashore at Castle Garden, an establishment for emigrants.[1] There our baggage was weighed, and customs paid. But now we had to get lodging as well as information about inland travel. That was not so easy as both of us were poor in English, and Emil did not know a word. We had with us a letter of introduction from Munch-Ræder (later Norwegian consul at Malta) to an American, but we did not find his address. Mr. James had promised to help us, but he went ashore before us, so we missed him. Eventually we found a boarding house—I don't remember who referred us to it—and we spent the night there. It was very plain, but inexpensive; we were served potatoes un-peeled in an earthenware dish and poor coffee. In the morning we went out to find the Swedish-Norwegian Consul Habicht and get him to help us. We found him all right, but he was anything but obliging, expressed his regrets that he did not have the time to take care of us, and referred us to a Methodist minister. No thank you, said we, and left. (This could be a contribution to the consulate issue!) [2]

As we were walking up and down the streets, we met the German craftsman, Jäger, and his wife, with whom we had sailed across the ocean. We agreed to keep company as they knew America. They were going to travel as emigrants, that is, on the emigrant train, and they advised us to do the same, both because it was cheaper and because then we could get our baggage on the same train.

We finally got on our way and were put with a number of German emigrants into an old railroad car, where we sat squeezed together. In the middle of the night, we were roused out and had to walk in the dark over rails and between engines as a German led the way with a lantern and shouted: *"Vorwärts!"* Like a flock of sheep we were herded aboard a ferry and then put on another train without knowing where we were or where we were going. Sleep was, of course, out of question. I forgot to tell that as we boarded the train in New York, Emil and I had to help Jäger carry a heavy box, which he otherwise could not have taken with him. We walked in mud so it splashed about us while an attendant led the way and shouted: "Go ahead, boys!" That was our entrance into America.

Next morning, a man came into the car with a big tin can, from which he poured into tin cups something that was supposed to be coffee but had only a scant resemblance to it—it was rather like dishwater. It was a horrible trip. Every once in a while, our train stopped and was switched onto a siding, where we had to wait for hours. This way we moved at a snail's pace . . . for several days and nights until we got to Niagara. At a nearby station we were shown into a car where human excrements, under favor, were found on one of the seats! It had been used as a toilet. That was going too far. Then we went on strike. We had already suffered so much from hunger and thirst that we were quite exhausted. For we never stopped at the regular stations, where decent food could be bought, but always on sidings, where shacks had been put up for the emigrants, and where the food was inedible. Once I was so hungry that I started to gnaw on a picked-off boiled old chicken that was set out. Changing clothes was out of question, and the nights were horrible. . . . Enough said, we could not take it any longer.

So we bought tickets to Chicago on the ordinary train but, of course, lost money since we had already bought emigrant tickets that far. We got a German to look after our baggage for the payment of one dollar, and then we found a room at the station where we could wash and tidy up some (we carried a suitcase with us). And when we got seated in the regular train, it was like a new life for us. We were back in civilization. At that time, the emigrants were treated like cattle—since then, of course, it has changed completely.

After two days we arrived in Chicago, which then had not yet developed into a real metropolis. It was before the big fire. Now [1903] they travel by express train from New York to Chicago in less than twenty-four hours.

So far, so good. We stepped out of the train, but where should we turn? Caja was carrying an accordion, which Staffeldt had given us, and which we had had out on the ship and were

stupid enough not to put in our crate. Emil and I were carrying
the suitcase, which was rather heavy, and he in addition an old
worthless rifle, which he had brought from Hovland. In this
procession we started on our way without knowing where to
proceed or how to get hold of our baggage when it arrived. We
were, however, lucky enough to come across a German boarding
house, where we found lodging, and where it was nice and clean
and pleasant to stay. We thanked God, who had guided us this
far safely, and prayed that He would continue to direct us.

That prayer was heard. The following day, we were wan-
dering through the streets—without our pack, however—and
arrived unwittingly outside a church, where the door was standing ajar, and from where we heard hymn singing: *Vor Gud Han
er saa fast en Borg* ["A Mighty Fortress is our God," in Nor-
wegian]. It was wonderful. I went in, and there I met a Norwegian, Torstenssen, who was having a confirmation class in the
Swedish-Norwegian church. The pastor, Unonius, was out of
town. When he [Torstenssen] heard who I was, he immediately
dismissed the children, and with great friendliness, even joy, he
accompanied us over to Unonius's house (which belonged to the
congregation) and put us up, assuring us that we could safely
settle down there as long as Unonius was away. We then gathered our chattels, took off from the boarding house, and moved
in there. But we had our meals with the Torstenssens.

I had to promise to give a sermon the following Sunday in
the church—it just happened to be my birthday, October 21st.
But I had no clerical garb as mine was in one of the crates, nor
did I even have a black cassock. So I donned a surplice, such as
the Episcopalian ministers use. (Unonius belonged to the Epis-
copal Church, with a little Lutheran supplement, so later on,
when we got acquainted with this friendly man, we used to call
him "Unionius.") But then Caja and I were stupid. I thought I
ought to have a clergyman's ruff, and what did we do? Well, Caja
sat down and sewed a ruff, starched it, and we fluted it with a
small iron cylinder that we found by the stove. But that didn't
go so well. The ruff was scorched, and we burned a hole in
the rug! And it was late at night. So that was the end of that
adventure. I had written the sermon word for word and read it
out—it wasn't grand, to be sure.

A couple of days passed, and then the baggage arrived.

Torstenssen helped us get it. And so we said good-bye to this kind man and left by railroad for Beloit in Wisconsin, where Pastor Dietrichson was to meet us. Sure enough, as we arrived there safely, Dietrichson was standing on the platform. I recognized him immediately from his resemblance to his cousin, Professor Dietrichson. He received us cordially and took us over to his carriage to drive us to his parsonage, Luther Valley, at Rock Prairie, which was half a Norwegian mile [about 3 English miles] from there. The baggage was to be picked up by people from Wiota as it went on to another station, Warren, which was closer to Wiota.

My surprise was great when it started to snow, and this in October at 42 degrees latitude! This I had certainly not imagined. And what a road! Up and down, now in deep mud, now up on the edge of the road, so we expected to topple any minute. But Dietrichson laughed and said that such were the roads in the West and that we should be prepared for much worse than this. And he was right, that I became fully aware of later. So we arrived in the evening at his home, where the lady of the house met us with great cordiality, and where we well could get a good rest after the long and difficult and very strenuous journey. They did everything to make us comfortable, and we stayed there for about a week.[3]

IN WIOTA

Now begins the grave period of my life. Yet I shall write down my memories of it, although they are not very cheerful, either to myself or to you, my dear children. For I was sorely and deeply disappointed in the expectations I had of a peaceful work as a minister in the free America.

The charge had been advertised by Dietrichson, surely in good faith, but without having been sufficiently informed about its true condition. It was composed of two parts situated far from each other, 3 1/2 Norwegian miles [about 25 statute miles] over desolate prairies, namely, Wiota or Hamilton, and Dodgeville. Wiota was again divided into three settlements: (1) Wiota, (2) the settlement on the Peccatonica (also called the Halling Settlement), and (3) Yellowstone, which were 3/4 mile [about

5 statute miles] apart but had one church together. It had been
very difficult to get a minister for them as there were some less
desirable elements who were asserting themselves there. Dodgeville was an older, Americanized settlement, which Preus had
served but was heartily fed up with and glad to get rid of.
Around the little spot Wiota were mostly people from Land,
who were fairly civilized but not very cordial. In Yellowstone
there was a drunkenness that was horrible because the annex
parish Lynner in Hadeland had sent their worst drunkards
there. They had even gotten people to join the congregation by
going around serving them drinks! The best conditions prevailed in the Halling Settlement, where many from Krydsherred
and Numedal were living, and where I had my best friends.

For all these mutually dispersed and discordant settlements
and elements was I, young man as I was, now to be a pastor!
Even before I left Norway I had received notice that it was not a
good place to be (I don't remember how), and I had written to
the Church Council [of the Norwegian Synod] about getting
another charge which then was free and much better in every
respect. At length came the reply that I had to follow the call I
had received.

I had been promised a parsonage, with a small piece of
land, a few hundred dollars in salary, pay for ministerialia, and
one bushel wheat and corn from each farmer, besides firewood
from a piece of woodland that the congregation had claimed
(but not bought). In Dodgeville, however, I would neither
receive pay for ministerialia nor corn, yet I *myself* had to assume
the cost of traveling back and forth! This I learned when I got
there. Had I known this, and had I had an idea of the distance
over the desolate prairies, then I would surely not have gone
there. But now it was too late.

One fall evening, driven by Dietrichson, we arrived in
Wiota after having traveled a terrible road. But the parsonage
(which consisted of two small rooms and kitchen downstairs—
indeed, the kitchen was actually just a closet—and one small
room upstairs) was far from finished. So they had rented space
for us with a neighbor, a grumpy old bachelor from Land, one
room, which also served as a kitchen, and a closet next to it. He
was staying below in the basement and fried bacon morning,
noon, and evening, so we had the smell of it almost all day—very

refreshing. He had ingratiated himself with Dietrichson, who had served the congregation, and he commended him highly. But we learned otherwise, for he was anything but pleasant. Well, there was nothing we could do about it, we had to stay there. We were sleeping in the "closet," and Emil in the kitchen-room, which was our parlor and dining room.

The church was close by, but it was not finished either. Thus the floor had not been laid but consisted of loose planks, and the draught came from all directions. Otherwise, the area had a pleasant appearance, only there was no lake or river, just a little creek running below the house.

There had been a big quarrel both about the parsonage and about the church, and one party stood against the other. As mentioned, they had claimed a piece of woodland, far away; but an Irishman had also laid claim to it as his and had threatened to "kil" anybody who came there to cut. For revenge, he had set fire to a good deal of lumber that the congregation had bought for the parsonage.

In all this mess I now got involved. It certainly was not easy. But I had a good supporter in my dear wife—had I not had her, I would surely have left there very soon.

We got our baggage and started unpacking. That, of course, was fun, and as we were young and healthy, it did not take much to cheer us up. We had a couple of rather friendly neighbors (although the nearest one was a loathsome person, who was not a member of the congregation, and who was plowing his field on Good Friday right under my nose).

On the first Sunday, I was "installed" in the congregation by Dietrichson and gave my first sermon, which was well received. Then Dietrichson went home, and we were alone.

Now I was going to Dodgeville but had neither horse nor carriage, so I got a farmer to take me on a lumber wagon [work wagon]. But the morning we were going to leave, I was ill, had a headache and a little fever. However, the service had been announced, and I had to go, no matter how poorly I felt. That trip I shall not easily forget. When I arrived at my lodging in Dodgeville late in the evening—it was dark—several people were gathered to receive me. But I felt poorly and had to ask for my room, and after a short supper I went to bed. The next morning, however, I felt better and was able to conduct services, etc., in

two places—in two schoolhouses as they had no church. It was a
relief to get back home, and Caja was happy to see me well
again. She had certainly prayed for me.

Later on, however, these "annex trips" became better as I
found two pleasant lodgings. One was with a storekeeper, Holmen (from Drammen), who was staying with his wife and children at a little spot called Linden, and who was both cultured
and very amiable. They also came down to see us in Wiota after
we had got a parsonage. The other accommodation was with a
man from Numedal, Lars Aasen, who lived a little distance from
Dodgeville, and where I also was comfortable.

But I would like to tell about a trip up there, which took
place much later. There was a well-to-do peasant family from
Telemark, who repeatedly had asked me to stay with them. As
they were living rather far from Dodgeville, I had repeatedly
declined. But finally I had to promise that I would come and
stay with them. It was a winter day, and rather cold. Per Fenne,
the sexton and my good friend to the end, was with me. After
having traveled all day, we finally arrived there late at night. I
had expected a good lodging as I knew they were well-off and
were older settlers. But I was thoroughly disappointed. They
had only one room, and in it were several urchins who had *freies
Leben*—to the degree that they sat down and "did" on the floor!!
For supper we were going to have sliced sausage, and the
urchins were allowed to handle the pieces, the woman did nothing about it. One can imagine that I did not touch it. But the
worst was yet to come. Eventually, we were going to bed and
were shown "upstairs." To where? To a cozy, warm bedroom?
No, sir! Up in the attic, a room had been partitioned off with a
sheet, where a double bed had been set up, and where we could
see through a hole in the roof up in the air. And it was icy cold.
This was what these well-to-do people had to offer. The sexton
and I lay down without undressing and each with his fur coat
on. And one can imagine that there wasn't much sleep. Oddly
enough, I did not take ill after this frosty night but was able to
conduct the divine service as usual. It was God's protection. But
I never went there again. Then it felt good to get home to
"Mother" and rest.

But I am getting ahead of the time. This, as I said, was
much later.

LIFE IN AMERICA

Wiota, or Hamilton, is situated in Lafayette County in the southwestern part of Wisconsin, under the same latitude as southern France. But the climate is quite different. The summer, certainly, is hot, and it starts earlier than at home in Norway. But the winter can be very severe, and we regularly had road conditions for sleighing. The spring comes rapidly during the latter part of March, and in April they plow and sow. As already stated, there may be snow in the latter part of October. But then, each fall there is a very pleasant time, the so-called "Indian summer," which may last for a week or two and brings mild air with some haze. The first year I was in Wiota, we had "Indian summer" early in December, and we had a Congregation Meeting on the lawn outside the church. But soon after that there was a severe frost. It is hard to drive in the winter when the snow has settled because it forms big drifts on the prairie, and they do not use snowplows. One must then always drive in the same tracks, which is possible because all sleighs have the same width. Usually they drive with two horses, so there is a ridge in the middle of the road. If only one horse is used, it has to be hitched up to the one side of the sleigh in a specially made trace. With shafts in the Norwegian manner it would be impossible to make one's way. The worst is when you meet somebody. Then you have to drive out into the deep snow and will easily overturn. That happened to me now and then—not that I overturned but that I had to step out of the sleigh and wade knee-deep through the snow.

It took a long time before I could afford to get myself a horse, I had to resort to the neighbors to borrow conveyance from them, and they were usually willing. Neither could I afford to get myself a rig until later, and then only a shabby old buggy.

My first sick call was rather arduous. It was a pitch dark November night, I was in my sweet sleep when suddenly there was a knock on the door, and somebody shouted for the minister. In a hurry I got some clothes on and opened the door, and in came two big fellows and asked me to come along to the Halling Settlement, where an old man was dying and wished to receive the Sacrament. Well, of course I had to go. They had a lumber wagon outside with two horses, and we rushed off in the dark. But they knew how to drive a team of horses, so everything went well, although the road was bad. One of the men was the same Norwegian-American, Even Glesne, who was here in Norway once and sold horses; in American his name was Mr. Ralsen. We arrived safely, and I spent the rest of the night until late morning with the sick man, who died a few days later. That was the only time I was called during the night. Later on, I married Even Glesne and this man's daughter, and I often went to visit them. It was in their cabin that Mama and I were sleeping in one bed, the married couple in another, and two fellows in a third one, so that Mama had to ask them to go outside when she wanted to get up. Another time, we were visiting a man, Lars Haugerud, whom I cherished greatly; then he and his wife and the wife's sister were sleeping in one bed, and we in another in the same room. That was all right.

The winter passed with no events worthy of note. We stayed in our kitchen-room, where I could stay erect only by walking lengthways between the beams. Emil stayed with us. It was rather cold later in the winter, and worst was the frosty breeze from the north, which often occurred. The Dietrichsons and we visited each other once in a while. However, only he came to us as we could not accommodate his wife. Each month I had my long trip to Dodgeville, and they went on without failure. I still had no horse and sleigh but had to borrow conveyance. I had a good time at Holmen's, and once Caja came along also. We bought our groceries from him, and the payment was subtracted from my salary. At home we had a Congregation Meeting now and then to deliberate about a barn and a stable at the parsonage, for they had not yet been built, and there was some doubt whether they would ever be built. It was a great error that the congregations in and around Dodgeville were not included in this. They did not want to have anything to do with it.

The spring came rather early, during the latter part of March, and then very suddenly, so that they could start to work the fields in the beginning of April. I had no cultivated land, only a "bottom" or pasture of a few acres. I had some of it plowed for potatoes and corn and planted a small vegetable garden.

Finally after Easter, or rather at Pentecost time, we could

move into the parsonage, where it was cramped and difficult as we did not yet have a kitchen—that was added on later. However, we were happy to be on our own and to get out of the smell of bacon. We laid out a flower garden outside our windows, and we got ourselves a cow, which stayed out on the prairie both day and night and came home mornings and evenings to be milked. We also got some chickens and geese and a dog, so we thought we were pretty well-off. Caja was quite in her element churning butter, keeping house, and making it cozy. Emil, too, was of great assistance. He helped us with firewood and went to the mill with the grain that we received in tithes.

That summer I traveled a lot. In June I preached for Brandt in Muskego as he was home in Norway to get married. Later on, Dietrichson and I joined forces and exchanged churches, which the people liked rather well. As Caja was "expecting," she was invited to come to the Dietrichsons and "lie in" there. She accepted the offer with gratitude, and it was at that time that Dietrichson and I were traveling about exchanging pulpits.

One beautiful day, we were driving up to the parsonage at Luther Valley, and behold, there was the flag flying, and on it Mrs. Dietrichson had sewn with tape: "The Princess has arrived." That was a nice surprise. I rushed inside, and there was Caja—from now on she is called Mama—smiling, and with the little princess at her side in a beautiful cradle, which we had bought before. Everything had gone well, and "Else" seemed to get along superbly. That I was *faderlig glad* goes without saying.[4] It did not take long before Mama was up again, and then we had some joyful days with the kind Dietrichsons.

Then Dietrichson and I were off again, up to Wiota, where he preached, then to a couple of his annexes, where I conducted the services, likewise at Dodgeville. After Else had been christened in Dietrichson's church, we returned to Wiota, conveyed by Dietrichson himself in his carriage. I had in the meantime bought a mare which, however, was rather sprightly, so I always had to have Emil with me when I drove her. I had also bought an old, wretched buggy, which often needed repair.

Thus the first summer went by. We were often bothered by the heat, especially at night. And then the dark evenings, which we were not used to, and the myriads of insects that came flying in, attracted by the lighted candles. But when the moon was shining and the firebugs were flying about in the green grass, then it was beautiful. Then we felt as if we were in the Mediterranean regions. We had much gratification from the fresh, cool spring right outside the house. We mixed the water with lemon juice and got a delicious lemonade. And I must not forget the splendid watermelons, which were highly refreshing. They grew outdoors where we had planted seeds. Toward the end of the summer, we could go out into a nearby wood and pick good plums. Wild grapes were also to be found. From them we could make good wine if we added some sugar. From a vegetable garden we had plenty of peas, beans, cabbage, etc. For the soil was deep and extremely fertile, so there was no lack of greens. But meat was a different matter, for the meat would not keep in the extreme heat. I remember Mama's birthday, the 14th of August; she was going to serve roast veal. She had a suspicion that it was not first class, but she thought that by washing it well, it should pass. But when it was brought in to the table and she started to carve, such a stench emerged that we were glad to get it out of there as fast as possible. Fish was seldom seen, and then mostly dried cod. Otherwise, we had wild rabbits, which were tasty. But the greatest feast was when we could get hold of some prairie chickens and, particularly, quails, which are the best game birds I have tasted (the Jews certainly did not suffer privation in the desert). Mama baked bread — partly from coarse wheat flour, partly from rye. We did not see much cheese, but we had plenty of butter; some Mama churned, some we were given.

Thus the days passed by, and as we kept our health, and as Else also was well, we were fairly comfortable. I was very busy, partly in Wiota, partly in Dodgeville, where I went each month, and partly, as mentioned, as I conducted services elsewhere. I had no Sunday free, besides, I spoke also on weekdays at Dodgeville and had Bible reading in various places, mostly in Green County (the Halling Settlement, where I had my best friends).

But in October 1856, we entered a time of stress and strain. In the course of the summer, the parsonage had become dangerous to live in as one corner had a poor foundation and was sinking. We then had to move out in the fall and were put up in an attic at Kristen Ruud's (a crabby old man from Land), where the rain came in on us, right into Else's cradle. I then developed a bad boil in the throat, which threatened to choke me. Caja nursed me as best she could, but we had no doctor, so—next to God's help—we resorted to brandy-and-salt. Finally, the boil broke, and I recovered gradually, but was of course faint. For three Sundays I could not conduct the services. As an example of the rowdiness of some people in the congregation I can mention that when the sexton, the worthy Per Fenne, prayed for me in the church, where he was going to read a sermon, someone in the audience shouted: "Aw, pray for yourself, you miserable wretch!"—Pretty!

On the 23rd of November, I could again start preaching in the Wiota church. We were then able to move back into the repaired parsonage, where on one of the Sundays in Advent I gave a sermon for a few as a snowstorm prevented the people from coming to church. These snowstorms could be dangerous, especially if you were on the prairie, where they raged with a violence just like in the high mountains at home. Then it was impossible to keep it warm in the parsonage. We had to hang rugs and fur coats in front of the windows, and even so we could barely stand it. We had none of those horrible windstorms—tornadoes—while I was in Wiota. But at Rock Prairie (Luther Valley) at Dietrichson's they had had a terrible one the year before we came. At that time, the roof blew off one of the buildings of the printing press, so the type was scattered through the air. Dietrichson described it as one of the most horrible natural phenomena he could imagine. After a sulky day in August, suddenly a black, yellowish cloud rose over the horizon, and all at once the storm broke loose with a roar as from a thousand bulls. It turned completely dark, only illuminated by the flashing lightning bolts, and they expected every moment that the storm would take the whole house. They had to resort to the basement. On one of my travels, I once saw a forest where the storm had cut down a wide path, where overturned trees were lying in a heap. Other trees had been twisted off at the root by the electric force. I have read somewhere that lately these devastating tornadoes have become more common, so both churches and houses have been destroyed. So living in America is not all pleasure either.

The most comfortable time of the year is the spring, in April and May, and in the fall, in September and also later, when there is "Indian summer"—its name is supposed to be derived from the fact that this was the best hunting season for the Indians.

By the way, concerning the Indians, there were none of them to be seen where I lived or where I went to my annex parishes. But across the land of the parsonage there was an Indian path, which was clearly visible. As is well known, they always walked in single file. In Green County, by the Peccatonica River (near the Halling Settlement), there had been a hard fight in the olden days between them and the new settlers. But that was long before our time. One time, when I was in the little town of Red Wing, by the Mississippi River, I saw a small band of Indians. They looked dirty and miserable, had long, shaggy, black hair, with no head covering, wrapped in their blankets, and smoked incessantly. They were quite peaceful.

This winter, 1856–57, everything went as usual. Christmas Eve, the Holmens came to visit and stayed with us through the holidays, which we enjoyed very much. Else got along well and was healthy and sound and sweet. She almost preferred to be with me. This was about the time when she splashed my face full of cracker-mush.

We went to Dietrichson's a couple of times during the winter, and they came to our place. Emil then had a job in the printing press, but he stayed there only for a year and then went to an American farmer to learn farming. Now and then he came and stayed with us to rest and to help us. This winter I got myself another mare, an old one, who was very steady, so I could drive safely. But a sleigh was a problem. I could not afford to buy one, for my income wasn't much, and I had debts to pay. Then it happened that I was going to Dodgeville one winter day. The sleighing was good. A farmer offered to make me a sleigh out of hickory wood and leather straps with wooden pegs, such as the Yankees used. Indeed, he got it put together, the old steady mare was hitched up, and we sat down in the sleigh and started on our way. Mama was standing there laughing at us. But what happened! We had gone about a mile or two when the sleigh gave a shocking groan, and down we went in the snow, and the sleigh to shivers. There was no choice but to turn around, leave the shattered sleigh behind, and walk back with the suitcase on the shoulders, driving the horse. In this procession we returned home, and then Mama had another laugh, and although the situation was sad as I could not get to the annex parishes, we had to laugh, too.

One day when the Dietrichsons were staying with us, there was perfect sleighing, and we were going to take a drive in Dietrichson's double sleigh with two horses. But as he drove out through the gate at our "bottom" he took too sharp a turn, and there we were, all four of us, tumbled in the snow, I with Mrs. Dietrichson in my arms, and Dietrichson with Mama in his. No one was hurt. The horses stayed put, and we got up again and continued the drive in the best of spirits. These visits with the Dietrichsons are among our most pleasant memories from our sojourn in America. Both winter and summer we got together, and we always had fun.

On the 27th of August [1857], I started out on a mission tour to pastorless settlements in Minnesota. I stayed away from home until the 21st of September and conducted divine services eleven times with many christenings and several weddings, etc. It was a rather trying but interesting trip, and from an economic point of view quite good. A man from Nordland accompanied me as a sexton. On that occasion, I also visited St. Olaf's Congregation [in Olmstead County], where Emil has stayed these many years as a farmer. I had quite a few experiences on that trip, and I shall tell about them as far as I remember them.

We traveled by railroad to Prairie-du-Chien—or, as the Norwegians call it, *Præri-Dusen*. It was a small town on the bank of the Mississippi, where we were going to take a steamship across the river. We arrived in the town at night, and it was a beautiful sight to see the big steamship lying there brightly lit. These river boats were flat-bottomed but built up high in several stories, so they made a grand sight, especially when they were illuminated. We got on board and bought our ticket, which consisted of a brass key to our stateroom—very practical. We had the stateroom to ourselves. We sailed down the river a while before we landed on the opposite bank. There we got an ox wagon—not exactly a comfortable conveyance—now at a foot-pace, now in a gallop downhill. But it went all right. Once we were driven by an Irishman, who had a whiskey bottle in his pocket and both drank himself and offered us. As I was afraid he would get drunk, I accepted the bottle, pretending that I would drink, but then poured the contents out beside the wagon. For this he got furious but did not dare go beyond abuses. Among other things, he said: "I thought all Norwegians were drinkers" —a pretty compliment!

One of the first settlements I visited was the beautifully located so-called "Norwegian Ridge" [Spring Grove, Houston County], which then was vacant. That charge I should have liked to have, but soon after they got a good-for-nothing minister there. From there we went to St. Olaf's Congregation, which had been organized by Clausen (the oldest Norwegian minister) but still was without a pastor. Many Norwegians were living there. This was where I had my busiest day on the whole trip. I think I have described it in a letter home.[5] But I shall tell it again as far as I remember it. I started by receiving communicants and registering christenings (in the house where I stayed, I also conducted the services). Then followed in rapid succession communion sermon, homily, christenings, and communion. Then it was dinnertime, and in the same room I then had dinner. Then at it again without any rest, registering confirmants, examining them, confirming them, and giving them the Lord's Supper. And finally a wedding. Then I was really tired—and then a pipe tasted awfully good, for I used to smoke then.

Another time . . . I had divine service in a small cabin with so many christenings that only the godmothers and the children could get into the room, and the congregation had to stand outside, while I gave the sermon from the door. During the christening ceremony there was so much crying from the many children, and so much hushing and lulling by the women that I hardly could hear my own voice.

We continued the tour through several settlements, and I regularly had to conduct services in the houses. They were often so low that I got many a good blow on my head when I went in or out of the door.

As an example of what could happen when I was out traveling, I can insert a little story about what occurred, not on this trip, but some time later. Together with Emil I was up in a small settlement situated in a grove. It was summertime, and on a Saturday night we came to a Norwegian family, who lived in a log cabin, where I was going to preach the following day. It was raining rather hard. All at once, the woman came in with her scrubbing pail and asked us not to take it amiss that she had to scrub the floor since it was Saturday—as far as I could see, it was needed, too. But where should we go? There was only this one room, . . . and we could not very well stay outside in the rain while she was scrubbing. So we had to take refuge in the stable, which was cramped and dark, and there we stood for about an hour until she had finished. Such a thing could hardly happen to ministers in Norway.

But back to the mission tour. At last we came to Goodhue County, high and beautiful near the Mississippi. There was a large and prosperous settlement, where I conducted service a couple of times. They had not yet built a church or a parsonage, but they had bought land for the latter and were about to start building. Later on they sent a delegation to me in Wiota to call me as their pastor, but I could then for several reasons not accept the call.[6]

At Red Wing, a small town by the Mississippi, we started our return trip. We went on board a big steamboat, which was going to bring us to the little town Warren, which was about one Norwegian mile [about 6 or 7 English miles] from Wiota. The trip was very comfortable in the beautiful September weather on board the magnificent ship. The day passed on, and the night settled in. But just as we were lying in our sweetest sleep, we felt a jolt which at once made us wide awake. The sexton was quicker getting into his clothes than I and rushed outside. But he soon came back laughing and said: "Now we can safely lie down, for we are lying in a forest." And that was about the truth. The flat-bottomed ship was grounded and had broken one of her wheels, which was lying on the bank at the edge of a dense forest. We calmly went back to sleep as we could not get any further for a while. This was early Saturday morning. All day Saturday we walked around in the woods and picked a few wild grapes, which were very sour but still refreshing. Sunday morning, another steamer came down the river, and it helped us off, then they tied on to each other alongside and went rather proudly on the way, each with one wheel in operation on the outside. In this way we arrived at Warren, where we went ashore, had a good meal, and then rented a fancy cover-buggy with two horses at the livery stable and went on to Wiota Parsonage in the best of spirits. When we drove up to the door,

Mama was not at home; she was visiting a neighbor woman with
Else, and when she saw the elegant carriage stopping outside the
door of the parsonage, she thought it was an American who had
come for a visit and became quite dismayed, for she wasn't very
sure of her English. Great was her joy when she came over and
saw me standing in the yard in the best of health. So that trip
came to a happy end.

About the following winter, 1857–58, I have nothing remarkable to tell. Clouds, however, were gathering in the congregation, which did not prognosticate anything good. Before my
arrival, they had been divided into parties as the various *Bygdelag* did not accord, and now this conflict appeared to be breaking
out again. It was concerned with expenses for the parsonage and
for a patch of woodland, which an Irishman had claimed before
the congregation bought it—he forbid us to cut there. And then
there were some—the drunkards and their friends—who were
discontented with the admonitions which had to be given, of
course. Yet, so far it was only smouldering, and the winter passed
in relative calm. In May—on the 15th—Thalie arrived, to the
great joy and surprise of little Else. We then got an adolescent
nursemaid and had also been lucky enough to get an adult
newcomer maid from Land, who remained faithful and loyal to
us. She was the one to whom Else said one evening when she
heard somebody outside: "There comes the thoemaker, Anne."
She blushed deeply and hurried out of the room. It was indeed a
shoemaker, to whom Anne was engaged. Else was a regular
joker. One evening when I was writing a letter home to Norway,
she came running over to me and tore the letter from me so it
got a long streak of ink across. I sent the letter anyway and
explained how the streak had got there. We made her a little
wagon from a sugar crate covered with colored paper, which she
was very fond of. We also had a dog, "Fido," who followed her
faithfully when she was pulled in her "stately carriage." The
poor dog was later shot in the leg by a mean Irishman because
he had got in on his farm. They were vicious people, these Irish.

The summer of 1858 passed in the usual manner. Together
with Dietrichson I had started to visit Chicago every other
month and organized a congregation there, which is still [1903]
in existence under the name of "Our Savior's Lutheran
Church." This summer a church was also finished on the prairie

near Dodgeville. Here happened in the fall, at the time of leaf-shedding, a rather remarkable event. We had decided that the church should not be used by anybody but the congregation who built it. But in my absence, the Methodists had been allowed to borrow it. When I returned there one Saturday afternoon, they told me that the church key—of brass—had been lost, and nobody knew what had become of it, though they had searched for it around the church. Sunday morning they started the search again, looking among the dead leaves lying on the ground, and a whole lot of people were searching everywhere about. But no key was to be found. "This is what you get for letting the Methodists have the church," I said to them, "they have of course mislaid the key; now you had better get an axe and break open the door, for we have to get in." And off we went, I leading the way in my clerical garb. But now happened the truly remarkable thing: Just a few steps from the church door, there lay the key, bright and shining, right by my feet. I bent down, picked it up, showed it to the crowd, and said: "Here you see who is supposed to enter the church." It was like a miracle, for on that spot many people had been searching and had not found it. But then there were those who said: The pastor was a shrewd one—he had the key in his pocket! Indeed, it really appeared as if that were the case. But it is still incomprehensible to me how it could happen.

I do not recall if it was that year—'58—or earlier that I took part in a big Synod Meeting at Pastor Koren's in Decorah in Iowa. All the pastors of the Synod were gathered, and there I preached in Koren's church. There it was decided to join with the theological school of the Missouri Synod—a fateful step that had far-reaching consequences. The Missouri Synod is German and known for its Lutheran scholasticism and narrow dogmatism with denunciation of such as think otherwise. This spirit also took effect in the Norwegian Synod and made itself felt by a servile imitation of the Missourian theology with its multitudinous "theses," which were to be adopted at the general meetings and provoked continuous strife. The well-known Formula of Concord, which our church community had been spared, was introduced—and woe to him who had a different opinion.[7] This extreme dogmatism with those multifarious, pointed theological theses did indeed after my return home bring about the great schism, which in the end led to the establishment of new Lutheran denominations. But even while I was there this tendency gained strength among the leading pastors of the Synod, and it was only Dietrichson and I who could not go along with it. This absorption into the German scholasticism also made Dietrichson and myself less favored and contributed in no small degree to our leaving America together.

There were also two other circumstances which made me decide to go home. The first one was that the situation in the Wiota and Dodgeville congregations caused me many difficulties and mortifications. As I have mentioned before, these settlements did not have the best reputation and had difficulties getting along. Besides, I was personally misjudged, even insulted, because I tried to introduce a somewhat better congregational order. In the window of my nearest neighbor, a puppet was put on display in Norwegian clerical garb, which was supposed to represent me and was the object of laughter from those who passed by. Close by my field was an English [i.e., American] school, and they used my field as a playground, although I repeatedly protested. There were also Norwegian boys and girls among them, who only laughed at me when I attempted to reprove them—and the teacher encouraged them in this. These constant chicaneries I got tired of. Besides, there was the long distance to Dodgeville, which made the trips there both cumbersome and sometimes dangerous in the wintertime.

The other circumstance which contributed no less to my decision to return home was the fact that lately I had suffered severely from nervous headaches, so that I regularly had to lie down and rest after the divine services. But even if this ailment had not been there, I would hardly have stayed because of my isolated position against the pastors who circulated with the Germans. Dietrichson wanted to go home in the summer of '59, and I would then have been alone. Because of my impaired health I did not feel strong enough to take up such an isolated position, and so we decided—Mama and I—to accompany the Dietrichsons home, which also would make our journey somewhat easier.

Let me just add that when I got home, Professor Caspari—who well knew the Missouri Synod with Walther at the head—declared: "There I would not have been tolerated one day!"

This was a great consolement to me, for I was soundly berated by the Church Council because I went home, and received abusive letters. Oddly enough, A. C. Preus himself was pelted with the same kind of abuse when he left the Synod some years later, although he was the hardest one in condemning me. For it was regarded as a "sin" to leave the Synod. Indeed, even the least deviation from their theories was a "sin."—Enough on that.

In the spring of 1859 we made all the preparations to go home. We sold our furniture, etc., by auction, and on the 1st of May I gave my farewell sermon in Wiota Church after having previously preached my farewell in Dodgeville. It grieved me, however, to leave my faithful settlement in the Town of Jordan (the Halling Settlement), where my best friends were living. But this little settlement could not support a minister alone, and we parted in sadness. The last night we spent with the honorable man, Ole Evensen Glesne; from there we continued to the Dietrichsons, with whom we set out on the journey home with our two little girls.

A GENERAL VIEW OF AMERICA

Before I leave America, I shall write down something about the conditions there as they were in my time, that is, well over forty years ago.

About the landscape and the climate I have spoken before, so there is not much more to say about that. The western country, where I was living, is very fertile. "It rolls along in hills and vale," [8] and was at least then well covered with forests of oak, maple, elm, and black walnut, besides hickory. However, they worked the forests hard, and the many prairie fires contributed to destroying them. Wisconsin is bounded on the east by Lake Michigan and on the west by the Mississippi and is regarded as one of the most beautiful areas of the West. Madison, the capital, has a lovely location surrounded by three lakes and by forest. The largest city is Milwaukee, by the Lake. It is mostly inhabited by Germans. There are many Norwegians in the state, and generally they are doing well. During my time, wheat was the main crop. Later on they seem to have been cultivating a lot of tobacco and have also been raising horses. Hay barns are not used, both the grain and the hay are put in stacks. The hay is then cut out with a big hay knife, and that was a work I often performed. Then the hay inside the stack was fresh and green. I had a neighbor mow and stack my hay for letting him keep half of it for himself. That was a good bargain for me as I had plenty of hay. The maize corn was left in the field until late in the fall, when it was *hasket* [American-Norwegian for "husked"], that is, the ears were taken out and the stocks were left until well into the winter. Cattle and pigs would eat these stocks and leaves. When the corn was husked, there usually was a "husking bee," when the neighbors were asked together to help. One time, the daughter of our neighbor Kobel came over to us, invited us for dinner, and borrowed our sterling spoons. Else, who was then two years old, was to come along. We dressed up in our best as we thought there was going to be a dinner party, not knowing that it was corn husking. But we soon learned the truth. For one after the other came in for dinner directly from the field, muddy and dirty, and sat down at the table like that. We were sitting there spruced up in our finery (Else had a red tulle dress on) and were the objects of everybody's smiles and murmurs and whispers. We understood very little of what they said to us (they were Irish), and we only wished to get away from there. The food consisted of a lot of boiled meat with kohlrabi and pota- toes, and then pie. Finally we escaped, and as we were leaving, the woman said to Mama: "That baby is fat as a hog; if she gets the croup, she will die immediately." Very friendly and consider- ate! That was the only time we went there.

The Norwegian language over there is famous. They hurry to mix it with English, and the more they can mix it, the better.

Concerning the social conditions, I need only remind you of the fact that the republican-democratic constitution is carried through into its most minute detail. All government functionar- ies, or "officers" as they are called, are elected by the people, from the president of the U.S. down to the lowliest county clerk. Each county has its various "officers," subordinate to the gover- nor of the state, who lives in the capital. All judges are elected. This gives the people great power and causes perpetual factional disputes—and often bribes. To the degree that the voters are immature and inarticulate, this system is a witness to its own weakness, as they easily become dependent on demagogues, with whom the candidates then will try to ingratiate themselves and are easily for sale. It was often disgusting to me to listen to the insolent swagger of immature Norwegians—and it happened quite often, to be sure, that liquor played a role in the elections. But nowadays it is not much better here at home. That the functionaries over there very often had low standards and were lacking in culture, is quite evident. For "justices of the peace" they regularly elected quite uneducated people. That it did not turn out any worse than it did in many places is probably due to the "common sense" which is peculiar to the American nation, and which the older settlers also picked up.

The relationship between master and servant is quite loose. The servants do not want to be called that, they are "helpers" or "hands." The servant maids are impossible—they will take up and leave at the least reproof as there is no determined "moving day." An example may illustrate this. There was going to be a ministers' meeting at A. C. Preus's, and they were very busy in the kitchen. The pastors arrived in the morning, and Mrs. Preus went out into the kitchen to make arrangements for dinner. To her horror she found the maid in the process of packing her suitcase and asked what this was all about. "Well, I am leaving." But why? "Well, the Missus did not introduce me to the pastors!" It sounds incredible, but it is true. However, nowadays the domestic servants have learned the same pretensions here at home, so it no longer seems so peculiar as when I first heard the story. Here at home we are quicker to learn the bad than the good in the American social life. It would be well if we also could learn the diligence and the quickness that the Americans show in their work.

It is also remarkable how the American national spirit is able to absorb and assimilate the many foreign elements that pour in there from the old countries, and who often seem poorly equipped to become good citizens. Among the emigrants, the Scandinavians, no doubt, are the ones who most easily adapt themselves to the free America, as even the Americans recognize readily. Indeed, several of them have recently held esteemed positions both as governors and as members of Congress.

In the West, most of the Norwegians are farmers, there are not many in other positions. During my time, there was much free land, which one only needed to settle down on and "claim," that is, have oneself registered as a settler, and which was then bought cheaply. One could also acquire land by pledging oneself to cultivate and plant it within a certain number of years. The land is divided into sections, and each section into quarter sections in even squares, so the divided land looks like a chessboard when it is plotted on a map. One quarter section is 160 acres, and that makes a big farm. Many have less. Most people want land that consists partly of prairie land and partly of woodland. Now they have to go far west to get usable land. But during my time, there was plenty of it.

When we left, Emil went to Minnesota and claimed a quarter section of good land in St. Olaf's parish in the southeastern part of the state. We gave him two horses and a colt, lumber wagon, and various tools and household utensils, and he was then very pleased. But later he is supposed to have complained that he thought he had got too little. We also gave him money for the trip. Eventually, he became a prosperous man. As long as Mama was living, he wrote to her and regretted that he could not return what we had done for him. But after her death he seemes to have changed his mind on the subject. This I have from Lagertha—but I am not inclined to think that badly about him, and I am writing this down *because* I do not believe it. Gossip we have had enough of. As long as he was with us, he was a kind and considerate boy.

Regarding the church situation in America, it is well known that the church is separated from the state, and that there are a host of church parties and sects. The state does not interfere in the business of the church as long as the church does not interfere with the state; moreover, in America there is a not inconsiderable religiosity, and the state maintains the Sunday and does not tolerate any desecration of religion—at least not public. But when I was there, the Norwegian settlers were not yet familiar with this order of things and had only little understanding of the rights and duties of a free congregation. The Christianity in name only, which they had brought with them from Norway, was very predominant, and only little by little have they learned to adapt to the new church situation.

The schools were separated from the church as "common school," where there was no teaching of religion but at most—although not everywhere—some reading of the Bible. But then parochial schools and Sunday schools were established. In the common school, the teaching was always in English except where there were so many Norwegians in a school district that some of the teaching was done in Norwegian. The American school is economically independent as there is land set aside, which belongs to the school, and which is everywhere sold to establish school funds. It is a very practical arrangement, whereby school taxes are avoided. From these school funds, the teachers are paid, and schoolhouses built. Each school has a board of supervisors, who are elected by the people. A larger school district also has a superintendent. As you known, there are also many higher schools and colleges, many of which have been established by private means.

It was quite usual that grown-up newcomers attended the common school to learn English. Men and women went together, and it is quite conceivable that they learned more than English in these so-called "spelling classes."

The schoolhouses were generally very simple and cannot be compared to the costly school palaces which are being built in our poverty-stricken country, and which so greatly increase our taxes. The same simplicity was also applied to railroad stations in the country. Most of the cost has been spent on the cars – contrary to what is the case among us. People here at home have no conception of the elegance and comfort of the American railroad cars. Particularly excellent are the so-called Pullman cars with their plate-glass windows and comfortable fittings as in a parlor.[9] They are more expensive than regular cars, which, however, are also very comfortable and roomy. I do not remember what the price was for regular fare, but I have the impression that it was very cheap, especially for more extended journeys. It was not necessary to buy the ticket beforehand – one could also do that – at least for shorter trips the conductor would collect the fare.

As known, the American money is dollar ($) and cent. One dollar is a hundred cents and about 3½ *Krone* [in 1903].[10] They mostly use paper money (of which there were many counterfeits in my time) , but also gold and silver. The most beautiful coin in the world is a twenty-dollar piece in gold. I brought a couple of those home with me, but unfortunately, they soon had to be exchanged. And since, of course, I have not seen them.

THE JOURNEY HOME

With the Dietrichsons and our two little girls we then traveled by railroad on the way to Quebec, where we were going to board a ship for Norway. It was the ship broker Holfeldt, who was living in Quebec, who had arranged it that way. He was a friend of Dietrichson and had usually spent some time each year at his place. He was a small hunchback, who was very "smart." We traveled through Chicago and on to Canada, to Montreal, a big and mighty city, and from there by steamship on the St. Lawrence River. Here we had to go down the rapids, where the mighty river rushes with a roar and high waves down the sloping, hilly riverbed. One place, in particular, is dangerous as there is a rock in the middle of the cascade, past which the steamship must maneuver at great speed. To keep the steerage-way it is necessary to put on full steam, and the ship shakes from bow to stern. An Indian is always at the helm. It was an exciting moment when with a tremendous speed we approached the black rock sticking out of the white foam and we suddenly had to bear away so the ship listed over. But it went well, and we felt relieved. "Well, we got safely down this time, too," said the purser when we got clear of the rapids. . . . The last leg to Quebec we went by a railroad which was slanting to one side so much that it looked as if we were sailing close-hauled, as a Norwegian sea captain said when he saw the train coming.

On invitation we, too, stayed with the Holfeldts, but it was somewhat discommoding as we could well perceive that it was for Dietrichson's sake that we had been included. But we were only too glad as we did not have much cash (as usual). We had to stay there well over a week, I believe, before we could sail. We had thought that we were going to have the company of the Dietrichsons also across the sea, and a prospect of this had indeed been held out. But as it turned out, there was no room for us. Dietrichson sailed with a Captain Grøntvedt (a Norwegian naval officer) and had a very comfortable voyage. We had to board a sailing ship from Sandefjord named *Ocean*. Captain Christensen was a very kind young man. But the cabin was cramped and poor and, worst of all, he had not thought of getting us some better provisions than the usual seafare—salt meat every day. . . . Besides, the ship was carrying a deck cargo, so we could not walk on the deck except in nice weather, of which we did not have much. Else, however, soon learned to wear sea legs and walked rather cleverly. We had much fun with her when we got home, asking her to "wear sea legs," and she readily obliged. We were four weeks on our way. The Dietrichsons made it in three.

Toward the end of our voyage, as we were approaching the coast of Ireland (the ship was bound for Belfast with lumber), we got a strong gale blowing onto the shore, so that the ship could carry only little cloth and was rolling terribly. We had some canvas stretched in front of the couch in the cabin, and there the little girls tumbled back and forth and did not mind the rolling at all. But for us, who understood the danger, it was terrible to see the Atlantic Ocean in such an uproar with the huge waves and the howling gale. Once the spanker gaff was bent so hard that had they not let go the sail, it would—according to the captain's statement—undoubtedly have broken, and then the fragments would have fallen through the skylight into the cabin and possibly crushed us. Another time, the ship nosed into the sea so the whole bow was engulfed by a wave and the greater part of the crew were floating around; it was a mercy none of them was washed overboard. After much struggle, we fetched up north of Ireland but had to spend a dark night tacking back and forth, getting our bearing from the lighthouses, before it became safe to set course for Belfast. I was up almost all night with the captain and the mate.

Finally we arrived safely in Belfast, where we docked. We stayed on board a couple of days before we continued on our way. During our stay in Belfast, we visited the Norwegian consul, Mynster. He and his family were very hospitable and obliging. We also had a trip down to his country house and traveled on one of the Irish char-à-bancs, which are so common but not exactly comfortable. He also helped me buy a new suit, which I needed badly, so I came home like a gentleman.

We traveled by steamship across the Irish Channel to Fleetwood, where we took the train through England to Hull. . . . There we found the Norwegian ship *Gangerrolf,* and Captain Gløersen (later harbor master in Kristiania). He received us cordially and took care of us in the best manner. There we got a

good glass of Norwegian beer, which I had not tasted for four
years. That was the first time I saw these beer bottles that are
now common but which were not in use when I left for America,
and I remember I found them ridiculous. We had a good time
on board together with some English travelers, who treated us to
champagne when they heard that we came from America.
There, too, Else was "wearing sea legs," to the general amusement.

So we arrived safely back in Kristiania. We stayed with
Mother, who was living in Johansen's house in Pilestrædet.
Mother was particularly fond of little Else, who both looked like
her and was named after her. But as they had cramped lodgings,
we did not stay long and then went to Hovland, where unfortunately all was not well as Falch was dying from cancer of the
stomach. The reuinion, therefore, was rather sad, and Mama,
who had been looking forward to seeing her dear ones again,
met only sorrow and tears. After about a week, I had to return to
Kristiania to look for a position. While I was there, Falch died,
and I had to rush back to Hovland to attend the funeral.

So it was a sad homecoming, and as I had no position, it
must be admitted that I regretted having left America and was
thinking of going back. We came home around St. Hans time
[June 24], Falch died in July, and we had to stay at Hovland
through the summer and fall—not precisely altogether pleasant.
Mrs. Falch was friendly as always, but we felt nevertheless that
we were an inconvenience.

On the 12th of September, 1859, Mama again gave birth to
a daughter, whom we named Ragna, and who was healthy and
sound from the day of her birth. Mama soon recovered. But
when I reflected that she in that condition had traveled through
America and over the ocean returning home, and courageously
endured so many hardships, then I had to admire her. Not many
would have suffered it like she did. But then she has always been
so bold, brave, and strong—the dear, dear Mama who is no
longer among us.

Social Class
and Acculturation

Social Class and Acculturation

by Peter A. Munch

THE LETTERS of Caja Munch were written during a period in the history of the American Upper Middle West which, in Pastor Munch's words, was "in all respects fermenting and unsettled." In 1855, when the Munchs arrived, the actual frontier had moved on to Minnesota Territory (soon to become a state), and in Wisconsin several cities had grown up, such as Madison, Beloit, and particularly Milwaukee, "which about thirty years ago consisted only of a couple of cottages and now is a city that in size is equal to, and in grandeur far surpasses Christiania," the capital of Norway. In Madison, the new capital of the young state, which with its ten thousand inhabitants had already won the reputation of being "a dangerous city" (at least in the eyes of Caja Munch), the University of Wisconsin was in its seventh year of operation, and in various other towns, several private colleges had already been founded, such as Milton, Beloit, Carroll, Lawrence, and Ripon. On the rolling prairies, settlements were fairly well-established, although scattered in places, separated from each other by large areas of virgin forest and wilderness, where deer, quail, and rattlesnakes were still ruling the ground, with an occasional band of miserable Indians roaming around like Gypsies. But small towns with a post office and a store (often combined in one), a sawmill, and an occasional flour mill were within reasonable reach of most of the settlements if one was prepared to spend a whole day or maybe two on a shopping trip by horse-drawn buggy or lumber wagon. As Caja Munch described it, "we can actually live like in the country at home and can get anything we want for money but for a few exceptions." But everything was new and fresh and immature, a haven for adventurers in more or less honest trades—indeed, as looked upon with European eyes, fermenting and unsettled.

Norwegian immigrants had by this time pushed on with the frontier across Wisconsin into Minnesota. According to the Federal census, in 1850 there were 12,678 Norwegians in the whole of the United States, more than 9,000 of them living in Wisconsin. And new waves of settlers continued to pour in as the European migration to America approached its first peak. By 1860, there were almost 30,000 Norwegians in Wisconsin alone.[1] Norwegian-Lutheran congregations with resident pastors—apart from government the only kind of local formal organization in these early settlements—had been established as far north and west as Manitowoc, Waupaca, Coon Prairie, and even at Springfield and Washington Prairie in Iowa. The center of cultural and religious activities among the Norwegians had moved from the early and ever struggling Fox River settlement in northern Illinois to the more prosperous Wisconsin settlements of Jefferson Prairie, Rock Prairie, Muskego, and Koshkonong. It was at this time, and in these settlements, that the first faltering institutions of an organized church and press took shape among the Norwegians in America. The first shortlived Norwegian newspaper in the Middle West, *Nordlyset* [The Northern Lights], emanated from Muskego in 1847, and in 1851 Koshkonong and Rock Prairie saw the establishment of the Scandinavian Press Association, which continued for several years publishing not only the newspaper *Emigranten* [The Emigrant] but also books and pamphlets in the Norwegian language. The first synodical organization of Norwegian Lutheran congregations came into being at Jefferson Prairie in 1846, when Elling Eielsen and his followers signed a document known as the "Old Constitution" to form what was henceforth referred to as "Eielsen's Synod," a church organization of decidedly pietistic orientation. And through several deliberations at Rock Prairie, Muskego, and Koshkonong, pastors of the State Church of Norway in 1853 finally organized The Norwegian Evangelical Lutheran Church of America, soon to be known as "The Norwegian Synod," with Pastor Adolph C. Preus of Koshkonong as its president.

It has been said that if you travel through rural Wisconsin and you get to a crossroad with two churches, one on each side of the road, you may be sure that you have entered a Norwegian settlement. Denominational strifes and cleavages are certainly not peculiar to the Norwegians in this area. But it is hardly an historical accident that, right from the outset, the Norwegians had two synodical organizations, separated from each other by a gulf which was as much social as theological in nature. It was a situation which had deep roots in the historical development of the Norwegian people during the fermenting period of national awakening and liberation of the eighteenth and early part of the nineteenth century. This is not the place for a detailed survey of the social and ecclesiastical history of the Norwegian people in Norway and America. But since this has a bearing on much of what is said in the letters of Caja Munch, and also on much that remains unsaid, a brief look at the salient points may be of interest.[2]

One of the most important social developments in Norway during the sixteenth, seventeenth, and eighteenth centuries was the emergence of a new elite of professionals and intellectuals to take the place of a weak and vanishing nobility. A similar development was taking place in other North and West European countries. But the impact of the new elite was greater in Norway, mainly because here it stepped unchallenged into a social and political vacuum. Having been for so long the political underdog in the Scandinavian family of nations, Norway had never had a strong feudal nobility, and by modern times it was practically nonexistent. Another factor, as the Norwegian historian Sverre Steen points out, and probably related to the first, was the fact that Norway at that time was in a state which today would have earned her the epithet of an "underdeveloped" country and therefore went through a more rapid development than most other European countries.[3]

By 1800 or so, the new elite was well-established and actually comprised two more or less vaguely distinct groups or "estates." The first group consisted of people engaged in various kinds of business. A few of them became industrial magnates on a small scale, establishing ironworks and glassworks and sawmills, others engaged in distribution and transportation, mostly in wholesale business or, particularly, in shipping, while some made their money from financing and banking. This was the money aristocracy of Norway, generally known as *Handelsstanden* or the commercial class. Most of them were certainly not great "capitalists" in the popular sense of the word. But this was the group that introduced the modern "spirit of capitalism" to Norway. Many of them engaged in land speculation and development on the side and became "proprietors," some of them dealing in city property, others buying up large tracts of forest land to feed their sawmills, others again setting up residence on comparatively large farms or estates on the outskirts of the cities or out in the country, pursuing agriculture and cattle breeding on a commercial scale.

The other group, usually described as *Embedsstanden* or the professional class, had less money but more prestige. They were the professionals, such as physicians, lawyers, architects and engineers, higher civil servants in state and municipality, and above all the *Embedsmænd*, officials of the Crown. The latter included not only the holders of high administrative offices and judges in the higher courts but also officers in the armed forces, bishops, deans, and pastors in the State Church, and—since 1811, when Norway got her own university—professors (but not faculty members of lower ranks). This was the core of the professional and intellectual elite of Norway, which also supplied most of the recognized artists and writers of the time.

There was no great social distinction between the two groups. They wandered pretty much in the same circles, and they were multifariously related by intermarriage and family ties. Together they formed a single leading class, the bourgeoisie, which even absorbed what little remnants there were of a feudal nobility. But this was not a privileged class in the proper sense of the word. Its social standing did not depend on inherited titles or royal decrees and favors. Nor was it entirely, or even primarily, based on wealth and economic power. It is true that for the mercantile elite a fairly prosperous and profitable business was an important factor in determining status, and the ability to invest money gave, of course, considerable power. But this did not apply to the professionals and particularly not to the crown officials, who mostly lived exclusively on their salaries which were far from exuberant. In fact, there was a notion that it was not quite proper for a professional, and especially not for a crown official, to engage in a profit-yielding business enterprise.[4] Extreme poverty was probably rare among them, although a widow with small children might sometimes find herself in a severe plight. But many of the crown officials had large families to support and often found it difficult to make ends meet while keeping up the standards expected of their station. Thrift and prudence became important virtues among them in a way that almost reminds one of Scottish and American puritan traditions, except that for the crown officials in Norway they were virtues of necessity.

Rather than on privilege or wealth, the status of the professional elite was based very predominantly on personal qualities achieved and accumulated through succeeding generations. A highly important qualification for membership in this class—if one can talk about "membership" in a group where belonging was so much a matter of degree—was a higher education aimed at acquiring competence and proficiency in the mercantile and professional occupations. Preferably it should be an academic education leading to an *Embedsexamen* or to a professional diploma from a university at home or abroad, and for a crown official this qualification was mandatory. But a prospective businessman could get away with a less prestigious "practical" business education, which usually involved a couple of years abroad as an apprentice in a business firm.

The most important distinguishing quality of this social elite, however, was neither education nor money nor, in fact, occupation but an intangible thing called *Dannelse,* precisely the same as the Germans call *Bildung.* It is rather surprising that the word has no exact equivalent in English, for the phenomenon is not lacking in British tradition. It may be rendered as "culture" or "breeding," but the best way to describe it is probably to say that *Dannelse* was that intangible attribute which turned a man into a gentleman, a woman into a lady. It was at the same time a quality, an attitude, and a style of life. It involved good manners, tact and dignity in conduct, neatness in grooming and habits, a home that bore evidence of taste, sense of style, and appreciation of the fine arts. In relation to others and to society at large it involved consideration and obligation rather than rights and privileges. It even involved a certain type of personality.

It was on the basis of such qualities that members of the professional elite would recognize another person as belonging to their circle by saying that he was a *dannet,* that is "cultured," person, while outsiders—the ones who were gratuitously referred to as *Almuen,* the common or general people—would mostly describe him as *conditioneret* or, as it sometimes was rendered in rural dialects, *konsenert.* And these were labels that tended to stick to him as long as he showed the personal qualities of his class, no matter what his occupation and economic status might be.

It was recognized by both insiders and outsiders that qualities such as these were not easily achieved except by growing up in a home that already had them. So the new elite soon became a rather secluded social circle, a self-sustaining group, where family background and a long and distinguished lineage were an asset and an important source of prestige. In fact, the whole social elite of Norway consisted in the main of a relatively small number of extended families or lineages, each with its distinct family name, often with its own family crest which, however, was usually adorned by a "bourgeois" helmet to indicate (with pride) that it was not of the old privileged nobility. These lineages were tied together by bonds of common interest and mutual recognition, but above all by a criss-cross pattern of intermarriage, in which cousin marriages became, if not common, at least not infrequent. In these circles, family loyalty and lineage pride became important values, richly symbolized in the homes by heirlooms, ancestral portraits, and a general family tradition. And these familistic values persevered well into the twentieth century in some lineages, only reluctantly giving way to more egalitarian principles.

This cultured elite—although few in number as could be expected in a small and sparsely populated country, "underdeveloped" at that, where about 85 per cent of the population were peasants [5]— was a dominant element in Norway throughout the eighteenth and far into the nineteenth century. It is not too much to say that this elite carried the political and intellectual life of the nation, and since crown officials as well as municipal administrators and officers were almost exclusively recruited from this group, they wielded considerable power. Of course, there were those who abused their power for personal gain as witnessed by many a just complaint submitted by peasants and other *Almuefolk* to bishops and high administrators as well as to the King in Copenhagen during the time of Danish rule, and there may have been many, many more who were never reported. But it is probably fair to say that, in general, the members of this cultured elite, including the crown officials, did not regard themselves as a "ruling class." Their attitude was rather that of a professional group, who saw the legitimation of their status and power— "influence" and "leadership" may be a nicer way to put it—not so much in their royal appointment as in their hard-earned professional competence, authorized by Europe's highest institutions of learning, which alone qualified them for appointment in the first place.

So the members of the professional elite naturally became leaders in national and communal affairs, liberal protagonists in political and cultural developments and, at the same time, conservative guardians of traditional values. And they were generally recognized and accepted in these roles—until the peasantry rose to challenge their exclusive position of leadership.

Just as important and interesting as the emergence of a professional elite in the seventeenth and eighteenth centuries is the rise of the peasant class in Norway during the nineteenth century. This development had even deeper roots in the historical past of the Norwegian people, and it grew into a powerful movement as the peasants, with their age-old traditions of freedom and independence, learned to embrace the new democratic ideas of national and individual liberty and human rights, which had been propagated and in part implemented by members of the professional elite.[6] While the peasant movement took firm shape as a political and cultural force in Norway only in the second half of the nineteenth century, the social and political fermentation that preceded it has a definite bearing on the early Norwegian emigration to America as well as on the struggles of the Norwegian Lutheran Church in this country.

For some generations the peasants of Norway had become accustomed to looking to their local crown officials, especially to the *Sogneprest* or parish pastor, for spiritual guidance as well as for community leadership. Stirrings of a more independent spirit had occurred during the latter half of the eighteenth century. But they were sporadic and mostly local in nature. In fact, when the new democratic Constitution of Norway adopted in 1814 put considerable potential power into the hands of the peasants by requiring that two thirds of the *Storting*, the Norwegian parliament, should come from the rural districts, the peasants continued for many years to elect local crown officials, particularly pastors, to represent them, which probably was partly due to an habitual deference to the prestige of the professional class but, in part at least, was a sincere expression of trust in the general honesty and competence of the elite.

The first important sign of an incipient emancipation of the peasants from the patronizing leadership of the crown officials came in the form of a religious movement. Since about the middle of the eighteenth century, pietism—with its emphasis on personal faith and lay activity rather than on doctrine propounded by orthodox pastors —had had a vitalizing effect on religious life among the people both in town and country. In its radical forms it often led to fanaticism and sectarianism, which in itself may be seen as an overreaction against the authority of the clergy. But in its more moderate form as preached by a new generation of pietist pastors it usually brought about a closer relationship between the pastor and at least part of his congregation, who became actively engaged in the affairs of the church.

Soon, however, still another generation of pastors took office, who had been brought up and trained in the spirit of rationalism, an intellectual trend that did not appeal much to the relatively unschooled *Almue* and tended to widen the gap between the learned pastor and his flock. While in the cities and towns this development often led to a growing secularization in the congregations, in the more conservative rural communities it created a chasm between the rather dry rationalism often served from the pulpit and a lingering pietism in the pews.

It was in this fertile soil of unfulfilled religious needs that Hans Nielsen Hauge started his activity of religious revival and created a significant movement of conventicle worship based on personal conversion and witnessing, and on lay preaching. Himself a peasant boy from Tune, not far from Christiania (Oslo), and brought up in the pietist tradition, in 1796 he experienced a religious awakening and became convinced of having received a call from God to preach the Gospel to the common people. During the following eight years, until he was arrested and put in prison for violation of the so-called "Conventicle Ordinance" which banned public prayer meetings (rescinded 1842), Hauge covered practically the whole of Norway, traveling from community to community, and his movement won a considerable following everywhere.

Although Hauge often identified himself—for instance, on the title page of many of the books and pamphlets that he published—as "a lowly peasant's son," which obviously contained an appeal to the common people over against the establishment, his movement was not essentially a peasant movement. It certainly did not become the rallying point for a consolidation of the peasant class. On the contrary, with its strong element of asceticism and otherworldliness the Hauge movement took a negative stand to many customs and usages which were firmly entrenched in the traditional peasant society; and with their rather exclusive self-identification as "Friends," the Haugeans tended to accentuate certain social differentiations and tensions already existing *within* the peasant communities, causing a cleavage rather than a unification.

However, it is hardly a mere accident that most of Hauge's followers were peasants, and—as most historians seem to agree—the considerable popularity that the movement enjoyed among this particular class was probably due, in part at least, to the fact that it had important social, economic, and even political implications, which were only emphasized by the strong opposition on the part of the authorities, particularly the clergy.

In the first place, although Hauge stayed loyal to the Church of Norway throughout his life and admonished his followers to do the same, his sharp criticism of the pastors, particularly in his early preachings and writings, was an open challenge to their professional competence. And the organization of conventicles with laymen preaching and leading the prayers, in direct violation of the "Conventicle Ordinance," was in fact an emancipation from the exclusive authority of the clergy in religious affairs.

Secondly, there was more to the Hauge movement than a religious revival. Hauge himself was an enterprising businessman, and in a spirit that reminds one more of Anglo-American puritanism than of Continental pietism, he not only engaged in various business enterprises himself, took out citizenship as a merchant in Bergen, and became a dealer in fish and grain, but he encouraged his followers to do likewise. He also organized and established cooperative sawmills and paper mills, a salt work, and even a printing press. This not only gave an economic independence to his followers that they had not known before; it also meant the beginning of an "occupational emancipation" of the peasant, a liberation from the idea that a peasant was forever doomed to be a tiller of the soil.

Finally, on the political scene it is significant that the leaders of the sharply increased political activity of the peasants in the 1830's, including the staunch protagonist of this movement, Ole Gabriel Ueland himself, were Haugeans. On the whole, the Hauge movement represented a forceful emancipation of the common people, particularly the peasants, from the control and dominance of the elite, and so it was an important manifestation, and a reinforcement, of the peasants' age-old, but dormant, and now reawakened quest for freedom and independence.

These are the elements of the Norwegian society which took the main leads in the drama of Norwegian settlement in America: a reluctantly retreating professional elite with a strong sense of responsibility for the preservation of the higher spiritual values in life, both religious and cultural; and a self-asserting peasantry in search of freedom.

"Freedom" had become a powerful idea—and an effective slogan —in the Western World during the eighteenth and nineteenth centuries. Wars and bloody revolutions were fought in its name, and it became the cornerstone of several newly written constitutions in many countries, including Norway. Freedom was espoused, praised, and proclaimed in every political declaration, in every chauvinistic speech, in every patriotic song all over Europe—indeed, the United States of America was far from the only country in the world that was pronounced "the Land of the Free." Yet few nations proclaimed freedom with quite as much fanfare as the young American nation did. And the trumpets were heard and applauded all over Europe, creating that indestructible image of America as the very champion of freedom.

There can be no doubt that this invigorated quest for freedom in Europe, coupled with the widely accepted image of America as a haven of freedom, became a most important factor in the enormous migrations of the nineteenth century.

But "freedom" meant different things to different people. To some it meant national liberation from political dominance, to others free enterprise, particularly free trade. To others, again, freedom was a democratic form of government, while some would look for it primarily in terms of freedom to dissent, particularly in religious matters. All these freedoms were fairly well-established in Norway by the middle of the nineteenth century, at least in principle. But then there were those to whom freedom first and foremost meant equality —equality of opportunity, particularly in an economic sense, but even more importantly, *social equality,* that is, freedom from conventional social differentiations. And it was not least in the latter sense that America was praised as a haven of freedom.

As far as Norwegian migration is concerned, it is not surprising, then, that the vast majority of Norwegian emigrants throughout the nineteenth century were peasants with their newly reawakened quest for freedom, and that "the emigration fever spread through our country districts like a disease." [7] The whole emigration movement may, in fact, be seen as one important aspect of the emancipation of the peasant class in Norway. It is significant that a great many, maybe a majority, of the early settlers in the Fox River settlement as well as in some of the Wisconsin settlements were followers of Hauge's religious emancipation movement.

As might be expected, these early Norwegian immigrants had strong feelings about their newly won freedom, and it is evident, without attempting to devalue the importance of purely economic considerations, that social equality loomed large in their appreciation of America. It comes out frequently in letters to relatives and friends in Norway. "Here it is not asked," says one letter writer, "what or who was your father, but the question is, what are you? . . . Freedom is here an element which is drawn in, as it were, with mother milk, and seems as essential to every citizen of the United States as the air he breathes. . . . This elevates the lowly and brings down the great." [8] Another states: "Farmers and artisans are just as good as merchants and officials. They all have practically the same manners, and the appearance and dress of people are usually the same as they are in Norwegian towns." [9] The new freedom is often described in direct contrast to conditions in Norway: "As proof of the high education of the [American] people it may be cited that the clergy is not regarded, nor indeed regards itself, as better than the common people. The minister dresses just like other members of the congregation. He wears no cassock in church, as in oppressed Europe, to call attention to differences of station in society." [10] Typically, the clergy is often singled out as the prime obstacle to social freedom and equality in the old country, and it shows considerable sensitivity on this point when even the clerical garb becomes a symbol of "oppression." An unnamed immigrant in Wisconsin states that "there are very few things that we can import from our old Norway which could be of benefit to us, and least of all Norwegian officials!" [11] It is quite evident that many of them were more concerned with "bringing down the great" than with "elevating the lowly."

So the fierce independence of the Norwegian peasantry, reinforced by American liberalism, joined hands with the devout pietism of the Hagueans to create an atmosphere of sensitive, sometimes supersensitive, egalitarianism. It is rather interesting to note, however, that this egalitarianism was specifically directed against social differentiations stemming from the old country. Like other settlers, the Norwegians apparently did not mind affording prestige and high social standing to a New World elite of Old American stock, equally conspicuous in dress and manners and an urbane style of life, who moved on the heels of the settlers into the new territories to establish business and banking—founding and naming such cities and towns as Madison, Stoughton, Blanchardville, Monroe, and even, on a smaller scale, Hamilton (Wiota) —and soon controlled the economic life of the area.[12]

It was in this atmosphere of limited but supersensitive egalitarianism that the sharply anticlerical Elling Eielsen, himself a forceful Haugean lay preacher from Norway, had a considerable influence and eventually (although reluctantly) became an ordained clergyman and the leader of a synodical organization of distinctly low-church inclinations.

It soon appeared, however, that, while Eielsen had a particularly strong position in the Fox River settlement with its predominant element from the Stavanger area, Norway's traditional "Bible Belt," his uncompromising anticlerical attitude was more than even the staunchest Haugeans in the Muskego settlement could take. And there was an increasing number of other Norwegian immigrants as well, who had little sympathy for Eielsen's revivalist form of religion, and whose fear of "pastoral overlordship" was overcome by their desire for order in their church affairs under the leadership and guidance of a properly trained and duly consecrated minister. So appeals were sent to Norway, both by letter and by personal visits of some of their leaders, "hoping to induce some ordained Lutheran Christian pastor to come over for the purpose of gathering the dispersed flock and nurturing it with the good things of God's house." [13]

At first, no ordained minister of the Church of Norway could be induced. Finally, a young Danish teacher and missionary answered the call and came to clear the ground for the organization of a Norwegian Lutheran church in America. C. L. Clausen arrived in Muskego in 1843, organized a congregation there, was eventually ordained by a German pastor, and conducted divine services according to the ritual of the Church of Norway in several Norwegian settlements, including Wiota.

Then came Johan W. C. Dietrichson, one of the most controversial figures in the history of the Norwegian Lutheran Church in America, "a barrel-chested proponent of ministerial authority and ecclesiastical order." [14] He was the first Norwegian pastor to come with a professional degree in theology from the Royal Frederik's University in Christiania (now the University of Oslo), and with an ordination by a Norwegian bishop. With financial support from a benefactor in Christiania, Dietrichson "strode into the comparative quiet of Muskego" in 1844 on what he himself described as a "missionary journey" with the stated purpose "to get information about the religious needs of the emigrant Norwegians, and to attempt to institute church order among them." [15] During the first year, he organized a number of congregations in Wisconsin. In 1845 he re-turned to Norway to recruit pastors for the newly organized congregations and came back the following year to serve as pastor of the two congregations organized by him at Koshkonong.

Induced by Dietrichson, other pastors followed. In 1848, Hans A. Stub arrived and became the pastor of Muskego after Clausen had moved to Rock Prairie, and Adolph C. Preus took over the Koshkonong congregations when Johan Dietrichson returned to Norway for good in 1850. The following year, 1851, three pastors arrived from Norway. Nils O. Brandt took charge of the congregations at Rock River and Pine Lake; Gustav F. Dietrichson released Clausen at Rock Prairie as the latter went to Iowa and organized a congregation at St. Ansgar; and Herman A. Preus became resident pastor at Spring Prairie. In 1852, Jacob Aall Ottesen arrived and took up residence at Manitowoc. These were the pastors who, in 1853, organized the Norwegian Evangelical Lutheran Church of America, commonly known as the Norwegian Synod.

That same year, 1853, Ulrik V. Koren arrived and became the first pastor ordained in Norway to take up residence west of the Mississippi, founding a congregation at Washington Prairie, Iowa. Olaus F. Duus joined the group in 1854 and became pastor at Waupaca, later at Whitewater. In 1855, Stub took over the Norwegian congregation at Coon Prairie after he failed to persuade the Haugeans in the Muskego congregation to join the Norwegian Synod. In the fall of that year, Johan St. Munch arrived and took up residence at Wiota. Peter M. Brodahl became the pastor at Black Earth in 1856, and in 1857 Peter Laur. Larsen took charge of the congregation at Rush River in Pierce County, which had been organized two years earlier but had so far been without a pastor, while F. C. Claussen became the first Norwegian Synod pastor in the Minnesota Territory at Spring Grove. In the meantime, Claus L. Clausen, the Dane among them, had taken leave from his ministry at St. Ansgar to become a member of the Iowa Legislature.

These Norwegian pastors had much in common both to tie them together as a group and to set them apart from the majority of the settlers. In the first place, all of them came from, and had been brought up in the traditions of, the professional elite of Norway. Some of them carried the names of prominent lineages who had distinguished themselves in politics, administration, or the professions in Norway, or they could claim relationship by kinship or marriage to other distinguished and well-known lineages. Even the forms and spellings of their names set them apart from the ordinary settlers, and everything in their conduct and manners, their taste and style of life, the language they spoke, served to identify them with the professional elite of Norway.

Also in keeping with the patterns and traditions of the professional elite, many of them were closely related by kinship among themselves. A. C. Preus and H. A. Preus were cousins; G. F. Dietrichson was a cousin of J. W. C. Dietrichson's father, and his wife was a sister of A. C. Preus and, of course, a cousin of H. A. Preus; Brandt married a double cousin of Ottesen; also Stub and Koren were related. And all of them were at least indirectly acquainted, with many common acquaintances in Norway.

More importantly, these pastors had this in common that all of them had gone through a thorough training in theology at the University in Christiania and, after further examination, had been ordained into the ministry of the Church of Norway. As theologians and churchmen and as curators of souls they had a professional concern for purity of belief as well as for proper organization and ritual in accord with the symbols or confessional writings of the Church of Norway, to which they were bound both by their oath of office and by the constitution of the Norwegian Synod. For this purpose, they deemed it necessary that their parishioners recognize the authority and responsibility of those who had both the professional competence (through a bona fide theological training) and the proper legitimation (through ordination and letter of appointment) to make decisions in matters of the church. Indeed, all of them were, if not barrel-chested, yet staunch proponents of ministerial authority and ecclesiastical order.

Here is not the place to pass judgment on character and ability. But the very fact that these Norwegian pastors chose to leave their home country, sacrificing the material, cultural, and social comforts to which their station had made them accustomed, to serve the pioneer settlements in a new land which, for all they knew, was still a wilderness, is at least an indication that they were men of strong faith and devotion to the cause of ministering to the religious and cultural needs of their countrymen. Although conflicting reports were in circulation in Norway concerning conditions in the Norwegian settlements in the Middle West, the pastors had not been without warning of the difficulties they might have to face. J. W. C. Dietrichson had published vivid descriptions both in his book, *Reise blandt norske Emigranter,* and in numerous letters to Norwegian newspapers. In a letter which appeared in *Bratsberg Amts Correspondent,* March 27, 1846, he writes:

> It is quite true . . . that the most important lack among the Norwegian emigrants is adequate church facilities and spiritual guidance from good and competent pastors endowed with with Christian strength and firmness in matters of ritual. . . . But it is likewise true that the economic condition of the Norwegian settlers is such that it is in no way correct to affirm, as Nærum does, that these ministers would be able to make a modest let alone satisfactory living for themselves, unless the churches of the emigrants receive support from their native country.[16]

And in his appeal to young clergymen in Norway to go as ministers to the Norwegian settlements in America, Dietrichson was quite frank in stating the almost superhuman qualities "to be looked for in the one who is to hold his own on the battlefield of controversy that awaits every honest Lutheran minister over there." [17] Both with regard to economic worries and with regard to controversy, some of the pastors—including Dietrichson himself—got more than they bargained for.

There can be no doubt that the great majority of the Norwegian settlers were quite happy and pleased with the arrival of the ordained pastors from Norway and highly appreciative of their work. In fact, to some if not most, it undoubtedly was a matter of prestige over their Haugean and Eielsenian neighbors to have a "real" pastor and a "proper" ritual as well as a "cultured" atmosphere in the parsonage. Even a hundred years later—and thirty years after the formation of a unified Norwegian-American Lutheran Church—when I was doing sociological studies of Norwegian settlements in Wisconsin and Minnesota, I found few exceptions to the rule that congregations and churches which formerly belonged to the Norwegian Synod claimed the highest prestige in the communities.

But to the Synod pastors, Eielsen and his followers remained a thorn, if not in the flesh, at least in the mind, particularly in the older settlements. And worse trouble was to come from elements within the congregations, who were no less fierce in their independence and no less sensitive to anything that smacked of "pastoral overlordship" than the radical Haugeans were, and far more impious in their modes of expression. Some of them were heavy drinkers, for which the Norwegians had won a probably well-deserved reputation in the settlements. This, however, was only part of the trouble and may have been more a symptom than a cause of a problem which, again, obviously had deep roots in the struggle of the Norwegian peasants for emancipation from an inferior social status, reinforced by vague and downright naïve concepts of American "freedom."

To these rowdy elements, as to the radical Haugeans, the very presence in the settlement of a Norwegian professional minister and his family, with their refined manners, speech, and dress, seems to have been a constant source of irritation and was even felt by some to be a threat to their newly won freedom. Obviously, it was a constant reminder of the settlers' own lowly origin, a thing that they had hoped to leave behind and forget about in the new country. Among these elements an attitude of supersensitive suspicion was present, in which the pastor's efforts to establish church order on the basis of ministerial authority easily were construed to be just another attempt to keep the common people "in their place." On this point, the Eielsen people and the rowdy elements—strange bedfellows as they were—indirectly encouraged and reinforced each other. In many congregations opposition groups were formed, which sought to create obstacles and hurdles for the pastor and his work. Often the pastor was exposed to abuse and name calling, and in a few settlements it even came to harassments, badgerings, and disturbances of the peace.

Johan W. C. Dietrichson appears to have had more than his fair share of this. Maybe it was because he was the first professional theologian and churchman to "stride into the comparative quiet of Muskego," where nevertheless the moderate Haugeans had rejected Eielsen and then refused to join the Norwegian Synod. Maybe the rowdy elements of Dietrichson's congregation at Koshkonong were more rowdy than most. Or maybe Dietrichson himself really was more imperious than most of his colleagues and therefore more provoking to his rowdy elements. Whatever the reason, Dietrichson fought an almost continuous battle against members of his congregation, was viciously attacked by an anonymous writer in the newspaper *Nordlyset,* and had the incredible experience of having a flagrant disturber of the peace acquitted in the courts of Dane County on the basis of a defense which declared "that the pastor, his congregation, and the Lutheran Church as a whole were a menace to our blessed freedom." [18]

But similar conditions prevailed in a number of other settlements, maybe in most of them, although they did not break out in the open to the same degree as they did at Koshkonong. Caja Munch's letters are revealing in this respect and are supported by Pastor Munch's own statements about the conditions in Wiota. And according to Pastor Munch, conditions were not much better in G. F. Dietrichson's congregation at Rock Prairie, which is confirmed by contemporary newspaper reports of disorders and vandalism both in and outside the churches at Luther Valley (Rock Prairie) and Jefferson Prairie.[19] Even the mild-mannered Olaus Duus stated that he was about to "become too satiated with all this lauded freedom and vulgarity," and although he personally had "no real ground for complaint, . . . it is exasperating to see so much ugliness prevailing here and hindering my ministry." [20] From Coon Prairie somewhat later we hear that A. C. Preus had troubles and "much disturbance" from drunkards as well as from lay preachers who "thundered against the State Church pastors with the long cassocks." [21]

The seriousness of the problems connected with the misconceived but widespread notions of "freedom" in the settlements is indicated by the fact that the editors of the Norwegian newspaper *Emigranten,* who saw it as one of their chief concerns to enlighten the Norwegian immigrants about conditions in the new country, found it necessary off and on to publish lengthy discussions of "the true nature and significance of freedom," in which attempts are made to explain to the readers the difference between "freedom under law and order" on the one hand and "license" on the other.[22] For the pastors who tried to introduce ecclesiastical law and order in the congregations, the situation was further aggravated by the fact that even the courts sometimes sided with the rowdy elements, acquitting obvious disturbers of the peace or even imposing fines on the pastor for trying to keep hecklers and disturbers out of his church during services, all in the name of "freedom." [23]

This was the general situation which was entered in the fall of 1855 by Pastor J. St. Munch and his young bride Caja, née Falch.

Caja Michaeline Falch was born August 14, 1830, at Hovland, near Larvik—or, as it was then called, Laurvig—in the County of Jarlsberg and Laurvig (now Vestfold) in the southern part of Norway. She died at Bestum, near Christiania (now Oslo), May 17, 1898. Her father was Friderich Wilhelm Stabel Falch (1807–59), proprietor and small shipowner, who had inherited the two adjacent farms,

Hovland and Faret, from his father, *Amtsforvalter* (County Adminis-trator) Michael Falch (1777–1838). Her mother was Thalie Falch, née Staffeldt (1809–87), a daughter of Bernhard Ditlev von Staffeldt (1753–1818), German-born officer in the Norwegian army, who had distinguished himself in war with Sweden, had advanced to the rank of lieutenant general, but was accused of treasonous conduct in the campaign of 1814, was sentenced to death by a controversial Supreme Court decision, and finally pardoned.

Caja was the oldest child in a large family of thirteen sons and daughters. They lived in patrician family style at Hovland, a short distance from town, had servants, of course, and took part in the social life of Laurvig, a small but thriving business town. But the economy apparently was far from affluent in the Falch household, and at an early age Caja learned to play her role as "daughter in the house" with diligence, thrift, and prudence, assuming her part of the chores and helping to take care of, even to bring up, her younger sisters and brothers—a responsibility which she continued in moth-erly fashion to discharge by letter even after she had left home.

The Falchs did, however, afford a tutor, or "candidate," for their many children, and one of the young men serving in this capacity at Hovland was to become Caja's husband.

Johan Storm Munch was born in Christiansand, on the southern coast of Norway, October 21, 1827, and died at Bestum August 11, 1908. He came from a lineage with strong family traditions, in which three generations before him had served as ministers of the Church of Norway. His father was Bishop Johan Storm Munch (1778–1832), of Christiansand Diocese, and his uncle, Edvard Storm Munch (1780–1847, grandfather of the now famous painter Edvard Munch), was Dean of the Diocese of Christiania. His grandfather, Peter Munch (1740–1802), had been a prominent pastor in the rationalist tradition at Vaage in Gudbrandsdal, later at Land, and was married to a daughter of his own predecessor at Vaage, Pastor Johan Storm (1712–76), after whom Pastor Munch's father was named.

There were literary and scholarly traditions in the family as well, entirely in the highly patriotic tone of national romanticism, dating back to Pastor Peter Munch's brother-in-law, the poet Edvard Storm (1749–94), who was one of the first to write poetry in Nor-wegian rural dialect and to proclaim the Norwegian peasant as the true and direct cultural heir of Old Norse traditions. Pastor Munch's father, "the Bishop" as he was usually called in the family circle, was himself a poet in his own right, even tried his hand as a playwright, but is probably best-known as the founder, editor, and (to a large extent) writer of a quarterly called *Saga,* devoted to studies in Norwegian history and language in the national romantic style. In Pastor Munch's own generation, his older brother, Andreas Munch (1811–84), was by the middle of the century a well-established romantic poet, and his cousin was the well-known historian, Professor P. A. Munch (1810–63), who is generally regarded as the founder of Norwegian national historiography.

Also on his mother's side there were ecclesiastical traditions. Pastor Munch's mother, generally referred to as "the Bishopess," was Else Petronelle Munch, née Hofgaard (1790–1879), a daughter of Pastor Andreas Hofgaard (1756–1826), owner of the Fornebo estate near Christiania, who in turn was the son of Pastor Ambrosius Flor Hofgaard (1713–86).

Johan Storm Munch was the youngest of eight children, one of whom died in infancy. He was only four years old when his father died in January, 1832.

> I was too young to comprehend the immense loss that we suffered at the too early death of my kind and highly regarded father. He was only fifty-three and a half years old. We then had to move from Christiansand, and my mother was alone with five sons and two daughters, of whom the eldest—the poet, Andreas Munch—then was only a young university student. And yet, in my childish fancy, I imagined it would be wonderful to travel on a steamship and to get to "the big city" Christiania. Among other things, I remember that when I heard them tell that in our lodging there we were going to have *Fløidøre* (double-leaved doors), I made it out to be *Fløielsdøre* (velvet doors) and was looking forward to such magnificence! (*sancta simplicitas*).
>
> So we moved to Christiania, which at that time was still a small town. Our first apartment was in a house that stood in a *cul-de-sac* in *Øvre Slotsgade*. It was quite a modest house, and there certainly were no *Fløielsdøre,* which was a disappointment to me.[24]

Indeed, the Bishop's widow and her children lived in poverty in Christiania, although a small pension probably kept the hunger from the door most of the time. Pastor Munch relates that he once contracted a serious case of typhoid fever because his mother could not afford to buy him an overcoat and he was ashamed to wear his sister's cast-off cloak. And he recalls with some bitterness how his favorite brother Edvard had suffered from cold while earning a pittance as an errand boy for a storekeeper, had contracted "consumption," and was buried in a paupers' cemetery, which was later leveled and turned into a market square.

After having completed school, young Johan—not quite 18 at the time—was preparing to enter the university.

> But then a turning point occurred in my life. Mother had little to live on, and I felt the pressure of this; it was also hinted to me off and on that now I had to lend a hand myself. Mother had had a supplement of 200 *Spdlr* to her annual pension until I was 18 years old. Now this supplement no longer applied, and that was severely felt. Then a tutorial post was advertized near Laurvig. It paid only 70 *Spd*, but especially Caroline pressed on that I should apply as it was so wonderful down there with the beech forest, she said. Lieutenant Staffeldt [Mrs. Falch's brother] was to make the appointment. And so I got the job with Falch at Hovland. . . .
>
> It was in the early part of March 1846, that I took off with the diligence to Drammen and from there on to Hovland. It was an unusually early spring, with no snow. I was met midway and arrived in the evening at Falch's. I shall never forget that entrance! It teemed with youngsters, who peeked through the doors to get a glimpse of the "teacher," as I was called. The eldest daughter was then only between 15 and 16 and very shy. . . .
>
> I was now going to be a "teacher." But—apart from the eldest daughter—it was a real bunch of impossible youngsters I had to deal with (I will, however, also except Lagertha, who was fairly good). It was a strenuous work for a young man of eighteen, and I probably was not mature enough to take it on. . . .
>
> At Falch's one day went as the other. There were never any guests save the nearest family, Mrs. General Staffeldt and daughters, with the exception of a Christmas ball, where several people from town were invited. Now and then I went along to the Staffeldts, where the old Mrs. General, Mrs. Falch's mother, always gave me a friendly reception. Once in a while Lieutenant Staffeldt was there for a visit, and then we played chess.

Already before this first visit to Hovland—obviously it was not the last—young Munch had decided to follow in the footsteps of his forefathers. He was to take up theology "according to tradition" although at that time he "did not actually feel a calling" for the ministry. He was, however, a serious young man, and while at Hovland he spent much time in deep meditation and self-examination.

> As far as my inner life is concerned, I was then rather vague about myself. I had read Kierkegaard and had particularly imprinted deeply in my heart his statement about the ethical point of view, which normally should be a transitional link from the aesthetic to the Christian-religious view. This appealed to me. I was going to lead an "ethical" life since I did not yet comprehend the life of faith. It was especially in the fall and the beginning of the winter of '46 that I got into this direction. I was going to live strictly according to the code of ethics in my innermost thought as well as in my outward life. I watched every word I spoke and kept a strict account of my daily life. For this reason I kept a diary, in which I wrote down in the evening everying that had moved inside me during the day. However, the prayer was only weak, although I did pray, but my own will power was going to do most of it. I was in the most literal sense under the law, but had no comprehension of grace. I tried to establish my own righteousness and did not have an eye for what I owed to Jesus as Savior and Redeemer. I certainly believed in Him and in what I had learned at school, and there was no thought of doubt or disbelief. But my faith was only an historical regarding-as-true, nothing more. I know that I meant it seriously; but of course, I got nowhere. There was no growth of life because there actually was no life.
> I kept this up for some time into the winter. But little by little I became laxer, neglected the diary now and then as well as the strict self-examination—and slid gradually back into the previous "aesthetic" carefree life, especially since there was no influence whatsoever from without in the direction of Christian earnest. The church here [at Hovland] is five miles away, besides there was an old, slack minister who would not be able to help me. I read in Wallin's Sermons, which they had in the house, but their flowery language had little effect on me. Kierkegaard's "Either—Or" was my favorite reading.

Munch was well-gifted and had always been at the top of his class in school. But lack of money and ill-health, including another attack of nervous fever, delayed his theological studies. On account of his widow mother's financial situation, which continued to be extremely difficult, he spent several years as a schoolteacher or as a tutor to children of patrician and professional families in the country.

This included two years at a girls' school in Christiania (which bored him) and another year with the Falchs at Hovland (which didn't). It was during this second year at Hovland, 1849–50, that he became engaged to Caja Falch.

Finally, in 1855 he finished his studies for the ministry, received a call from Wiota and Dodgeville congregations in Wisconsin, was ordained by Bishop Arup in Christiania, got married, and sailed for America. He had to borrow money for his fare from his father-in-law.

The settlement where the Munchs were to set up residence for the next few years was Wiota, in Lafayette County, also known at that time as Hamilton's Diggings, or simply Hamilton, named after Colonel William Stephen Hamilton, Alexander Hamilton's youngest son, who started lead mining in the area in 1828. Some time in the 1840's the place was named Wiota, presumably by Hamilton himself. But the old name stuck for some time.

To the Norwegians in the southern Wisconsin settlements, Hamilton's Diggings soon became an important stopping place, where newcomers could earn some money in the lead mines before settling down as farmers. In his "guide-book" for Norwegian emigrants, Reiersen encourages this.

> In the lead-mining region, which comprises parts of Illinois, Missouri, Iowa, and Wisconsin, the foremost opportunity is to engage in active business as diggers, miners, and smelters. Wages range according to ability, and vary from fifteen to forty dollars a month, besides board. At a place in Wisconsin called Wiota, I discovered some Scandinavians who mined partly on their own account and partly for others. At the smelting-shack there, which belonged to a Colonel Hamilton, there were only Norwegians, who earned between twenty and twenty-five dollars a month and board.[25]

In his official report of 1847 to the government of Norway concerning Norwegian settlements in America, Consul General Adam Løvenskjold lists "Hamilton, or Wiota," where "there is now a little settlement of about ten or twelve families from Voss and Sogn."[26] It was a small and transient population, unstable in more than one sense—surely not the best foundation for the establishment of an organized and orderly church. This was clearly recognized by Pastor Clausen, who was the first Lutheran minister to work also in this area. On February 13, 1844, he gave the first two Lutheran services in the settlement, "in the morning in K. Knudsen's house in

Wiota, and in the afternoon in Peder Davidsen's house about 5 miles from Wiota."[27] But he did not, for various reasons, attempt to organize a congregation there.

There is a report that at this time a joint Letter of Call was issued by several smaller settlements in southern Wisconsin, including Hamilton, offering a minister's salary of three hundred dollars besides a parsonage and eighty acres or even a quarter section (160 acres) of land. This Letter of Call, which is supposed to have originated in Wiota, is said to have been submitted to Bishop Sørensen of Christiania and is claimed to be the first Letter of Call to be sent to Norway from any Norwegian settlement in America. Reiersen reports this to have happened during his visit (he spent Christmas 1843 in Wiota), and Holand dates it on the basis of oral tradition in the congregation to February 1844, adding that the action was initiated by Knud Knudsen, blacksmith in Wiota and a prominent person in the settlement, who was the first emigrant from Drammen, Norway, in 1839. Holand's account places the drafting of the letter exactly at the time and place ("K. Knudsen's house") where Clausen gave his first divine service in Wiota. However, no official record or document has been found either in Norway or in the United States to confirm the report, and particularly since the event is not mentioned by Clausen in his official record of developments in Wiota, the authenticity of the report remains doubtful, in spite of support from Reiersen's contemporary account.[28]

Later that same year (1844) J. W. C. Dietrichson, who was more aggressive than Clausen, and also perhaps more optimistic, "took the initial step toward laying the foundation" (Clausen's cautious words) of a Norwegian Lutheran congregation in Wiota. This was done by presenting the following "general conditions" which had to be accepted by each one who wished to become a member:

1. Do you wish to belong to the Norwegian-Lutheran congregation here?
2. Will you submit to the church order determined by the Ritual of our Church of Norway?
3. Will you accept and recognize the rightly called and properly ordained Norwegian-Lutheran minister who becomes your soul curate as your ecclesiastical authority in what he requests in accordance with the Ritus of the Church of Norway, your Fatherland?
[4.] Will you by signing your name here, or by having it signed,

acknowledge that you enter the congregation as a member on the above conditions? [29]

Thus organized, the congregation issued in November 1845 a Letter of Call to "the permanent minister and soul curate of the Norwegian-Lutheran congregation at Rock Prairie, Rock County, W.T." to serve Wiota six times a year for a payment of six dollars each time. This Letter of Call, according to Clausen, was signed by each member on joining the congregation and was submitted to Clausen after he had decided to move to Rock Prairie, probably in 1846. It was a five-year appointment, with certain restrictions.

> Should the congregation at this place prior to the expiration of the five-year period find itself satisfied to be served by the Rock Prairie pastor less than the stipulated six visits, then 6 dollars shall be deducted for each of the visits thus eliminated, and if the congregation is pleased not to have the pastor come at all they have the right to discontinue his services with the stipulation that the pastor shall be notified at least two months before the contemplated change is made.[30]

Indeed, it looked like a rather reluctant "call" to say the least! Although he must have had his doubts about the future of this congregation, Clausen accepted the call as of June 24, 1846. But the relationship did not last through his stay at Rock Prairie. It was discontinued by Clausen himself for reasons which he has conscientiously entered in the Church Record.

> In the spring of 1845 the congregation had 95 members, children included, but in the course of the summer that year, so many went away that for a time it had only a little more than 50 members. . . . Not only was the congregation very small from the beginning, but it consisted for the most part of members whose sojourn in this settlement was quite uncertain and usually of short duration, and there was reason to fear that if the lead-digging, with which the livelihood of most was directly connected, should cease, then both the settlement and the congregation would soon also cease to exist or at least become too few in number to carry the necessary expenses for visits by the pastor. This fear might perhaps gradually fade away as it appeared that the settlement was increasing each year and gaining a more stable character by the fact that many new emigrants arrived from Norway and settled down there as farmers. However, these new arrivals did not hasten to join the congregation. Besides, there was another fear which soon, with good reason, was in evidence, namely,

that churchly order would end there because of the complete
indifference, even resistance, on the part of the members to
every means and step for the promotion and confirmation of
true Christianity and churchly order among them. Also, there
was an altogether too general and prevalent addiction to
drunkenness and other vices therewith connected.

They could not agree to conduct a religious school, although
this gradually appeared to be uncommonly necessary. . . .
Not infrequently the contention was expressed that if the
pastor wanted the children to receive the religious training
of our Church, then he would have to get the books translated
into the English language, catechize and confirm the children
in English, etc., etc. On the whole, the members showed a
total indifference for the Christian teaching of the youth,
which the pastor certainly had their permission to promote,
but without any help being rendered or any burden or expense being assumed by those concerned.

A house for the people to gather for divine service and common prayer was also badly needed in this congregation, and
the people themselves felt this need insofar as they repeatedly
held meetings for the purpose of deciding upon the erection
of a church edifice among them. But even these attempts broke
down because of their mutual repugnancy, the people dividing
into different parties, each wanting the church built at their
place and with their own materials, and no one wanting to
yield to the other.

The payments for my visits were also presented with great
irregularity.

In a nucleus, here were all the problems present which were to
tear the Norwegian Lutheran Church in America asunder in continuous struggle and strife for decades, nay, generations to come. A
hundred years later, looking at the early history of this congregation,
a prominent churchman remarked:

Here you have the problems involved in transiency, with
us today on a more massive scale than ever before; alcoholism,
not country club style, but lead-mine and lumber-jack style;
here is "America fever" running wild; here the language problem with a vengeance; here the reactions of the "newcomer"
being withdrawn from close fellowship with his own and exposed to the propaganda and the proselytizations of a mixed
community.[31]

At a meeting on November 11, 1849, Pastor Clausen presented
the Wiota congregation with an ultimatum. He would not visit the
congregation again until the most pressing needs had been recog-

nized, steps had been taken to establish a religious school and to erect a church, and the congregation's debts to the pastor had been paid. Evidently, this was his last visit to Wiota.

Such were the shaky beginnings of the Norwegian-Lutheran congregation at Hamilton's Diggings. After Pastor Clausen had severed relations with this troublesome "annex parish," there is no evidence that it was visited by any pastor for almost five years. Although the pastors of the Synod frequently went on "mission trips" to congregations who were without a resident minister, this place appears to have been shunned by all.

However, in 1851, without the aid of a pastor, the congregation came to life. On February 7 that year, the congregation was incorporated in accordance with the Incorporation Act of the State of Wisconsin, and a Board of Trustees was elected, with one Ole Knudsen as Over-Trustee, all duly entered on the first page of a new minute book entitled:

RECORD

*for Den Norske Evangeliske Lutherske kirke
og Menighed i og omkring Wiota, Laffayett County, State of
Wisconsin.*

The first concern of this newly reorganized and apparently revitalized congregation was the building of a church. The opening paragraph of the By Laws ELLER REGLEMANG (Bylaws or Regulations) adopted February 15, 1851, reads as follows in its poorly spelt Norwegian mixed with English:

§ 1th

*Beslutet at Vi ufortövet Skride til opretelsen af en kirke
Bÿgning eller Mitting Hus.*

In translation: "Decided that we forthwith take steps toward the erection of a Church Edifice or Meeting House." And subsequent paragraphs give detailed directions concerning the size of the church and the organization and financing of the work. Even deadlines for completing the work are incorporated in the "bylaws." One paragraph reads: "The church shall be started by the master mason on the 15th April and shall be finished by same by the 15th June, 1851. The rest shall be completed by the 1st August next."

Financing of the work was done by voluntary subscriptions, and what more was needed was assessed against each member according to the value of his property. The amounts subscribed and assessed could be paid in cash or rendered in the form of material or labor, and meticulous records were kept of the contributions of each. The whole bears witness to a community spirit which is really amazing in a settlement that used to consist of transient sojourners. By this time (1851) the center of the mining activities seems to have moved to the area around Mineral Point and Dodgeville,[32] and we get the impression from the Wiota Church Record that the majority of the 83 original subscribers are settled farmers rather than miners, and most of them probably family heads, which would give the congregation a total membership of some estimated 250 or more. It is quite understandable that the reading of these records could bring a present-day pastor to the following eulogy:

When it is read that the cost of the church was $933 . . . and measure dollar value then and now, the effort made today is puny and small. Think of it—men who labored on the church building and [were credited] $1.56 for 2½ days labor, and then subscribed $40 to the building. Another man received $3.12½ for 5 days labor and subscribed and paid in full for the church fund the sum of $30. No other explanation for this can be entered, save the fact that they realized their need, and [that] of their children, of a place to worship their Creator and feel the fellowship of their Savior, for which no cost was too great.[33]

Unfortunately, the enthusiasm was not of long enough duration to complete the work. When the Munchs arrived in the fall of 1855, the church was not yet finished.

The next problem, of course, was to get a pastor to serve the congregation. That proved to be not an easy task. Not that they did not try. According to the Church Records, Pastor Stub had been approached. He was then probably quite unhappy with the Haugean elements at Muskego and later moved to Coon Prairie. But a Letter of Call drafted by Stub was rejected by the Wiota congregation because his requirements were too stiff, particularly with regard to the erection of a parsonage. Attempts were made to get together with the Dodgeville settlements further north and particularly with the nearby Blue Mounds settlement for the purpose of getting a pastor from Norway, and it was decided to do this by writing directly to Norway rather than going through the Church Council of the Norwegian Synod. At one point it was even considered writing to Professor W. M. Reynolds, of Capital University in Columbus, Ohio, to inquire about the possibility and costs of having a Scandinavian trained for the ministry there. Capital University belonged to a German Lutheran body known as the Ohio Synod.

From the days of Pastor Clausen, Wiota was vaguely considered an "annex parish" to Rock Prairie, and that congregation had recently been taken over by Gustav F. Dietrichson, who arrived from Norway in 1851. He, too, however, was apparently quite reluctant to serve the ill-reputed congregation of Wiota. In the Record for the "annex parishes," which had been begun by Clausen and was still kept at Luther Valley, the parsonage at Rock Prairie, we find the following entry in Dietrichson's unmistakable (and almost illegible) handwriting:

> After repeated requests from Hamilton Congregation, I finally decided to take over temporarily the management of this congregation and conducted divine service there for the first time on the Sixth Sunday after Epiphany, 1854.

According to an entry in the Wiota Church Records (also in Dietrichson's handwriting), the pastor agreed to serve the congregation until June 24, 1855.

It was probably Dietrichson who persuaded the Wiota congregation to decide on the building of a parsonage. He also took effective steps to procure a pastor from Norway and had announcements placed in Norwegian newspapers. In this effort the Wiota congregation went together with the recently organized congregation at Dodgeville. Dietrichson was then a member of the Church Council of the Norwegian Synod, and it may be assumed that he was instrumental in bringing the Wiota congregation "back into the fold" by having a Letter of Call issued through the Synod rather than independently, although the congregation had not yet formally joined the Synod.

These were the events which in the end led to a Letter of Call being issued to Pastor Johan St. Munch. It is dated *Luther Walley* [sic] *Præstegaard*, Wisconsin, January 18, 1855, and is signed by the members of the Church Council, Pastors A. C. Preus (Chairman), G. F. Dietrichson, and H. A. Preus, and by Lay Members Lars Josephsen Lie, I. Ingebrigtsen, and H. Ommelstad.[34]

Pastor Munch and his young bride had in the meantime arrived safely in Beloit. There they were picked up by Dietrichson with his landau and taken to the Luther Valley parsonage, where they spent some time resting before they continued on to Wiota. Pastor Munch recalls:

> One late fall evening—driven by Dietrichson—we arrived in Wiota after having traveled a horrible road. But the parsonage . . . was far from finished. So they had rented space for us with a neighbor, a grumpy old bachelor from Land. . . . He was staying below in the basement and fried bacon morning, noon, and evening, so we had the smell of it almost all day—very refreshing.

It was a widely dispersed charge that was given to Pastor Munch. Wiota and Dodgeville were about twenty-five miles apart, and each of them consisted actually of several smaller settlements. Pastor Munch reminisces that "had I had an idea of the distance over the desolate prairies, I would surely not have gone there."

The Wiota settlement was located in the township of the same name, in Lafayette County. The old stone church, which is still standing and is now referred to as the "East Church," is situated near the present U.S. Highway 78, about three miles east of the unincorporated town of Wiota. The old parsonage used to be just across the road from the church.

Further north was the Yellowstone settlement, also in Lafayette County, occupying parts of Argyle and Blanchard Townships between the Yellowstone River and the East Branch of the Peccatonica River (just east of the present Yellowstone Lake). Then there was the "Halling Settlement," so named because of the preponderance of settlers from Hallingdal in Norway, which was situated in Cadiz and Jordan Townships, Green County, north of the present town of Browntown. During Munch's stay at Wiota this settlement was organized into an "annex parish" under the name of Jordan. In addition to these settlements, Munch also served a small settlement in the northern part of Adams Township, Green County, west of the Daugherry Creek.

Even in the Dodgeville area were several small Norwegian settlements, which were here more interspersed among other nationalities. There seems to have been a concentration of Norwegians in and around the little town of Linden, northwest of Mineral Point, and another one north of Dodgeville, between the two tributaries to the Wisconsin River, Otter Creek and Mill Creek. Once a month, Munch made a trip "to Dodgeville"—actually he hardly ever went to the town itself but mostly stayed in Linden. The first trip up there was made on a lumber wagon and was Pastor Munch's first experience with this contraption, which Caja describes as "looking just about like our box carts, but twice as long and with four wheels—we sit on a board with our arms around each other to keep from falling out, and the shaking is terrible." Later he was able to afford a young mare of his own and "a wretched old buggy, which often needed repair."

About the people in these settlements, Pastor Munch did not have flattering words, and his memories confirm the testimony of the unfinished church that the flash of community spirit that had suddenly made its appearance four years earlier was indeed of short duration.

> It had been very difficult to procure a minister for them as there were some less desirable elements that prevailed there. . . . Around the little spot Wiota were mostly people from Land, who were fairly civilized but not very cordial. In Yellowstone, there was a drunkenness that was horrible because the annex parish Lynner [now Lunner] in Hadeland had sent their worst drunkards there. They had even got people to join the congregation by going around serving them drinks! The best conditions prevailed in the Halling Settlement, where many from Krydsherred [now Krødsherad] and Numedal were living, and where I had my best friends. For all these mutually dispersed and discordant settlements and elements was I, young man as I was, now to be a pastor!

Norwegian peasants had a strong feeling of identity with their local districts or *Bygdelag*, which might even override their national identity. This probably had a connection with the extreme isolation of rural communities in Norway, mainly because of the topographical conditions of the country, with uninhabited mountain ranges separating one district from the other. When these peasants settled down in the Middle West, they had a tendency to flock together not only with fellow Norwegians but with people from their own valley or their own local district. In this way some rather well-integrated, homogeneous settlements could be formed.

Not so around Wiota. Here came people from all parts of Norway to earn some money in the lead mines. Although most of them moved on to other settlements, some lingered in the area, with the result that the settlements around Wiota were probably more "mixed" than most Norwegian settlements in the Middle West. There were indeed pockets of settlers from Land, Hadeland, and Hallingdal; but these were too small to be self-sufficient in any form of community organization, and to bring these "mutually discordant elements" of fiercely independent settlers together in any durable form of cooperation proved to be a formidable task.

> Before my arrival they had been divided into parties in that the various *Bygdelag* did not accord. . . . There had been a big quarrel both about the parsonage and about the church, and one party stood against the other. . . . They had claimed a piece of woodland far away; but an Irishman also laid claim to it as his and had threatened to "kil" anybody who came there to cut. For revenge he had put fire to a good deal of lumber that the congregation had bought for the parsonage.
> In all this mess I now got involved. It certainly was not easy. But I had a good supporter in my dear wife—had I not had her, I would surely have left very soon.

Pastor Munch took up with considerable vigor the task of bringing order into the "mess" that he had entered. Much of his effort was motivated by the desire to preserve the religious, spiritual, and cultural heritage of the Old Country on American soil. This, apparently, was not so much an "issue" to him as it was a matter of course, an obligation that he felt, not only as an ordained minister of the Church of Norway but particularly as a member of the cultured professional class. On this point he shared the view of the rest of the early Norwegian Synod pastors and their concern for their countrymen who, in the pastors' opinion, abandoned and even denied their personal and cultural identity in a misguided attempt to find freedom and independence. To him, as to many others even outside the little circle of Synod pastors, awareness of national identity "must be as dear to every Norwegian living here, and to his descendants, as the awareness of his personal freedom," as he wrote later in an article in *Emigranten.* In this he was vividly supported by his wife, who frequently in her letters expressed disgust with the Norwegian settlers who were so quick to imitate the crude "Yankee manners," peppered their language with English words, and Anglicized their names as if to conceal rather than assert their identity. To the culturally and intellectually more sophisticated immigrants, freedom and identity were inseparable and complementary values. What Munch and the other Synod pastors were trying to do was not to combat the values and achievements of the American society, as they were often accused of doing, but simply to provide leadership and guidance in filling what they considered a cultural vacuum. That this leadership and guidance, for the time being at least, had to be offered in the Norwegian language was to them a matter of expediency rather than of principle. The important matter to them was the content of the cultural tradition rather than its form.[35]

Surely, like most of the high-church Synod pastors—indeed, like most of the professional elite in Norway—Pastor Munch looked with concern upon the mass migration to America. In 1857, during the severe economic crisis of that year, he wrote in a letter to his mother that "it is *madness* that so many emigrate; thorn and thistle grow as abundantly here as in Norway." And he blasted the newspaper *Aftenbladet* in Christiania and its editor, Ditmar Meidell, who previously had showered the world-famous violinist Ole Bull's colonization project in Pennsylvania with satire but now was taking a more liberal stand on emigration.

However, although Munch was critical of certain aspects of American customs and social life and mildly amused at others, he did not have an all-out negative attitude to America. On the contrary, with all his warm patriotism for Norway, he found much to admire in this "fermenting and unsettled" new nation.

For one thing, he was strongly in favor of a free church in contrast to the situation in Norway, "where the Church slumbers sweetly in the arms of the State"—an attitude which came to full expression in his later life, when he became an admirer of the American revivalist and free church protagonist Dwight Moody and eventually (1875) broke with the State Church of Norway, establishing himself as a celebrated evangelist in Christiania.

But he had no patience with those who confused liberty with license, be it in moral, theological, or organizational matters. He was as staunch a proponent of professional ministerial authority and ecclesiastical order as any of the other Synod pastors at the time. It was almost inevitable, therefore, that he should get into conflict with the rowdy elements of his congregation with their unsophisticated concept of "freedom" and high sensitivity to any form of authority imported from the Old Country.[36]

It is characteristic that one of the first issues to be taken up by Pastor Munch in Wiota was that of a Norwegian school. This was before the time of the great school controversy among the Norwegians in America. But to the immigrants who, like the Munchs, had benefited from the rather advanced school system and high level of education in Norway, the inefficiency of the American common school was quite evident. To the Munchs there was living proof of it right at their doorstep, for a schoolhouse was located close to the Wiota church, and Caja Munch writes about the absence of discipline and lack of respect for material as well as ethical values displayed by the children, who "do not know what it is to respect their parents," adding with sarcasm that "they live in a free country, and they are supposed to have freedom to do as they please."

Munch seems to have visualized something more than a Sunday school to teach the "Catechism" and the "Explanation." His school was to have a broader base, something on the order of the early rural "ambulatory schools" of Norway, where a number of teachers would move around from one community to the other holding classes, now here, then there. Financing of the teachers' salaries was to be sought through a special subscription which was not to be limited to the congregation—attempts were made to interest Norwegians living in Monroe in the project as well.

Already in December 1855—a couple of months after Munch's arrival—Peder Fenne, a member of the Wiota congregation, was "called" temporarily to be precentor and schoolteacher, a combination of functions that used to be common in the rural areas of Norway. But the ambition was to have the position filled by a *Seminarist,* that is, a person trained at a *Seminarium* or teachers' college in Norway. In August 1856, it was decided in a congregation meeting that one "Seminarist Hans Olsen from Sandvær" was to be "called" to the position. This, apparently, had negative results, and for a while Munch was teaching school himself until Peder Fenne was reappointed and later replaced by two other members of the congregation, Iver Fenne and Hans Schjager.[37] In January 1858, we find three teachers, who received a remuneration of twelve to fourteen dollars a month each. At that time another attempt was made to get a trained teacher. A meeting of the congregation decided unanimously to announce the position of precentor and schoolteacher in *Emigranten* as well as in Norwegian dailies and at the same time to write to one Ole Andreassen Rødbergsæteren, asking him to apply.[38] Even this attempt appears to have been in vain.

If Munch had moderate success with the school (at least he got it started), his attempts to bring order into the economic and financial affairs of his congregations met with utter frustration. The issue

centered around the problem of firm organization which was indeed
an essential part of what all the early Synod pastors meant by
"churchly order." Pastor Munch seems to have gone about this task
with the same vigor as he did in the school case. During his first year
at Wiota, he had ten meetings of the congregation or its elected
trustees. Soon after his arrival, a committee of twelve was appointed
to meet with the pastor and work out a proposal for new bylaws,
which were adopted by the congregation December 1, 1856, and
contained detailed provisions concerning the privileges and obligations of the members and their elected officers, particularly in financial affairs, including provisions for dealing with members who were
delinquent in their payments of assessed or subscribed contributions.
Quite significant is the opening paragraph of these new bylaws.

> § 1. Only the outer, secular affairs concerning the congrega-
> tion shall be dealt with in the Congregation Meetings and be
> ruled by these Bylaws. All else is submitted to the Congrega-
> tion Council (that is, the Pastor and his Assistants) and the
> Norwegian-Lutheran Synod for decision, presuming that the
> congregation joins the Synod.

Obviously, here is an attempt to distinguish between, and to
separate the domains of, a *verdslig Øvrighed* (secular authority) and
a *geistlig Øvrighed* (ecclesiastical authority), a distinction which has
been rigidly adhered to in the State Church of Norway as a safeguard
against government interference in church affairs, particularly in the
professional theological matters of doctrine and ritual. This distinction has generally worked well under the firm and centralized organization of the State Church. Under the loose congregational organization of the fermenting new settlements in America, with their strong
emphasis on local and individual self-determination, it did pose some
problems.

Pastor Munch soon learned—if he did not know it already—that
passing a new law or introducing new rules was not enough to
establish a well-structured organization among a group of basically
individualistic and mutually repugnant Norwegians still under the
intoxication of their newly won freedom. At the outset, of course,
everything went well, and in November 1855, only a few weeks after
their arrival, Caja Munch writes home that "Munch will, if we can
judge from our short stay so far, get along very nicely with his
congregation. . . . It is pleasant to see how peaceable they are, and
Munch gets approval of everything he wants." However, getting

approval is one thing, getting it done is quite another, as young Caja bitterly recognized when, about a year later, she wrote: "Promising is honest, but keeping is hard."

Within the first year of Munch's stay in Wiota, it became evident that the congregation was either unable or unwilling to meet its obligations to the pastor. "He is not at all getting from the congregation what they promised him. . . . They come and tell us that they are so poor and that they do not have anything, so what can the minister do?" However, there had already been indications that this was not only an economic problem, that it was part of a tension that was building up between the pastor and the rather predominant rowdy elements of his congregation.

Pastor Munch recalls that once he had a bad throat and could not officiate for three Sundays, and

> as an example of the rowdiness of some people in the congregation I can mention that when the sexton, the worthy Per Fenne, prayed for me in the church, where he was going to read a sermon, someone in the audience shouted: "Aw, pray for yourself, you miserable wretch!" Pretty!

In this connection, complaints had been voiced—the church records do not reveal how or by whom—about the pastor neglecting *his* obligations to the congregation by missing services, "and as the Pastor could not accept this complaint, he declared that he resigned as the Congregation's Minister as of June 24, 1857, unless the complaint was withdrawn or the complainers were expelled from the Congregation." [39]

There is no record of any action taken by the congregation in response to this declaration, which seemed rather harsh in relation to the relatively mild complaint. It is obvious that the accusation had touched Pastor Munch's professional pride as a conscientious minister of the church. But in the end he did not resign this time.

It is apparent, however, that the tension was steadily increasing, and it became more evident as time went on that the main issue was the extent and limit of ministerial authority. Caja Munch tells about a man "who was wealthy and had great influence," that he "always tried to harm Munch and opposed him on every occasion; finally he became a Methodist, but even so, out of love for his countrymen, as he explained, he had to attend their congregation meetings to give them guidance so that the minister should not get too much power over them." [40]

Pastor Munch had originally agreed to serve the congregation for five years, and he felt himself bound by this agreement in spite of the congregation's delinquency in the payment of his salary, which put him in a difficult economic position and made it impossible for him to pay his debt to his father-in-law. One important consideration appears to have been his own professional reputation in Norway as well as in America. But in May 1857 a plan was developed by Munch and Dietrichson, whereby Munch would spend the last year of his contract, 1859–60, at Rock Prairie, taking care of Dietrichson's congregations as well as his own (or what was left of them by then), while Dietrichson would go to Norway in search of replacement for both charges.[41]

The following summer, however, it came to a crisis. The following entry in the Church Records is in Munch's handwriting but is signed, as usual, by the trustees of the congregation.

> Year 1857, the 15th June, a regular Congregation Meeting was held in the church, where the following items were discussed (the meeting was conducted by Pastor G. F. Dietrichson as chairman):
>
> *1)* Pastor Munch presented a complaint to the effect that the congregations in Wiota and Dodgeville had not met their obligations—unanimously adopted: *The Congregation must admit that neither this nor the Dodgeville Congregations have met the obligations which are contained in the Letter of Call.*
>
> 2) The Congregation was then repeatedly urged to declare if it had found any faults with Pastor Munch's discharge of his office as a whole, that is, as a preacher, as a soul curate, and as an administrant of the Sacraments—whereupon *unanimously* was adopted: *The Congregation hereby declares that Pastor Munch as a preacher, a soul curate, and an administrant of the Sacraments in every respect has worked as behooves a faithful and zealous servant of the Lord.*

After thus having established that the contract contained in the Letter of Call had been unilaterally broken by the congregation, Pastor Munch declared that he regarded the Letter of Call as void.

> 3) . . . and as his economic condition does not permit him to remain any longer with his charge unless a change to the better occurs, he must resign his office as of June 24, 1858, unless by that time a new congregation is formed which offers, and pledges itself, to pay what is needed so that the minister will not be forced to leave it.

At the same time, the congregation was informed of a "charity offering" from all five of Dietrichson's congregations in the amount of $188.90, which alone made it possible for Pastor Munch to stay another year—without it he would have had to resign by June 24, 1857.

This confrontation was obviously designed and well prepared by Pastor Munch. The opposition seems to have been taken by surprise. Unaccustomed as they were to public appearance, and inept in polished diction, they evidently preferred to acquiesce rather than to take up a debate with the eloquent pastor. The meeting decided "with great majority" to issue a new Letter of Call, which was to be signed by every confirmed member of the congregation, and six men were "unanimously elected" to canvass the settlements for signatures. It was also decided that only those who signed would be regarded as members, which in fact made it practically impossible to dissent.

The result of the canvass must have been passably satisfactory, for at a Congregation Meeting November 9, 1857, Pastor Munch declared himself willing to accept a call for another year, beginning June 24, 1858, provided no other pastor could be found by that time to serve the congregation. His conditions were that the congregation pay its debt to him by January 1, and that Yellowstone (the drunkards' nest) be set off as a separate congregation.

It may have been about this time that Munch thought he had "pulled the poison-fangs" of the opposition, as he expressed himself in a letter to Norway (now lost). In his memoirs, he writes that he has "nothing of note" to tell about the following winter, 1857–58. "Clouds, however, were gathering in the congregation, which did not prognosticate anything good. . . . Yet, so far it was only smouldering, and the winter passed in relative calm."

One problem, however, was the increasing number of people who resigned from membership in the congregation or—even worse —let their memberships lapse in apparent indifference. In January 1858, Caja Munch writes that "most of Munch's annex parishes have dissolved since New Year's but for a few honorable Christians." She also writes about "gossip and slander circulating about us and always ill will and opposition and grumbling and an ungodly way of living everywhere."

Harassments, too, were on the increase, although of a milder kind than those experienced by J. W. C. Dietrichson at Koshkonong ten years earlier. Munch does not give much detail about these harassments, either in his letters or in his memoirs, and he did not, like the Koshkonong pastor, enter them in the Church Records. But Caja Munch hints about them several times in her letters. A couple of times she reports that drunkards would come uninvited to the parsonage while Munch was away and make themselves at home, claiming that it was their house since they and not the pastor had paid for it. And she adds that "Munch is having many similar annoyances." Some of the incidents could possibly be regarded as pranks and insignificant practical jokes if it were not for the general atmosphere of ill will in which they occurred. On the whole, in his memoirs, Munch seems to have played down his struggles with his congregations—as he said, they were not very cheerful memories. But he does mention that he was "misjudged, even derided" for his attempts "to introduce a somewhat better congregational order," and he gives as one example the incident where a puppet dressed in Norwegian clerical garb was put on exhibit in a neighbor's window, to the laughter and amusement of passersby, adding that he got "tired of these constant harassments." Incidents of heckling and snickering in church seem also to have occurred. Obviously, the "poison fangs" were showing again.

By this time, the focus of the issue had evidently shifted somewhat from the question of church organization to that of church discipline, which probably had been an underlying issue all along. The opposition apparently wanted the pastor's activities restricted to the formal official functions of preaching and administration of the sacraments within the church building, and any interference in their private lives was regarded as a transgression of the pastor's ecclesiastical authority and a threat to their individual freedom. Pastor Munch, on the other hand, could not relinquish his role as the guardian of morals in his congregations and emphasized his duties as *Sjælesørger* or curator of souls. He was undoubtedly a "faithful and zealous servant of the Lord," as the Church Record states, and conscientious to the extent of being uncompromising, not only in his efforts to establish church order but also in his fight against drunkenness and other forms of rowdiness so prevalent in his congregations. He was a strong personality and a forceful preacher, who was apt to call a spade a spade, and he attempted to exercise "church discipline" —or, as it was called with a somewhat harsher Norwegian word, *Kirketugt*—by denying the Sacrament of the Altar to those who in his judgment were living in vice and sin unless, in private confession, they showed genuine signs of repentance.

On this issue, Caja Munch notes a "considerable victory" for Pastor Munch when he presented to the congregation a written statement "about a minister's work and duties as a *curator of souls*" (her emphasis), which met with "universal approval." [42] Mrs. Munch is apparently referring to the Congregation Meeting of February 8, 1858, where Pastor Munch accepted the call until June 24, 1859 for the Wiota congregation only. At this time, the Dodgeville and Otter Creek congregations had either completely dissolved or formally separated themselves from the Wiota congregation. However, Munch committed himself to enter into negotiations with these congregations for a reunification with Wiota, even if his resignation would be required. An interesting little detail in this agreement—and this could perhaps be regarded as a "victory" for Munch—is that these negotiations were to be conducted, not by the Congregation Meeting or the Board of Trustees, which held secular authority only, but by the Congregational Council and the Church Council of the Norwegian Synod, representing ecclesiastical authority.

It appears, however, that the long hot summers—then as now—tended to bring existing conflicts to a head. The summer of 1858 saw another climax in the conflict between Pastor Munch and his unruly congregation. At a Congregation Meeting July 5, 1858, Pastor Munch called on those who were dissatisfied with his services to withdraw from the congregation. Five men, then and there, rose to resign, and this time some of the more prominent leaders of the congregation were among them, such as Even Kronborg, the "grumpy old bachelor from Land," who had played host to the Munchs when they first arrived in Wiota, and Hans Schjager, who had been the congregation's overtrustee during the first two years of Munch's service and also a teacher in the parochial school.[43] Soon there were more withdrawals, including Kristen Ruud (or C. Rood, as he signed his name), who also had taken the Munchs under shelter when the parsonage needed repair, and even Ole Monssen, whom Caja Munch had described with such enthusiasm as one of the pillars of the congregation. And "just before Christmas, the storm broke loose with American fury."

It now appears that this group of renegades, with Hans Schjager as one of the ostensible leaders, tried to reorganize the congregation independently of ministerial authority. A so-called "peace list" was circulated in the settlements, soliciting signatures to a statement which apparently urged unification and the removal of certain "malpractices" in the congregation but in reality resulted in a manifest split. It appears that this group even called an independent Congregation Meeting (without, of course, notifying the pastor), where the question of calling another minister had been discussed. Unfortunately (but quite understandably), none of the activities of this group, including the Congregation Meeting that they are supposed to have called, has been entered in the official Church Records, which were usually kept at the parsonage. The only documentary evidence we have of these activities is found in the minutes of a regular Congregation Meeting January 12, 1859, where the whole affair came up for discussion. There is also mention of a letter to Pastor Brandt, the contents of which, however, are not known. But it is a matter of record that Schjager resumed his activities as a schoolteacher, possibly in an attempt to organize an independent parochial school.

Naturally, in his attempts to exercise church discipline, Pastor Munch acquired many enemies, especially among the rowdy elements of his congregation, who for revenge or for other personal reasons would gladly join Schjager's independence movement. Nevertheless, it is probably fair to say that to Schjager and the other leaders, the movement was a genuine attempt, and an organized effort, to assert the "secular authority" of the congregation and its elected officers over against what was felt to be an intolerable "pastoral overlordship." That this was indeed the issue is also confirmed by a letter of appreciation sent to Pastor Munch after he had left Wiota. Reviewing the case in a half-ironic style, the letter states, "and if you were unfortunate enough to have something to say in external church affairs, then you were 'meddling in things that were not your concern.' " [44] This, undoubtedly, is a quotation of an argument frequently heard in the congregation at the time.

Munch, on the other hand, could only regard it as downright revolt against the minister's "ecclesiastical authority" and reacted accordingly. He demanded that those who had signed the "peace list" should either withdraw their names from the list or resign from membership in the congregation. As only two members reacted favorably to this demand by having their names removed from the list, Munch again resigned from his pastorate as of June 24, 1859, and this time, "because of received information about the disruption of the congregation," his resignation was accepted. [45]

This was Pastor Munch's final resignation. But the case was not closed. The apparent revolt in Wiota could not fail to attract the attention of the Church Council of the Norwegian Synod, particularly since rumors of it apparently had reached professional circles in Christiania and Laurvig and had echoed back, presumably in a somewhat distorted form, to members of the Church Council.[46] A. C. Preus, the Chairman of the Council, acting in his capacity of Bishop according to the Ritual of the Church of Norway (although the title was never used in America), came to Wiota, and on January 12, 1859, a Congregation Meeting was held under his direction. Gustav Dietrichson, although no longer a member of the Council, also attended. Both sides were asked to present their case, and this time the opposition came prepared. Hans Schjager and Erich Erichsen Fosse each brought a written statement, which was read to the assembly.[47]

The meeting was an anticlimax. Whether by design or because of ineptness in articulating their case, the opposition leaders apparently did not touch on the central issue of "secular" versus "ecclesiastical" authority but limited themselves to personal attacks on Pastor Munch for his *Skjændeprædikener* or "tongue-lashing sermons" and for having refused to accept in his confirmation class a child who was receiving religious instruction from Schjager after he had resigned from membership in the congregation. Munch put his finger on the issue by denouncing the "peace list" and other activities of the opposition as attempts to remove certain churchly affairs from being dealt with by the pastor. And in condemning this, he had, of course, the full support of Preus and Dietrichson. In the end, the meeting adopted a resolution (against seven votes) that it would be desirable if Pastor Munch continued as the minister of the congregation.

So the Wiota congregation was once again brought "back to the fold" of the Norwegian Synod. Munch's resignation, however, was irrevocable.

The conditions in the Wiota Congregation may have been an important reason for Munch's resignation and return to Norway. But it was not the only reason, not even the most important one according to Munch himself.

During his stay at Wiota, Pastor Munch took part in three synodical conferences—at Koshkonong in June, 1857, at "Little Iowa" (Washington Prairie, near Decorah, Iowa) in October the same year, and at Luther Valley (Rock Prairie) in October 1858. The conference at Koshkonong was not an official Synod Meeting, but all the Synod pastors were there for the dedication of the West Koshkonong church.

Apart from Laur. Larsen, who arrived in 1857 (but too late in the year to take part either in the Koshkonong dedication or the Iowa meeting), Munch was the youngest of the group, which may in part explain why he seems to have played a relatively modest part in these conferences. There was one issue, however, on which he appears to have thrown himself into the debate with all he had. That was the issue of the future recruitment of ministers for the Synod.

So far, the Norwegian Synod had relied exclusively on pastors who had received their theological training in Norway, and the number of young Norwegian theologians who had answered the calls from their emigrated countrymen had been encouraging. In 1850, there were only two Norwegian-trained pastors in America. By the end of 1857, the number had increased to twelve in a relatively short time. However, it was far from enough to meet the growing need for more pastors both in the already settled congregations in Wisconsin and in the new settlements west of the Mississippi, and it was soon recognized that in the future the Synod would have to rely increasingly on recruitment from some Lutheran theological seminary in America. The issue was whether to seek an affiliation with one of the already established German Lutheran theological seminaries or to build a separate Norwegian seminary.

On this issue the Synod was divided. There was general agreement that the best solution would be for the Norwegian Synod to have its own seminary. But the majority of the Synod pastors were of the opinion that this goal was out of reach within the foreseeable future and recommended an affiliation with one of the German Lutheran synods for the use of its educational facilities, at least as a temporary, perhaps as a permanent arrangement. Gustav Dietrichson and Munch were strongly opposed to this view and proposed that a greater effort should be made to recruit pastors from Norway until such time as a Norwegian Lutheran theological seminary could be established. They argued that national identity was the strength of Lutheranism among the Norwegians in America and feared that giving up this identity would open the Norwegian settlements to all kinds of non-Lutheran influences. Besides, they were opposed to what Munch described as the "scholasticism and narrow dogmatism" of the German bodies, particularly of the Missouri Synod.

The question of an affiliation with one of the German Lutheran bodies had been up for discussion among the Norwegian high church pastors several times since January 1852. At that time, Professor W. M. Reynolds, of Columbus, Ohio, had suggested that the Norwegians unite with the Joint Synod of Ohio, which would give them access to the educational facilities of Capital University. The offer was rejected at that time, against the recommendation of A. C. Preus. But in June 1855, shortly before Munch arrived, it was decided in the Norwegian Synod Church Council to send out two delegates on an inspection tour of three German Lutheran seminaries, Concordia Seminary in St. Louis, Capital University in Columbus, Ohio, and Martin Luther College in Buffalo, New York. Pastors Brandt and Ottesen were selected as delegates, and in January 1856, Preus issued an appeal to the Norwegian pastors and congregations to contribute to the travel expenses of the delegates, estimated to the amount of four hundred dollars.[48] The six months' delay in issuing the appeal as well as the fact that it took a year to raise an amount that was seventy dollars short of the goal is probably an indication of the controversial nature of the issue.

This appeal from the President of the Norwegian Synod became the occasion for the temporary editor of *Emigranten,* Knud J. Fleischer, to open the columns of his paper for a public discussion of the issue. For this he was sharply reproached by Preus, who regarded the subject as "exhausted" and closed, and declared that the promotion of a separate Norwegian theological seminary at this time would only mean a delay in the solution of the immediate and pressing problem of recruitment of pastors.[49] This was a challenge to the opposing minority within the Synod, and the first one to take it up was Munch.

In a lengthy article published in *Emigranten,* Pastor Munch spoke with warmth of the achievements already made in establishing a distinctly Norwegian Lutheran body on American soil and argued that it would be better to broaden the foundation already laid rather than to abandon the impressive results obtained so far by "throwing ourselves into the arms of the Germans." For this, he predicted, would be the end of national identity as well as of an autonomous, self-governing Norwegian Lutheran Church in America. On this basis, he strongly opposed an affiliation with any German or other "foreign" Lutheran body, advocated an immediate pursuit of funds for a separate Norwegian theological seminary, and suggested that the collected funds, until they were large enough to support an institution, should be used to intensify the recruitment of young pastors from Norway by granting low-interest loans to meet the considerable travel expenses connected with the acceptance of a call in America.[50]

Also Dietrichson, "on behalf of the minority," attacked the

proposed affiliation with a German Lutheran body and explained
why he had voted against the sending of delegates to the three
German seminaries.[51] He openly declared, as did two of his congregations, that they would not contribute anything to the travel fund for
the delegates.

From the other side, the debate was entered by C. L. Clausen,
H. A. Preus, and particularly by A. C. Preus, the President of the
Synod, who was engaged in a continuous battle of the pen on several
fronts. Editorial comments favoring the views of Dietrichson and
Munch were scattered throughout the debate.[52]

The debate was conducted with politeness and restraint as befit-
ting the station of the debaters (the language of *Emigranten* was not
always that civil). Whether private exchanges of a more vicious
nature followed the public debate is not known, but Pastor Munch
wrote to his brother a year later that in this discussion "both Preus
and I had gone rather too far, and an unpleasant relationship had
developed." Anyway, out of the whole debate concerning the affiliation with a German Lutheran body, the Norwegian Synod emerged
clearly divided into two camps. The still dominant group, orthodox
and with heavy leanings toward German Lutheranism, had its center
in Koshkonong with A. C. Preus remaining its strong man, at least
for the time being, effectively supported by H. A. Preus, Ottesen, and
Koren. The other camp, with a more liberal theology, and with a
deep concern for the identity of a Norwegian Lutheran Church in
America, had its center in the Luther Valley parsonage at Rock
Prairie, with Dietrichson and Munch as its hot-headed spokesmen,
and with strong moral support from the little circle of Norwegian
intellectuals formed by the editorial staff of *Emigranten*. It was
indeed a loss to the opposition within the Synod when, in 1857,
Emigranten was taken over by Carl Fredrik Solberg, moved to
Madison, and completely divorced from the church.

In the spring of 1857, Brandt and Ottesen made their trip to the
three German institutions, including also a visit to Concordia Seminary at Ft. Wayne, Indiana, and in August that year they submitted
to the Church Council of the Norwegian Synod a report which
contained a profusely enthusiastic presentation of the Missouri
Synod and its Concordia Seminary in St. Louis. What appealed to
them particularly at this school was its "Old Lutheran" orthodoxy.[53]
The question of possible affiliation was to be taken up at the following Synod Meeting in Iowa.

At first, it seems that Munch did not plan to attend the Iowa meeting, partly because he could not afford the long trip, partly because his congregations had not yet formally joined the Norwegian Synod. But, as Caja Munch puts it, since "Munch's own proposal concerning a separate educational institution" was to come up for debate, he decided to go, and after Caja had patched up his suit as best she could and persuaded him to buy a new overcoat, he left "looking fairly decent and respectable."

At the Synod Meeting, Pastor Herman A. Preus presented a resolution which obviously originated in the Church Council and expressed the view of the Koshkonong group. It recommended the use of Concordia Seminary in St. Louis for the education and training of Norwegian Lutheran ministers and suggested the establishment of a Norwegian professorship at that institution. The professor's salary was to be raised from the interests of a fund, which was to be set aside and eventually used for the establishment of a separate Norwegian seminary unless the Synod should decide to use it for an expansion of the activities at Concordia Seminary.[54]

Apparently, the meeting was divided over the acceptance of this resolution, and a committee was appointed consisting of Pastors Hans A. Stub (chairman) and J. St. Munch (secretary), and three lay representatives. After some deliberation, the committee presented a report containing a slightly revised resolution, which was unanimously adopted.[55]

The difference in the wording of the two proposals is not great. Even the committee report recognized that "the present conditions do not allow" the establishment of a separate Norwegian seminary "for the time being" and remarked that valuable "insight and experience" could be gained by a temporary affiliation with the German institution. On one point, however, it introduced a significant but, as it turned out, inconsequential revision. While Preus had proposed the establishment of a Norwegian professorship at Concordia and only incidentally mentioned the possibility of a separate Norwegian institution in the future, the committee report presented a resolution which in its opening sentence firmly states: "The Synod decides to establish a separate Norwegian-Lutheran educational institution among us," thus emphasizing the temporary nature of the Concordia arrangement. In this revision we may possibly see Pastor Munch's hand. However, it must be put on the account of Caja Munch's pride in her dear husband when she reported home to her parents that

"Munch's idea was victorious." At best it was a half compromise, which in essence vindicated the view of the Koshkonong group. The close affiliation of the Norwegian Synod with the German Missouri Synod, which was to have serious consequences, was sealed.

Looking back at the events some fifty years later, Pastor Munch has this to say:

> I do not recall if it was that year—'58—or earlier that I took part in a big Synod Meeting at Pastor Koren's in Decorah, Iowa. . . . There it was decided to join with the theological school of the Missouri Synod a fateful step that had far-reaching consequences. The Missouri Synod is German and known for its Lutheran scholasticism and narrow dogmatism with denunciation of such as think otherwise. This spirit also took effect in the Norwegian Synod . . . and it was only Dietrichson and I who could not go along with it. This absorbtion into the German scholasticism also made Dietrichson and myself less favored and contributed in no small degree to our leaving America together.

Another contributing cause for Munch's departure was his health. Lately he had suffered much from nervous headaches, which undoubtedly may have been brought on in part by the frustrations and harassments that he experienced in Wiota.

> But even if this ailment had not been there, I would hardly have stayed because of my isolated position against the pastors who circulated with the Germans. Dietrichson wanted to go home in the summer of '59, and I would then have been alone.

So the Munchs packed up and left with the Dietrichsons. Pastor Munch gave his farewell sermon in Wiota May 1, 1859.

All this made up Caja Munch's world during the three and a half years that she stayed in Wiota. Although she seldom moved out of the confines of the parsonage and the church except for several visits to the Dietrichsons at Rock Prairie, and although in her letters she seldom gave details of what happened in the congregation or of anything else in her husband's work, and she never tried to explain what she did not fully comprehend, the ups and downs in her husband's career are clearly reflected in her letters by changing moods and attitudes, up to the point where Adolph Preus, who was "a nice and pleasant man" the first time she met him, becomes a villain who "never suffers any one to have an opinion"—she probably met him only two or three times. But this turbulent world was filled with deep meaning and naïve joy from the buoyancy of her own personality.

In her letters, she bubbles over with anything that comes to her mind, shifting from deep depression in her loneliness when Munch is away to hilarious joy over letters from home. In one instant she may strictly forbid her mother to sacrifice her precious sleep for writing to her, and in the next, a cry from the abyss of desolation—why don't you ever write! She can go from pious devotion to silly pranks, with no transition whatsoever, and her faith in God is firm and strong, of the kind that regards misfortune as God's loving chastening when it afflicts her dear Munch, and as the Lord's righteous punishment when his enemies are stricken. Through it all runs a deep and never faltering loyalty and devotion to her husband and his work, so that one could well put as a motto for her letters and for her life what she once exclaimed: "How wonderful to be a pastor's wife!"

Caja took for granted the values of her upbringing. Loyalty, gracious living, and professional competence were to her not so much a mark of distinction as an ethical demand, be it in her husband's ministerial work or in the performance of her own duties as a housewife. And this was the scale by which she tended to judge others. Finding so little of these virtues in America outside of her own little circle of friends and associates, it tended to color her picture of the country and its people in a rather gloomy hue. She was horrified at the disrespect of children, the disloyalty of servants, the sloppiness of many farmers' homes, the professional incompetence of self-established doctors and clergymen, and she would rather live in poverty than have her husband engage in land speculations that might endanger his undivided loyalty to his calling. She was amused, and a little irritated, at those who could not understand that being a professional's wife entailed certain obligations with regard to standards and style of living.

These standards put rather restricted limits on Caja's social life. It is hard to imagine the loneliness of a housewife in a Middle West parsonage in those days, especially during the long days and weeks when the husband was away on a journey that might take him over desolate prairies which the wife could only picture in her imagination, and through the unaccustomed violence of the weather. Like the rest of the early Norwegian pastors, Munch traveled extensively during his stay in the Middle West, not only to his own "annex parishes" but also to other settlements where a regular service by a resident minister was lacking. There was also considerable exchange of pulpits between the Synod pastors. Thus in June 1856, Munch preached in Muskego for Brandt, "who was home in Norway to get married." Later that summer, Munch and Dietrichson exchanged churches, "which the people liked rather well." In January 1858, the two pastors went together to Chicago and organized a congregation among the Norwegians there, which was later known as Our Savior's Lutheran Church. They continued to serve this congregation, taking turns in alternating months to go down there to preach, until both of them returned to Norway in May 1859.[56] But Pastor Munch's most extensive journey was his mission trip to Norwegian settlements in Minnesota Territory in August and September 1857, of which he has given a lively description in a letter to his brother.

During those endless weeks and months, Caja Munch was utterly alone in the parsonage at Wiota. At first she had the company of her younger brother Emil, who had gone with the Munchs to America. But he seems to have been a strange and reticent boy, and he soon left the Munch home to take a job at the Norwegian printing press at Rock Prairie, later in the "dangerous city" of Madison, which caused Caja some motherly worries.

It was indeed different after daughter Else was born. From now on the little baby filled Caja's life as it filled her letters home. But there was no one to talk to. Occasionally there would be servants in the house, at least a little nursemaid for the baby; but they were of a different world. Not even the most isolated rural parish in Norway could be as lonely as this, for there, in Norway, would at least be a district doctor and a *Sorenskriver* (judge) and perhaps a *Fogd* (magistrate or bailiff), who would be cultured and educated people with whom one could visit, exchange ideas, and cultivate common interests; and there were even well-to-do peasants, who in their own traditional style well knew the art of gracious living. But here, there was nothing of the sort for miles.

No one knew this better than Elisabeth Koren, Pastor Koren's wife, who lived "out west" in splendid isolation from other people of her kind, and who in her diary and letters often sighs for the company of cultured people.[57] There are striking similarities in the experiences and reactions of these two pastors' wives. Both had experienced the wants and privations of pioneer life as they had to find lodgings with some farmer in his log cabin while their parsonages were being finished—and both complain about the smell of fried pork. Both had friendly relations with people in their congregations but were lonely in their company. Says Mrs. Koren:

> I can indeed talk to them, and do so, too, and it is probably my own fault that I find these conversations of so little interest. This is not always true, to be sure; but at times the wish to have a cultured person to talk to becomes very strong. My thoughts prefer to linger elsewhere, and find it intolerable to have to turn back to cattle and swine.[58]

Also in Caja Munch's letters we find the same longing and sighing for people with whom she could feel at home. There were, of course, the other Synod pastors and their families. But they lived far apart, and the wives hardly ever saw each other. Caja Munch knew Elisabeth Koren from childhood, for the Falchs and the Hysings were acquaintances from Laurvig. But it is with some irony that Mrs. Koren writes to her father, Ahlert Hysing, that "Munch will now be our nearest neighbor," explaining that "it will take us more than three days . . . to reach his home, but then we shall not have much more than a day's journey left to Spring Prairie." [59] Not once during her stay in Wisconsin did Caja see her friend, nor did she ever meet any of the other pastors' wives except Mrs. Dietrichson at Rock Prairie, which was only a day's journey from Wiota, and Mrs. Stub, who once came to the Dietrichsons while Caja was there.

Social distances were of no less importance than the physical ones, and this applied not only to the farmers, most of whom were *Almuefolk*. There were other Norwegian pastors around. Eielsen and Ole Andrewson were living at Jefferson Prairie, not far from Rock Prairie, and Peter A. Rasmussen, although his home was in far-off Lisbon, Illinois, was serving a small congregation in Green County, Wisconsin, not too far from the Munchs. But they were not of the Synod, and they, like the farmers, belonged to a different social world. As far as Caja is concerned, she hardly even knew that they were there. Once she went with her husband to a Synod Meeting at Rock Prairie, and she writes home about it. She names and describes each of the Synod pastors whom she met there, including "a young but serious and outspoken man" named Larsen (who later became president of Luther College in Decorah, Iowa). She also mentions the presence of the two German Professors Walther and Crämer without, however, naming them. But from her account one should never have suspected that the two Norwegian Pastors Rasmussen and Thalberg were also present at the meeting, and very prominently so.

It was not that the Munchs or the other Synod pastors were "snobbish" or had contempt for the peasants. On the contrary, under the influence of the romantic trend of the time, the professionals generally admired the peasant for his independence, his dignity, and his colorful customs and traditions. The "cultured" professionals and the *Almuefolk* simply represented different styles of life, and each felt somewhat awkward in the other's company.

In Pastor Munch's congregations there was one family with whom the Munchs had more than an official association. That was the family of Mr. Holmen, who had a general store in Linden. The Holmens were described by the Munchs as cultured people, and Pastor Munch used to stay with them when he visited his Dodgeville congregations. But Caja's contacts with them were rather limited. And even here a certain social distance was present as indicated by the fact that Holmen's wife, however pleasant and nice, did not quite rank as a *Frue* but was referred to by Caja as *Madam* Holmen.

However, when the Munchs first arrived in Wisconsin, they were at once introduced to one of the cultural centers of the Norwegians in the Middle West. Ever since the days of the remarkable Pastor Clausen, the parsonage at Rock Prairie, or Luther Valley, as it was named by him, had been a busy center not only for religious but also for secular intellectual activities. And Gustav F. Dietrichson continued in the same spirit. It was largely because of the presence of these two men that Rock Prairie became the first location of the Scandinavian Press Association, which attracted a number of gifted and interesting people. And all of them came frequently to the Dietrichsons.

Upon their arrival at Luther Valley parsonage, the Munchs met Knud J. Fleischer, the temporary editor of *Emigranten,* who lived with his family in a house close by the parsonage. And Johan Holfeldt, the first secretary-treasurer of the Press Association, arrived with his wife from Quebec, "where he makes money in the summer, but every winter they have their lodgings with the Dietrichsons." There followed a combined party to celebrate Mrs. Dietrichson's birthday and a christening at the Fleischers, and among the guests was "a Norwegian by the name Suckow, who could sing and play the guitar and commenced at once on mine"—undoubtedly Bertol W. Suckow, who later moved to Madison and started publication of *Billed-Magazin,* the first Norwegian illustrated magazine in America.

Thus the Munchs developed lasting friendships with the Fleischers, the Holfeldts, and particularly with the Dietrichsons, whom they visited several times and also entertained as guests at the parsonage in Wiota. Luther Valley became the social center and a second home to the Munchs, where particularly Caja could find relaxation and cultural and mental nourishment, cultivating her music on Dietrichson's piano while Mrs. Dietrichson sang, and frolicking to her heart's delight. Among the interesting people whom she met there she also mentions "a very nice young man named Solberg"—none other than Carl F. Solberg, the noted journalist and editor—and the famous Dr. Søren J. Hanssen and his wife Alberta, née Ulfers, who was "kind and nice and straightforward but a little bombastic in her ideas, it was plain to see that she had been a governess for several years." It was also at the Dietrichsons that Caja met all the other Synod pastors, whom she describes in vivid colors and with mixed praise.

But it was mostly in the lonely hours at the Wiota parsonage, while her "dear Munch" was away on one of his long and strenuous journeys, that Caja Munch wrote her letters. In her loneliness, she found consolement in "talking" to her mother in her writing, and in many instances it obviously cheered her up chatting away about this and that.

In 1882, Pastor Munch received another call from America. In the meantime, he had been leading a rather stormy life in Norway as a protagonist of church reform, had angered his Bishop, embarrassed the Minister of Church, and earned himself the labels of a "rebel" and a "troublemaker." Finally, he broke with the State Church of Norway, resigned from his office at Horten, and laid down the cloth. But preaching the Gospel was a thing he did not intend to give up. In the fall of 1875, he moved to Christiania with his family of nine children. His fame had preceded him. When he announced that he would give a sermon in the Klingenberg Dance Hall, of all places, since the churches were closed to him, the hall was so crowded with people that he could hardly get in. From then on, he was established as a celebrated evangelist in Christiania.

In America, the Norwegian Synod had by then acquired its own theological school, Luther Seminary, located in Madison, Wisconsin, where the teaching went on fully in the Missouri Synod tradition. Most of Eielsen's followers had consolidated to form a synodical organization known as Hauge's Synod and had likewise established their own theological school, Red Wing Seminary, in Red Wing, Minnesota. But between the extreme dogmatism of the Norwegian

Synod and the extreme pietism of Hauge's Synod, a liberal church movement had sprung up, partly under the influence of a new generation of immigrant pastors graduated from the University in Christiania. By 1870, this movement had crystallized into an organization known as the Conference for the Norwegian-Danish Evangelical Lutheran Church under the leadership of none other than Pastor Claus L. Clausen, the old veteran from the early days of the Norwegian Synod. Among the forceful leaders of this rapidly growing, "middle way" organization were the two Norwegian-born and Norwegian-reared professors at Augsburg Seminary in Minneapolis, Sven Oftedal and Georg Sverdrup, both of them stemming from well-known lineages in Norway, and both of them with strong free church leanings. Even within the Norwegian Synod, strong anti-Missourian sentiments were beginning to assert themselves, which eventually led to a so-called Anti-Missourian Brotherhood splitting away from the Synod and later joining the Conference to form the United Norwegian Lutheran Church.

What happened was that a new leadership, emanating from the rank and file of the Norwegian community in America and reinforced by offshoots from a liberal movement within the professional elite of Norway, established itself in competition with the old elite of the Norwegian Synod. Liberal in its basic attitudes, the new leadership stood closer to the people and gave articulation and direction to the "fermenting and unsettled" elements within the Norwegian community, thereby opening the road to true acculturation—the emergence of a Norwegian community which formed an integral part of the American society.

The congregation which had issued a call to Pastor Munch in 1882 was Scandinavia, in Waupaca County, Wisconsin, which had previously been served by Pastor Duus. It was described by Pastor Munch as having the largest Norwegian church in America. He decided to take a trip and look at the situation, whether it would be advisable to emigrate with his whole family. He was accompanied on the trip by his oldest son Johan. As they arrived in Chicago, however, the heat was unbearable, Pastor Munch took ill, and this became an excuse for canceling the trip to Waupaca. Nothing came of the emigration plans.

One of the reasons for Pastor Munch's apparent coolness at the prospect of emigration at this time may have been that the Scandinavia Congregation, to which he was called, was then still a member of the Norwegian Synod. In his memoirs, he remarks that "it was perhaps just as well" that he did not emigrate, "for if I had accepted the call, I would have got involved in unpleasant doctrinal controversies." Pastor Munch is referring to the bitter "election controversy," which shook and split the Norwegian Synod during the 1880's as the issue of the acceptance or rejection of the German-Missourian Formula of Concord came to a head.[60] It was as a result of this controversy that the Anti-Missourian Brotherhood split away from the Synod.

There is no doubt which side Pastor Munch would have taken in this controversy. It is interesting to note that during his second short sojourn in America, he did not visit any of his former colleagues in the Norwegian Synod. Of the ten Synod pastors whom he had known and worked with during his stay in Wiota, four had by this time returned to Norway for good. Gustav Dietrichson, as mentioned, left with Munch in 1859, and later that same year, Duus followed. Brodahl returned in 1868, and Adolph C. Preus left in 1872 and died as dean of Øvre Nedenes, Norway, in 1878. But Koren was still at Washington Prairie, and in Decorah were now also Brandt and Larsen, the latter as president of Luther College, which had been established by the Norwegian Synod in 1861. Stub, who had returned to Norway for a few years, was now administering several congregations northeast of Decorah. Herman A. Preus, president of the Norwegian Synod, was still at Spring Prairie, and Ottesen was at Koshkonong.

Arriving in New York on this second visit, Munch was entertained by the local Synod pastor, whom he describes as "very pleasant and obliging although he belonged to the buttoned-up synod." But from Chicago, instead of going to Waupaca, he went straight to Lisbon, Illinois, where he spent about a week with Peter A. Rasmussen, a former follower of Eielsen, who had been stamped as an heretic at the Synod Meeting at Luther Valley in 1858 because of his liberal view on laymen's activities in the church—Munch was present at the meeting and apparently acquiesced to the decision. Rasmussen had later been accepted by the Synod and joined it only to become a prominent member, along with Clausen, Muus, and others, of a liberal faction within the Synod, in sharp opposition to the established leadership, H. A. Preus, Koren, Ottesen, and Larsen. Of course, Pastor Munch visited his former congregation in Wiota, but he cut the visit short to make a special trip all the way to Minneapolis to see none other than Professor Georg Sverdrup, then president of Augsburg Seminary and a prominent figure in the liberal church body, the Conference.

Neither is there any doubt that Pastor Munch would have become "involved" in the controversy with heart and soul, had he stayed on in America. Although it may be too harsh to say that he was a man of strife, he never backed away from a fight when his conscience demanded that he take a stand.

In the family, however, he was a tender husband and father, and whatever battles he fought—and lost, in his memoirs he never failed to acknowledge with warmth the strength, the support, and the understanding he received from his wife Caja. The heaviest decision of his life, by his own recollection, was to lay down the holy office of the church. "But during all these calamities, I had a faithful assistant in Caja, who firmly stood by my side and gave me strength, expressing her full agreement with my action, and her willingness to suffer with me. . . . Then, as always, she was my consolement and my support. Blessed be her memory!"

REFERENCES AND NOTES/INDEX

References

Manuscripts

Caja Munch, née Falch, Letters from Hamburg, Chicago, Rock Prairie (Luther Valley), and Wiota, Wisconsin, August 1855–March 1859, containing 14 letters to Thalie Falch, née Staffeldt (2 fragments), 1 letter to Mrs. Staffeldt (February 1857), and 1 letter to Henriette and Caroline Munch (February 1857), with supplements by J. St. Munch. University Library, Oslo, Norway.

J. St. Munch to Else Munch, née Hofgaard, July 16, 1857. Peter A. Munch, Carbondale, Illinois.

J. St. Munch to Andreas Munch, November 16, 1857. Peter A. Munch, Carbondale, Illinois.

Peder Fenne, Elev Johnsen, and Guldbrand Wang to J. St. Munch, Wiota, May 8, 1859. Peter A. Munch, Carbondale, Illinois.

J. St. Munch, "Vita Mea," autobiography written for his children, 1903. Peter A. Munch, Carbondale, Illinois.

Peter A. Munch, "Slegten Munch," 1928. Peter A. Munch, Carbondale, Illinois.

"Forhandlings-Protocol for Wiota Norsk-Lutherske Menighed," 1856–79. Archives of Wiota Lutheran Church.

"Kaldsbrev" [Letter of Call] to Johan St. Munch, from "de norsk-evangelisk-lutherske Menigheder i Wyota, Lafayette Cty og Dodgeville, Iowa Cty, Wisc.," dated "Luther Walley Præstegaard d. 18 Januar 1855." Peter A. Munch, Carbondale, Illinois.

"Kirkebog for de norsk-lutherske Menigheder paa Jeffersons Prairie, Long Prairie, Rock Run og Hamilton." Archives of the Norwegian-American Historical Association, Northfield, Minnesota (photostatic copies of excerpts in the Archives of Wiota Lutheran Church).

"Record for Den Norske Evangeliske Lutherske kirke og Menighed i og omkring Wiota," 1851–6. Archives of Wiota Lutheran Church.

"Skoleprotocol for Wiota Menigheds Skolecommission," 1856–60. Archives of Wiota Lutheran Church.

Books and Articles

Anderson, Arlow William. *The Immigrant Takes His Stand: The Norwegian-American Press and Public Affairs 1847–1872.* Northfield, Minn.: The Norwegian-American Historical Association, 1953.

Barton, Albert O. "Norwegian-American Emigration Societies in the Forties and Fifties," *Norwegian-American Studies and Records,* 3 (1928), 23–42.

Bergh, J. A. *Den norsk lutherske Kirkes Historie i Amerika.* Minneapolis: Augsburg Publishing House, 1914.

Blegen, Theodore C. *Norwegian Migration to America.* 2 vols. Northfield, Minn.: The Norwegian-American Historical Association, 1931–40.

—— ed. *Frontier Parsonage: The Letters of Olaus Fredrik Duus, Norwegian Pastor in Wisconsin, 1855–1858,* tr. Verdandi Study Club of Minneapolis. Northfield, Minn.: The Norwegian-American Historical Association, 1947.

——. *Land of Their Choice: The Immigrants Write Home.* Minneapolis: University of Minnesota Press, 1955.

Clausen, Clarence A., and Andreas Elviken, eds. *A Chronicle of Old Muskego: The Diary of Søren Bache, 1839–1847,* tr. Clarence A. Clausen and Andreas Elviken. Northfield, Minn.: The Norwegian-American Historical Association, 1951.

Dietrichson, G. F. "Et Ord i Delegat- og Universitetssagen fra Minoriteten," *Emigranten,* April 18, 1856.

Dietrichson, J. W. C. *Reise blandt de norske Emigranter i "De forenede nordamerikanske Fristater."* Stavanger, 1846 (reprinted Madison, 1896).

Fleischer, Knud J. "Tidsaanden" (editorial), *Emigranten,* August 18, 1855.

——. "Til Medlemmerne af vor Synode" (editorial), *Emigranten,* May 9, 1856.

Gjerset, Knut, ed. "An Account of the Norwegian Settlers in North America," tr. Knut Gjerset, *Wisconsin Magazine of History,* 8 (September 1924), 77–88.

—— and Ludvig Hektoen. "Health Conditions and the Practice of Medicine Among the Early Norwegian Settlers, 1825–1865," *(Norwegian-American) Studies and Records,* 1 (1926), 1–59.

Gullixson, T. F., and J. C. K. Preus. "Focal Point of History: Luther Valley," in: *Norsemen Found a Church: An Old Heritage in a New Land,* ed. J. C. K. Preus, 57–81. Minneapolis: Augsburg Publishing House, 1953.

Halvorsen H. *Festskrift til Den norske Synodes Jubilæum 1853–1903.* Decorah, Iowa: Den norske Synodes Forlag, 1903.

Haugen, Einar. "Pastor Dietrichson of Old Koshkonong," *Wisconsin Magazine of History,* 29 (March 1946), 301–18.

——. "The Struggle over Norwegian," *Norwegian-American Studies and Records,* 17 (1952), 1–35.

————. *The Norwegian Language in America: A Study in Bilingual Behavior*. 2 vols. Philadelphia: University of Pennsylvania Press, 1953.

Høibo, Gudrun Johnson. *Slekten Falkener Falch Falck*. Oslo: Otto Falchs Boktrykkeri, 1962.

Holand, Hjalmar Rued. *De Norske Settlementers Historie*. Ephraim, Wis.: Privately published, 1908.

————. *Coon Prairie*. Minneapolis: Augsburg Publishing House, 1927.

Hovde, B. J. *The Scandinavian Countries, 1720–1865: The Rise of the Middle Classes*. 2 vols. Ithaca, N.Y.: Cornell University Press, 1948.

Koht, Halvdan. *Norsk bondereising*. Oslo: H. Aschehoug & Co., 1926.

Larsen, Herman Astrup. "Day of the Laymen: Fox River, Chicago," *Norsemen Found a Church: An Old Heritage in a New Land*, ed. J. C. K. Preus, 23–56. Minneapolis: Augsburg Publishing House, 1953.

Larsen, Karen. *Laur. Larsen, Pioneer College President*. Northfield, Minn.: The Norwegian-American Historical Association, 1936.

Larson, Laurence M. *The Changing West, and Other Essays*. Northfield, Minn.: The Norwegian-American Historical Association, 1937.

Løvenskjold, Adam. *Beretning om de norske Setlere i Nordamerika*. Bergen: Trykt i C. Rudolphs Officin, 1848 (tr.: see Gjerset, Knut).

Malmin, Gunnar J., ed. *America on the Forties: The Letters of Ole Munch Ræder*, tr. Gunnar J. Malmin. Minneapolis: University of Minnesota Press for the Norwegian-American Historical Association, 1929.

Mossin, P. L. "Frihedens sande Væsen og Betydning," *Emigranten*, May 2, 1856.

Munch, J. St. "Hvorledes kan den norsk-lutherske Kirke i Amerika sikres Bestaaen?" *Emigranten*, March 28, 1856.

Munch, Peter A. "Social Adjustment Among Wisconsin Norwegians," *American Sociological Review*, 14 (December 1949), 780–87.

————. "Segregation and Assimilation of Norwegian Settlements in Wisconsin," *Norwegian-American Studies and Records*, 18 (1954), 102–40.

————. "The Peasant Movement in Norway: A Study in Class and Culture," *British Journal of Sociology*, 5 (March 1954), 63–77.

————. *A Study of Cultural Change: Rural-Urban Conflicts in Norway*. Oslo: H. Aschehoug & Co., 1956.

Nelson, David T., ed. *The Diary of Elisabeth Koren, 1853–1855*, tr. David T. Nelson. Northfield, Minn.: The Norwegian-American Historical Association, 1955.

Nelson, E. Clifford, and Eugene L. Fevold. *The Lutheran Church Among Norwegian-Americans: A History of the Evangelical Lutheran Church*. 2 vols. Minneapolis: Augsburg Publishing House, 1960.

Norlie, O. M., ed. *Norsk lutherske prester i Amerika, 1843–1913*. Minneapolis: Augsburg Publishing House, 1914.

————. *Norsk Lutherske Menigheter i Amerika, 1843–1916*. 2 vols. Minneapolis: Augsburg Publishing House, 1918.

Ottesen, Jacob Aall, and Nils O. Brandt. "Indberetning fra Pastorerne Ottesen og Brandt om deres Reise til St. Louis, Missouri, Columbus, Ohio og Buffalo, New York," *Kirkelig Maanedstidende*, October 1857.

Paulson, Arthur O., and Kenneth Bjork, eds. "A School and Language Controversy in 1858: A Documentary Study," *Norwegian-American Studies and Records,* 10 (1938), 76–106.

Preus, A. C. "Vort Kirkesamfunds Delegater," *Emigranten,* March 7, 1856.

——. "Videre om Universitetssagen og vor Kirkes fremtidige Stilling," *Emigranten,* April 25, 1856.

——. "Tilsvar i Anledning af Hr. Pastor Dietrichsons Indsendelse om Delegaterne," *Emigranten,* June 20, 1856.

Preus, Caroline. *Linka's Diary on Land and Sea, 1845–1864,* tr. and ed. J. C. K. Preus and Diderikke Preus. Minneapolis: Augsburg Publishing House, 1952.

Preus, H. A. "Om Delegatsagen," *Kirkelig Maanedstidende,* May 1856.

Preus, J. C. K. "The Widening Frontier: Koshkonong," in: *Norsemen Found a Church: An Old Heritage in a New Land,* ed. J. C. K. Preus, 83–128. Minneapolis: Augsburg Publishing House, 1953.

—— ed. *Norsemen Found a Church: An Old Heritage in a New Land.* Minneapolis: Augsburg Publishing House, 1953.

Qualey, Carlton C. *Norwegian Settlement in the United States.* Northfield, Minn.: The Norwegian-American Historical Association, 1938.

Reiersen, Johan R. *Veiviser for de norske Emigranter til de forenede nordamerikanske Stater og Texas.* Christiania, 1844.

——. "Norwegians in the West in 1844: A Contemporary Account," tr. and ed. Theodore C. Blagen, *(Norwegian-American) Studies and Records,* 1 (1926), 110–25.

Rohne, J. Magnus. *Norwegian American Lutheranism up to 1872.* New York: The Macmillan Company, 1926.

Semmingsen, Ingrid. *Veien mot vest.* 2 vols. Oslo: H. Aschehoug & Co., 1942–50.

——. "The Dissolution of Estate Society in Norway," *The Scandinavian Economic History Review,* 2/2 (1954), 166–203.

Solberg, Carl Fredrik. "Reminiscences of a Pioneer Editor," ed. Albert O. Barton *(Norwegian-American) Studies and Records,* 1 (1926), 134–44.

Steen, Sverre. *Langsomt ble landet vårt eget.* Oslo: J. W. Cappelen, 1967.

Tavuchis, Nicholas. *Pastors and Immigrants: The Role of a Religious Elite in the Absorption of Norwegian Immigrants.* The Hague: Martinus Nijhof, 1963.

Wiota Lutheran Church, 1844–1937. Privately Published, 1937.

Wiota Lutheran Church: 125 Years Of Grace, 1844–1969. Privately published, 1969.

Wiota Lutheran Congregation 1844–1944. Privately published, 1944.

Notes

The Voyage to America and the First Year in Wiota
1855–1856

1. *Robert le Diable,* opera by Giacomo Meyerbeer (1791–1864), built on tales and legends about Robert II, Duke of Normandy (d. 1033), also called "the Devil."

2. The principal monetary unit in Norway at that time was *Speciedaler,* mostly abbreviated *Spdlr* or *Spd,* which equaled about $1. There were 5 *Mark* (sometimes called *Ort*) in a *Speciedaler,* and 24 *Skilling* in a *Mark.*

3. October 31, Thalie Falch's birthday.

4. Swedish-Norwegian consul in New York at that time (1855) was Claus Edvard Habicht. Caja Munch mistakenly (but consistently) calls him Heierdal.

5. Probably meaning the Hudson River at Albany. At that time, it appears, there was no railroad bridge across the Hudson River at this point.

6. Qvelsogn, now Kvelde, is a parish in Hedrum, just north of Larvik.

7. During the nineteenth century, Scandinavians were—and still are to a lesser degree—quite formal in the way they address each other. When two persons of the professional class first met, they would use titles and last names and say *De* (you) to each other. The first step in removing this self-imposed social distance is to "become *Dus*," which means that the titles are dropped, and they will say *Du* (thou) to each other; but they would still use last names. This is the stage of intimacy between Pastor Munch and his father-in-law, which is the reason why Caja Munch always refers to her husband as "Munch" (although she would, of course, address him as "Johan"). That this stage was reached immediately between Munch and Dietrichson is mentioned here as an indication of how cordial the meeting was.

8. This could possibly be the same blacksmith, Knud Knudsen, at whose house Pastor Clausen gave the first divine service in Wiota in 1844.

9. In the peasant culture of Norway, no social distinction is made in addressing another person. Everybody is addressed with *Du,* be he a lowly cotter or the King himself. Among the professional elite, in accordance with the trend of National Romanticism, this was generally recognized as simply a difference in custom and was even admired as an expression of the proud

independence of the peasants. Hence the reproach that Pastor Munch apparently gave his wife for complaining about it. However, this approving attitude applied only to the "genuine" peasants, such as, particularly, the mountain peasants, and did not extend to the townspeople, for whom it was still regarded as improper to address a member of the elite with *Du*. And the use of the first name, which even among the professionals themselves was reserved for the more intimate relationships such as within the family circle, was in this case an insult. No doubt, the settlers knew the rules as well as the pastor and his wife did, and when some of them would address the minister's wife as *Du*, Caja, it may have been an explicit expression of their refusal to recognize social distinctions from the Old Country any longer, which was indeed Caja Munch's interpretation. Hence her indignation.

10. *Fru Winsnes* refers to a famous cookbook by Hanna Winsness (1789–1872), a minister's wife who wrote novels, poetry, and children's books under the pen name Hugo Schwarz as well as, under her real name, a textbook in home economics and the cookbook, which was a standby in every professional home.

11. Obviously referring to a quilt (unknown in Norway).

12. Captain Hageman was a friend of the Falchs and the Staffeldts, with whom Caja appears to have had an ongoing joking relationship involving Caja's being teased as having a "cat's paw" (with hidden claws?).

13. This letter has no signature and is probably incomplete. The contents of the following letter also shows that something is missing.

The Second Year 1856–1857

1. That letter has not been preserved. And there certainly must have been a letter, now lost, to Caja Munch's parents telling about the birth of her first child, Else, who was born at the Luther Valley Parsonage August 20, 1856 (a week ahead of Emilie Falch's third birthday).

2. Reference is to a sleigh made of hickory wood held together by leather straps and wooden pegs, no nails, screws, or angle irons, which provided a flexible vehicle well-adapted to travel on uneven and unplowed roads.

3. Reference is to the unsuccessful attempt to establish a Norwegian colony in Pennsylvania (not Ohio), which was designed and promoted by the world-famous Norwegian violinist Ole Bull (1810–80). The colony was to be called "Oleana." Carl Solberg's father emigrated with his family to Oleana in 1853 and became the "director" of Ole Bull's project. When the project collapsed, Carl Solberg eventually came to Beloit and then to Rock Prairie, where he was employed by the Scandinavian Press Association. His father settled in Minnesota. Also Bertol W. Suckow and Johan Holfeldt had been connected with the Oleana project, Suckow as a secretary to Ole Bull, and Holfeldt as his agent in New York.

4. Topical poems, occasional songs, or—as some would say—*vers de société* played a large part in the social life of the Norwegian professional class during the eighteenth, nineteenth, and far into the twentieth century.

In particular, there was hardly a wedding without at least one such topical poem, mostly several of them, written for the occasion to a well-known melody, printed, and performed in unison by the wedding guests. "Our wedding song" obviously refers to such a song.

5. Caja Munch is here obviously referring to a Norwegian translation of Ludwig Hofacker's sermons, published in Christiansand, 1852. Hofacker was born in 1798 and died in 1828—only thirty years old—from typhoid fever. At the time of his death, he was serving as pastor of Rielingshausen parish in Würtemberg. His sermons were published posthumously by his brother and later translated into Norwegian.

6. That letter, which is lost, probably told what happened to the parsonage in Wiota. Pastor Munch recalls: "In the course of the summer, the parsonage had become dangerous to live in as one corner had a poor foundation and was sinking. We then had to move out in the fall and were put up in an attic at Kristen Ruud's (a crabby old man from Land), where the rain came in on us, right into Else's cradle."

7. Brandy-and-salt consisted of boiling hot water with brandy and—indeed—salt. It was an old standby in those days for colds or any kind of throat and chest trouble, and the patient usually recovered quickly, if for no other reason than to avoid having to swallow another dose of the stuff.

8. Caja's sister, Nanna, married the captain of one of her father's ships, Fredrik Ellegers, in May 1856. They went on a honeymoon trip to the Baltic Sea. Nanna came home as a widow. Four years later, she married Peter Christian Munch, an older brother of Pastor Munch.

9. The child was named after Pastor Munch's mother, "the Bishopess," who was known as a very beautiful lady, particularly in her younger days, but also in her old age.

10. In those days, no license was required to practice medicine in Wisconsin.

11. This episode is mentioned in Mrs. Preus's diary, where there is also a brief reference to the fact that Dr. and Mrs. Hanssen were staying with the Preuses; *Linka's Diary On Land and Sea, 1845–1864,* translated and edited by J. C. K. Preus and his Wife, Diderikke Margrethe, née Brandt (Minneapolis, 1952), pp. 270 ff.

12. In 1835, Friderich W. Falch (Caja's father) had taken over the two adjacent farms or estates of Hovland and Faret from his father. He later sold off parts of the combined estate, which at one time had been the second largest in the area.

13. "Runtom" (meaning "round about") is apparently the name of a place at Faret, perhaps a cotter's farm with a vacant house, possibly used as a summer place.

14. Ditmar Meidell, the editor of *Aftenbladet,* was living in an apartment just above the Munchs in "Saabygaarden," Pilestrædet, Christiania.

The Third Year 1857–1858

1. The letters from the Munchs were apparently sent off in bundles, possibly to save postage. This particular bundle of eleven letters may have contained several communications addressed to people other than the Falchs at Hovland, possibly including Pastor Munch's letter to his mother of July 16, 1857. It probably contained several sheets of Caja Munch's own letters to her parents, possibly dating as far back as May—hence the apology for being so late in getting "this letter" sent off.

2. In Scandinavian cities, particularly in the old Christiania (now Oslo), a house, or *Gaard*, was usually named after its owner. Thus, Saaby is in this case the name of the owner of the house, *Saabygaarden*, in the street or avenue called *Pilestrædet* (still a prominent street in Oslo), where Bishopess Munch was living with her unmarried children Herman, Caroline, and Henriette. At this particular time, Andreas Munch, who was a widower, also stayed there with his little boy, Johan.

3. Andreas Munch spent his early childhood at Sande Parsonage, where his and Pastor Munch's father served as pastor 1812–17.

4. The two were Peter Laur. Larsen, who later became the Norwegian professor of theology at Concordia Seminary in St. Louis and then president of Luther College in Decorah, Iowa, and F. C. Claussen, who went to Spring Grove in Minnesota and remained there until his death in 1870.

5. This obviously has reference to a *Snittemaskin* ("slicing machine"), a simple device, turned by hand, to slice French beans, up to the present a matter-of-course household tool in every Norwegian home.

6. The first half of this letter is missing. From the contents it is obvious that it was written some time during the spring of 1858, probably in March.

7. In Norway during the heavy emigration of the nineteenth century, a person who had been to America, who was even contemplating going to America, was called an "American."

The Last Year in Wiota 1858–1859

1. The letter of August 1858, frequently referred to here, has been lost. There probably was even another letter between this and the preceding fragment of March 1858, which must have contained information about the birth of Pastor and Mrs. Munch's second daughter, Thalie, born at Wiota Parsonage, May 15, 1858.

2. In Norwegian, "saloon captain" is used contemptuously about a sea captain who spends most of his time in the ship's saloon, flirting with the lady passengers, rather than on the bridge, then figuratively about any person who slights his responsibilities, approximately like "carpet general" in English.

3. Shortly after this was written, Pastor Laur. Larsen, the "young but serious and outspoken man," was offered, and soon accepted, the position as Norwegian professor of theology at Concordia Seminary in St. Louis.

4. It may be of interest to note in this connection that of the eleven ministers who had come over from Norway up until 1856, seven eventually returned to Norway, including the two Dietrichsons and A. C. Preus.

An American Adventure

1. Castle Garden had just that year (1855) been opened as a receiving station for immigrants—Ingrid Semmingsen, *Veien mot vest*, I, 150.

2. Pastor Munch is here referring to the Norwegian demand for a separate consular service, which in the 1890's became a hot issue in the tottering union between Sweden and Norway and eventually led to its dissolution in 1905. According to Caja Munch's letters, the consul was out of town when the Munchs called on him.

3. According to the letters, the Munchs stayed for a month with the Dietrichsons while Pastor Munch made several short trips to Wiota. There are several minor discrepancies between the letters and Pastor Munch's memoirs written fifty years later. Some of them are undoubtedly due to a slipping memory on the part of Pastor Munch. Others seem to stem from Caja Munch's limited knowledge of certain things. In some cases it appears that Mrs. Munch, as a young woman, was actually protected from knowing exactly what was in fact going on in the world of the men.

4. A pun on *faderlig,* which means both "fatherly" and "tremendous."

5. See Pastor Munch's letter to his brother, Andreas Munch, November 16, 1857.

6. Holden Congregation in Goodhue County, Minnesota, was organized in 1856 but did not have a resident pastor until Bernt J. I. Muus arrived in 1859.

7. By 1530, the faith and belief of the Lutheran Reformation had crystallized into the two basic confessional "symbols" of the Catechism, by Martin Luther himself, and the Augustan Confession, formulated by Melanchthon and endorsed by the Lutheran princes of Germany at the Diet of Augsburg (also called the Augsburg Confession). These were also the confessional symbols of the Church of Norway, as formally established by King Frederik II of Denmark-Norway in 1574. After Martin Luther's death in 1546, however, the Lutherans in Germany had fallen into a confessional and doctrinal strife, which rapidly produced more than twenty different substitute and supplementary confessions. Doctrinal unity among the Lutherans in Continental Europe was finally reestablished in 1580 by the so-called Formula of Concord, which was a compromise not only in name and appears to deviate on certain points from the Augsburg Confession. But the Formula of Concord was never adopted by the Scandinavian churches, hence the doctrinal differences between the (German) Missouri Synod and the Church of Norway, whose doctrines had till then been embraced by the Norwegian Synod. Without going into the finer theological points of the debate, it can be stated that the most controversial issue was concerned with the election for salvation by faith (Augustana) or by grace alone (Concordia).

8. This is a quotation of a line from the Danish National Anthem.

9. Pastor Munch may here be guilty of an anachronism. George Pullman did indeed operate as a contractor in Chicago in the 1850's and had started to experiment with remodeling a couple of railway coaches into sleeping cars. But the first regular Pullman sleeping car was developed in 1863, and a parlor car did not come into being until 1875. Pastor Munch may have ridden in one of these cars—or at least seen or heard about them —on his second short visit to America in 1882.

10. In 1875, Norway introduced a decimal monetary system, with *Krone* (Crown) as the principal unit (1 *Krone* = 100 *Øre*).

Social Class and Acculturation

1. Carlton C. Qualey, *Norwegian Settlement in the United States* (Northfield, 1938), pp. 40 ff. and Appendix.

2. The most outstanding work on the Norwegian settlement in America and its Old World background is still Theodore C. Blegen, *Norwegian Migration to America,* 2 vols. (Northfield, 1931–40), from which much of the following has been gleaned. See also Ingrid Semmingsen, *Veien mot vest,* 2 vols. (Oslo, 1942–50).

3. There is to my knowledge no comprehensive and definitive historical presentation of the role and significance of the professional class in Norway during the eighteenth and nineteenth centuries. But the importance of this elite stands out clearly in any historical work concerned with the period. See, e.g., Halvdan Koht, *Norsk Bondereising* (Oslo, 1926); B. J. Hovde, *The Scandinavian Countries, 1720–1865* (Ithaca, N.Y., 1948); Ingrid Semmingsen, "The Dissolution of Estate Society in Norway," *The Scandinavian Economic History Review,* II, No. 2 (1954), 166–203; Sverre Steen, *Langsomt ble landet vårt eget* (Oslo, 1967), pp. 147–58.

4. This notion, which according to Steen (*Langsomt,* p. 150) was present already in the eighteenth century, finds expression in one of Caja Munch's letters, where she criticizes some of the Norwegian pastors in America for buying land and getting involved in land speculation, even making money on it.

5. In 1815, the population of Norway was 907,000. By 1855, it had increased to 1,479,000.

6. On the Peasant Movement in Norway, see particularly Halvdan Koht, *Norsk Bondereising* (Oslo, 1926). An attempt at a sociological interpretation of the movement may be found in Peter A. Munch, "The Peasant Movement in Norway: A Study in Class and Culture," *British Journal of Sociology,* 5 (March 1954) 63–77; also his *A Study of Cultural Change: Rural-Urban Conflicts in Norway* (Oslo, 1956), especially pp. 30–63.

7. *America in the Forties: The Letters of Ole Munch Ræder,* trans. and ed. Gunnar J. Malmin (Minneapolis, 1929), p. 65.

8. A member of the Voss Correspondence Society of Chicago to "our dear Fatherland and old Norwegian friends," January 1, 1849, quoted in

Albert O. Barton, "Norwegian-American Emigration Societies in the Forties and Fifties," *Norwegian-American Studies and Records*, 3 (1928), 31 ff.; see also *Land of Their Choice: The Immigrants Write Home*, ed. Theodore C. Blegen (St. Paul, 1955), p. 203.

9. Nils Hansen Nærum, at Muskego, Wisconsin, to J. H. Nærum, Porsgrund, Norway, November 16, 1845, published in *Bratsberg Amts Correspondent*, March 5, 1846, trans. Blegen, *Land of Their Choice*, p. 199.

10. Carl Thorsteinsen, in Milwaukee, Wisconsin, to his father, July 19, 1853, published in *Morgenbladet*, November 28, 1853, trans. Blegen, *Land of Their Choice*, p. 275.

11. Blegen, trans. *Land of Their Choice*, p. 198.

12. See Peter A. Munch, "Social Adjustment Among Wisconsin Norwegians," *American Sociological Review*, 14 (December 1949), 780–87; "Segregation and Assimilation of Norwegian Settlements in Wisconsin," *Norwegian-American Studies and Records*, 18 (1954), 102–40, particularly p. 126.

13. *A Chronicle of Old Muskego: The Diary of Søren Bache, 1839–1847*, trans. and ed. Clarence A. Clausen and Andreas Elviken (Northfield, 1951), p. 88.

14. E. Clifford Nelson and Eugene L. Fevold, *The Lutheran Church Among Norwegian-Americans: A History of the Evangelical Lutheran Church*, I, 1825–90 (Minneapolis, 1960), 95.

15. Nelson and Fevold, *The Lutheran Church*, p. 97, 99, the quotation translated from J. W. C. Dietrichson, *Reise blandt de norske Emigranter i "De forenede nordamerikanske Fristater"* (Madison, 1896), p. 42. Dietrichson's account of his travels among the Norwegian emigrants was originally published in Stavanger, 1846.

16. *Land of Their Choice*, p. 144. The letter was in response to a previously published letter by Nils Hansen Nærum (quoted above), in which Nærum states that ministers "would be able to make a decent living if, supplementary to their clerical office, they owned some land" (*ibid.*, p. 200). Even ten years later, Dietrichson's statement proved to be true for some settlements, as Pastor Munch found out.

17. The letter appeared in *Morgenbladet*, August 16, 1845, trans. Blegen, in *Land of Their Choice*, p. 143.

18. About J. W. C. Dietrichson and his battles, see particularly Einar Haugen, "Pastor Dietrichson of Old Koshkonong," *Wisconsin Magazine of History*, 29 (March 1946), 301–18. Dietrichson was obviously misunderstood and perhaps misjudged, not only by his contemporaries but also by the early church historians, who present him as a deliberate powermonger and an enemy of freedom. He has often been misquoted, and translations of his words into English gave occasions for subtle twists. As an example may be mentioned Rohne's possibly unintentional mistranslation of the words *geistlig Øvrighed* in Dietrichson's famous "Four Points," which he presented to every new congregation that he organized. Dietrichson was clearly referring to "church authority" as opposed to the "secular authority" of civil government, in full accordance with the separation of church and state.

Rohne renders it as "spiritual rulership," a subtle but significant difference; J. Magnus Rohne, *Norwegian American Lutheranism up to 1872* (New York, 1926), p. 69. It is regrettable that this mistake as well as the rather biased picture of Pastor Dietrichson have been accepted unchecked and perpetuated in more recent historical accounts as, for instance, Nelson and Fevold, *The Lutheran Church,* pp. 96–119, especially p. 105. For a more sympathetic and undoubtedly more objective appraisal of Pastor Dietrichson and his work, see J. C. K. Preus, "The Widening Frontier—Koshkonong," in *Norsemen Found a Church: An Old Heritage in a New Land,* ed. J. C. K. Preus (Minneapolis, 1953), pp. 83–128, especially pp. 89–104.

19. *Emigranten,* March 28, 1856.

20. *Frontier Parsonage: The Letters of Olaus Fredrik Duus, Norwegian Pastor in Wisconsin, 1855–1858,* trans. Verdandi Study Club of Minneapolis and ed. Theodore C. Blegen (Northfield, 1947), pp. 17 ff.

21. Hjalmar R. Holand, *Coon Prairie* (Minneapolis, 1927), p. 71.

22. See, for instance, *Emigranten,* August 18, 1855 and May 2, 1856.

23. A couple of cases involving J. W. C. Dietrichson are cited by Einar Haugen, "Pastor Dietrichson of Old Koshkonong"; see also *Emigranten,* March 28, 1856, about disorders during divine service in Rock Prairie and Jefferson Prairie and subsequent court procedures.

24. This and the following quotations, unless otherwise stated, are from an unpublished autobiography, "Vita Mea," which Pastor Munch wrote for his children in 1903. The handwritten document is now in the editor's possession.

25. Johan R. Reiersen, *Veiviser for norske Emigranter til de forenede nordamerikanske Stater og Texas* [Guide for Norwegian emigrants to the United States of North America and Texas] (Christiania, 1844), p. 49, here quoted from Carl O. Paulson's translation in *Wiota Lutheran Church, 1844–1937* (privately published), p. 8. Reiersen, a liberal Norwegian newspaper editor interested in promoting emigration from Norway, visited the United States and Texas during 1843 and 1844.

26. "An Account of the Norwegian Settlers in North America," translated from the Norse by Knut Gjerset, *Wisconsin Magazine of History,* 8 (September, 1924), 77–88, "from a report by Consul General Adam Løvenskjold to the Norwegian government, October 15, 1847, describing his visit the preceding summer to the Norwegian settlements in the western districts of the United States, printed in Bergen, 1848."

27. "Church Record for the Norwegian-Lutheran Congregations at Jefferson Prairie, Long Prairie, Rock Run, and Hamilton." These were the "annex parishes" served by Clausen during his stay at Rock Prairie. The "Church Record" is now in the Archives of the Norwegian-American Historical Association, Northfield, Minnesota.

28. Reiersen, *Veiviser for norske Emigranter,* chapter 10, trans. and ed. Theodore C. Blegen in *Norwegian-American Studies and Records,* 1 (Minneapolis, 1926), 114; Hjalmar Rued Holand, *De Norske Settlementers Historie* (Ephraim, Wis., 1908), p. 180; J. A. Bergh, *Den norsk lutherske Kirkes Historie i Amerika* (Minneapolis, 1914), pp. 34 ff.; Nelson and Fevold, *The Lutheran Church,* p. 94.

29. These are Pastor J. W. C. Dietrichson's "Four Points," which he presented to every new congregation to be organized by him. The wording apparently varied slightly from time to time, and from place to place. The above version is translated from the official "Church Record of the Norwegian-Lutheran Congregations at Jefferson Prairie, Long Prairie, Rock Run, and Hamilton," which was kept by Pastor Clausen.

30. T. F. Gullixson and J. C. K. Preus, trans. "Focal Point of History—Luther Valley," *Norsemen Found a Church,* pp. 60 ff.

31. *Ibid.,* p. 62.

32. A decline in the mining activities at Hamilton's Diggings is also indicated by the fact that Colonel Hamilton left for California in the gold rush of 1849.

33. *Wiota Lutheran Congregation 1844–1944* (privately published, 1944), p. 4. The booklet is written by Pastor G. M. Gunderson, who served Wiota at the time of the centennial in 1944.

34. The original *Kaldsbrev* is in the writer's possession.

35. The view of the early Norwegian Synod pastors on culture and education among the immigrants is clearly expressed by A. C. Preus in his reply to an attack by a Danish schoolteacher, Rasmus Sørensen, in *Emigranten,* November 29, 1858; see Arthur C. Paulson and Kenneth Bjork, "A School and Language Controversy in 1858," *Norwegian-American Studies and Records,* 10 (1938), 76–106. Not until a decade later, after the Civil War had added its impetus of intensified patriotic feelings, was the issue sharpened into a real conflict by the emergence of an aggressive "Americanization" movement which, in turn, created a more militant kind of Norwegianism in which precisely the *form* of culture—customs, food habits, and particularly language—became the all-important symbols of identity. See particularly Einar Haugen, "The Struggle over Norwegian," *Norwegian-American Studies and Records,* 17 (1952), 1–35, later published as chapter 10 in Einar Haugen, *The Norwegian Language in America,* I (Philadelphia, 1953), 233–60. See also Laurence M. Larson, *The Changing West and Other Essays* (Northfield, 1937), pp. 116–46.

36. A recollection of this fiercely independent attitude of the Norwegian settlers has been retained in numerous jokes and anecdotes circulating in the Norwegian settlements. Particularly characteristic is a story that was told to me in Wiota in 1949—in Norwegian, of course. It is concerned with Pastor Munch and his efforts to introduce a proper atmosphere in the church. There was a parishioner from Sogn, a fjord district on the west coast of Norway, who used to chew tobacco in church. This was the time when the church in Wiota was not quite finished—the floor consisted of loose planks, and our Sogning had his regular seat next to a big knothole, which served very conveniently as his spittoon. His aim was perfect, so there was no problem on that account. His conduct, however, did not quite measure up to Pastor Munch's idea of propriety during divine services. He decided to talk to the man about it, and since the Sognings had a reputation even among Norwegians of being particularly fierce in their independence, he took along the sexton for moral and—if needed—physical support. After Pastor Munch had presented his view on the impropriety of chewing

tobacco and spitting in church and had admonished the man to refrain from this unseemly practice, the Sogning looked at him and said, nodding first to the pastor, then to the sexton: "Neither priest nor prophet will tell me where and when to spit."

37. In the Church Records, the name is usually found in its Norwegian form, Skjæger. But he always signed his name Hans Fr. Schjager. Later on, the family changed the spelling to Shager.

38. Minutes of Congregation Meeting, February 8, 1858.

39. Minutes of Congregation Meeting, November 21, 1856. This is obviously the meeting that Caja Munch is referring to in one of her letters (February 23, 1857), where she tells that "at a congregation meeting they even stood up and abused him," reproaching him for missing the services, "and when Munch told them that he was sick, one of them said: 'You could have come anyway!'"

40. Caja Munch's letter of June 1, 1857.

41. See Caja Munch's letter of May 3, 1857.

42. Caja Munch's letter of March 1858 (undated). Unfortunately, the written statement that she is referring to has not been preserved.

43. On a later occasion, Even Kronborg claimed that he had not withdrawn and wished to stay in the congregation.

44. The letter, which is in the present writer's possession, is dated Wiota, May 8, 1859, and is signed by Peder Fenne, Elev Johnsen, and Guldbrand Wang.

45. Minutes of Congregation Meeting, December 20, 1858, and January 12, 1859.

46. See Caja Munch's letter of October 28, 1857, where allusions are made to "gossip and slander," which may possibly be assumed to have been about Munch's conduct as a pastor in Wiota.

47. Unfortunately, again, the written statements by Schjager and Fosse were not copied into the official Records but were "attached to the minutes" and have since been lost.

48. The appeal is dated January 31, 1856, and appeared in *Emigranten* February 8, 22, and March 1.

49. A. C. Preus, "Vort Kirkesamfunds Delegater," *Emigranten,* March 7, 1856.

50. J. St. Munch, "Hvorledes kan den norsk-lutherske Kirke i Amerika sikres Bestaaen?" *Emigranten,* March 28, 1856.

51. G. F. Dietrichson, "Et Ord i Delegat- og Universitetssagen fra Minoriteten," *Emigranten,* April 18, 1856.

52. Contributions by Clausen and by A. C. Preus appeared in *Emigranten,* April 4, 25, June 20, 1856. H. A. Preus's contribution was published in *Kirkelig Maanedstidende,* the official paper of the Norwegian Synod, May 1856, and was extensively quoted and commented on in *Emigranten,* May 9. Other editorial comments appeared in the issues of March 14, 28, April 25.

53. The report was published in *Kirkelig Maanedstidende,* October 1857, and is extensively quoted in J. A. Bergh, *Den norsk lutherske Kirkes Historie i Amerika,* pp. 138–44.

54. Bergh, pp. 144 ff.

55. H. Halvorsen, *Festskrift til Den norske Synodes Jubilæum, 1853–1903* (Decorah, Iowa, 1903) , pp. 125 ff.

56. Our Savior's Lutheran Church, on the corner of May and Erie Streets, Chicago, continued in existence until 1925, when it merged with two other congregations to form the present United Evangelical Lutheran Church of Oak Park; see Herman Astrup Larsen, "Day of the Laymen—Fox River—Chicago," in *Norsemen Found a Church*, p. 52.

57. *The Diary of Elisabeth Koren, 1853–1855*, trans. and ed. David T. Nelson (Northfield, 1955) .

58. *Ibid.*, p. 159.

59. *Ibid.*, p. 303.

60. Concerning the Formula of Concord, see note 7, "An American Adventure."

Index